The Army is known as the number one repository for Foreign Area Officers (FAOs), but when I met Air Force Major Bill Baker when I taught Russian at the US Air Force Academy and he taught Arabic, I knew I was working with a FAO of no equal when it came to Arab-Israeli and Middle East matters. That was forty-years ago; he has only gotten better.

Bill's *The Israel Narrative* is a compelling, historically sound, captivating, first-hand rendering of the Israeli experience. Post-World War II Soviet literature of the 1950s and 1960s had a wartime genre called "Okopnaya Pravda (Trench Truth), known for its "I was there in the trenches" style. Bill was in the trenches of the *The Israel Narrative*. His account reflects it, i.e., an excellent interpretation of what occurred, why it happened, and what it means today. A great read and reference source, with superb explanatory footnotes for those who want to dig deeper. This book is a must-read for students and practitioners of Israeli and Middle East geopolitics.

Edward S. Pusey
Colonel, USA (Ret.)
Soviet/Russian Foreign Area Specialist
Military Attaché and Chief of Task Force Russia (POW/MIA) Moscow, USSR/ Russia
Principal Director, Deputy Assistant Secretary of Defense (Ret.)
Senior Analytic Service, CIA

Bill and I served at the US embassy in Tel Aviv, Israel, from 1988 to 1991. We had several occasions to work together, but one assignment in particular stands out. An American humanitarian aid worker had been kidnapped by a would-be terrorist in Gaza City. I was directed by the Ambassador to choose one person and go to Gaza to help negotiate and secure the aid worker's release. Without hesitation I chose Major Baker. No one in the embassy could come close to Bill's ability to articulate natively between the Arabs and Israelis, both linguistically and with cultural acumen.

In this book Bill has broken down what is normally a difficult and complicated subject into an easy-to-follow account. He presents the Jewish-Israeli narrative as one continuous story and makes the Arab-Israeli conflict clear. If I were to buy one book which simplifies and declutters the story of the Jewish people and the Arab-Israeli dilemma of the past century, this book would be it. *The Israel Narrative* is a must-read for any serious student, foreign service officer, diplomat, member of the armed forces, and all who want to understand the Middle East today.

Alan O. Bigler
Special Agent in Charge (Ret.)
Senior Regional Security Officer
American embassy New Delhi, Beirut, Tel Aviv, and Cairo
Diplomatic Security Service
United States Department of State

I began working with then Captain William (Bill) Baker in 1980 at an Air Force headquarters command current intelligence briefing unit. As a First Lieutenant Baker was chosen from all Air Force officers to be the Arabic interpreter for the US Air Force Chief of Staff during an official visit by a senior Arab Air Force commander to the Pentagon. Lt. Baker was again chosen to accompany the Air Force Chief as his interpreter and intelligence briefer on an official visit to six Middle East and north African countries, making him the most junior Air Force officer to be a member of the Air Chief's entourage. Over the next decades Bill continued to excel as a valuable intelligence officer, military attaché, Middle East expert, and university professor. This book represents the culmination of that career and educational journey.

The Israel Narrative provides what anyone trying to decipher events in the Middle East needs most – valuable historical context and keen cultural insights. I base this judgment on my experience as a regional office chief within the Defense Intelligence Agency and from evaluation of intelligence products sent to our nation's most senior leaders as part of my duties in the Office of Director of National Intelligence. Logically organized and easy to use, Professor Baker's book is an absolute required addition to any professional's bookshelf or a university undergraduate Middle East course reading list.

James (Jim) D. Marchio, Ph.D.
Colonel, USAF (Ret.)
Professor Emeritus and Associate Dean
College of Strategic Intelligence
National Intelligence University

THE ISRAEL NARRATIVE

From Genesis to Regenesis

WILLIAM G BAKER

THE ISRAEL NARRATIVE
FROM GENESIS TO REGENESIS

iUniverse books may be ordered through booksellers or by contacting:

iUniverse
1663 Liberty Drive
Bloomington, IN 47403
www.iuniverse.com
844-349-9409

ISBN: 978-1-6632-2476-7 (sc)
ISBN: 978-1-6632-2477-4 (hc)
ISBN: 978-1-6632-2478-1 (e)

Library of Congress Control Number: 2021916985

Print information available on the last page.

iUniverse rev. date: 10/28/2021

To my family, without whom my life's journey in the Near East could not have been the great adventure that it has been, and consequently, without whom this book could not have been written.

Contents

Foreword

William (Bill) Baker is an accomplished and eminently qualified Near East expert, university professor, retired military intelligence officer, native Arabic and Hebrew linguist, and author.

Professor Baker, the son of American Christian missionaries, was born in the United States but taken as an infant to the newly independent Jewish state of Israel, where his parents took up residency in the southern Galilee region. Bill spent his early childhood attending an all-Arabic instructional school in the city of Nazareth and his high school years at the American International School north of Tel Aviv, where he developed a proficiency in Hebrew second only to his proficiency in Arabic.

Being the only active-duty US Air Force officer with native reading, writing, and speaking fluency in both Arabic and Hebrew, Professor Baker served for twenty-seven years as a career military intelligence officer, a Middle East geopolitical expert, an assistant professor of Arabic at the US Air Force Academy, an Arabic intelligence briefer and interpreter for the US Air Force Chief of Staff, and a US Air Force attaché and military diplomat to three Middle Eastern countries. His early personal history in the bilingual Israeli culture, combined with his years of military service in the Middle East, prepared him well for his second career as a senior lecturer in Arabic and Middle Eastern studies at Baylor University—a position he held for twenty years following his retirement from the military.

This book is an authoritative, concise history of the people of Israel from their earliest appearance and historical mention in Egyptian New

Kingdom inscriptions of the late second millennium BC through the millennium-long biblical period and the two-millennia-long Jewish Diaspora, culminating in the reconstitution and establishment of the modern state of Israel in the twentieth century. The narrative continues with a discussion of today's Israeli cultural character, government institutions, regional geopolitics, conflicts, and the "eight-hundred-pound gorilla in the room," known as the "Palestinian question." How is Israel to accommodate its growing Arab population? Professor Baker considers possible options facing Israel as this question becomes more pressing. The nearly four-millennia-long saga of the commonwealth of the Hebrew-Jewish people, dispersed from and returned to their ancestral homeland, could only be found by consulting several sources until Bill set this story of national determination and survival into one inclusive book. *The Israel Narrative* will undoubtedly be an important single source for all students of the Jewish people, Israel, and the modern Middle East.

Daniel J. Reilly
Former Professor of Arabic, Baylor University
Independent Scholar of the ancient Middle East and Biblical Languages
Former Arabic Interpreter with the US Army in Iraq

Preface

This book is the outgrowth of an upper level/graduate course I taught at Baylor University from 2013 to 2020 under the broad rubric of "Readings in Middle East Studies." In this book, as I did in the course, I examine the Jewish narrative from its beginning with the Hebrew-Jewish patriarch Abraham through the Hebrew-Israelite ethnogenesis in Canaan; the establishments of the various Israelite and Judahite kingdoms; their tenacious attempts to hold on to self-rule in the face of conquering regional and outside superpower empires, including the Assyrians, Persians, Babylonians, and Greeks; and their eviction from the land of Israel by the Roman Empire and the beginning of the Jewish Diaspora. I then briefly follow the Jewish people as they fell victim to state-sponsored European anti-Semitism, culminating in Hitler and the Nazi "Final Solution to the Jewish Problem"—the attempted extermination and genocide. I move next to the establishment of political Zionism, the call for an independent, self-governed Jewish nation in the Jewish ancestral homeland of Israel-Palestine, and the resurrection of Hebrew as a modern spoken language, which had only been a liturgical language for the previous two thousand years. I chronicle the British intervention in the Near East between the two world wars and the attempt to resolve the modern Arab-Jewish conflict that Great Britain created through the multiple conflicting agreements and promises it made to the Arabs (through the McMahon-Hussein Correspondence), to the Jews (through the Balfour Declaration), and the secret colonial pact it signed with France (the Sykes-Picot Agreement). I then detail the four major Arab-Israeli Wars that took place as the Jewish state of Israel reconstituted itself in Israel-Palestine in the heart of the Arab Middle East over the objections of the pan-Arab and Muslim world. The book examines the ingathering of millions of Jews from one hundred different countries into a cohesive, new, contemporary Jewish-Israeli society and its development of a strong military, which has made Israel today the conventional and nonconventional regional superpower. The book examines the Palestinian narrative and Palestinians' objections to not having their nationalistic aspirations realized, notwithstanding the peace treaties between Israel and two of its former adversaries, Egypt and Jordan. I briefly discuss the recent rapprochement between Israel and non-neighboring Sunni Arab and Muslim countries and address the new and changing strategic and economic alignments between former adversaries occurring in part, and even primarily due to, Arab Gulf countries' concerns over Iranian Shiite threats and its regional hegemonic aspirations—"the enemy of my enemy is my friend." The book concludes with Iran emerging as the new leader of the previously Arab confrontation state vowing Israel's destruction. In the final chapter, I propose a starting point for discussions of possible options for resolving the Palestinian-Israeli conflict.

I developed this material because there was previously no single text that covered the historical span of the Hebrew-Israelite-Judahite-Jewish-Israeli narrative from its ethnogenesis in antiquity to its regenesis in modernity. Had I not developed this material I would have had to require my students purchase multiple textbooks to cover the same material. I complemented the course curriculum with historically specific movies and documentary videos. With the exception of the first four historical chapters, which discuss the well-chronicled Jewish ethnogenesis and rule in the Land of Israel in antiquity, the material in this book is based on my firsthand, direct observations of and often participation in the facts as they occurred.

Acknowledgments

I want to first thank my parents, Dwight and Emma Baker, who moved our young family to the Near East in 1950, before my first birthday. In my early childhood, I lived in the all-Arab city of Nazareth, in the Galilee region of Israel, and during my teen years, I lived in the predominantly Hebrew-speaking region of Israel near Tel Aviv. As we traveled the world to and from the Near East, my parents unwittingly gave me the priceless gift of being raised as a citizen of the world, trilingual and tricultural. I could not have obtained this gift and education in any university for any amount of money. Thank you, Mom and Dad, for this priceless gift and my global understanding and pan-worldview.

Secondly, I would like to thank my wife, Carol Sue (Robinson) Baker, for her support and accommodation of my profession as I carried her and our children, Brent, Scott, and Holly, through a twenty-seven-year career in the United States Air Force. Thank you, Carol, for providing a warm, stable, and safe home for our children as I pursued my global military career while you suspended yours.

I would like to give special thanks to my friend and teaching colleague Daniel Reilly, who provided substantive material and mechanical editing to this manuscript. He is a scholar of the ancient (and modern) Near East and an expert in biblical and Near Eastern languages. He has translated and taught biblical Greek, Hebrew, Aramaic, and Arabic. Dan is a former lecturer in Arabic at Baylor University who speaks colloquial Levantine Arabic and modern Hebrew. Mr. Reilly worked as a civilian Arabic interpreter in Iraq with the US Army and Marine

Corps for two years during Operation Iraqi Freedom. Dan is a six-year veteran of the US Navy.

Finally, I would like to articulate a big thank you to two of my former undergraduate students of Middle East studies whom I taught at Baylor University during the spring 2020 semester, Ms. Bahna Miller and Ms. Corrie Shrock. Their keen editorial eyes found errors in the manuscript after it had been edited by three other people. Bahna and Corrie are not only great editors but two of the brightest and most enthusiastic students of the Middle East I have had the privilege of teaching. Thank you, Bahna, and thank you, Corrie, for your ever-present optimistic, can-do spirit and your exemplary character and integrity. You are true ambassadors of your generation and the best the US has to offer.

Introduction

Most of this book is a firsthand accounting of the reconstitution and development of the modern country of Israel, a nation established to give world Jewry a protected safe haven from global anti-Semitism and persecution. I initially produced this material in a PowerPoint format as the curriculum for an upper level/graduate course I taught at Baylor University and then later developed the material into a manuscript. This book is most helpful for any student of the modern Near East and Israel, as well as State Department foreign-service officers serving in the Near East and military forces deployed to the Near East. The book is also of benefit to anyone interested in the development of the modern Near East since the end of World War I and the fall of the Ottoman Empire, specifically as it relates to the Levant, the establishment of the state of Israel, and the Arab-Israeli conflict.

Beginning with the ethnogenesis of the Hebrews in antiquity, the material traces their evolution as Israelites, Judahites, and Jews, their establishment as a people in Canaan, and their fight for survival in the face of regional and external empires, culminating in their eviction from the Land of Israel by the Romans. The next section traces the two-thousand-year Jewish Diaspora and European persecutions, culminating in their reconstitution in Palestine as the nation of Israel in the twentieth century. The final section is a firsthand chronicle of the Arab-Israeli Wars; ongoing conflicts and subwars; the development of Israel's modern society, its demographics, religions, language, education, social character, physical features, water concerns, social concerns, and government; the status of Jerusalem; and Israel's economic miracle, trade, rapprochement with Arab countries, social services, infrastructure, housing, and new existential threats. It concludes with options for a peaceful Arab-Israeli dialogue.

Some spellings in this book are nonconventional. As a native Arabic, Hebrew, and (American) English speaker, I write the non-English Arabic and Hebrew words in as close to their native-language spelling and phonetic pronunciation as possible to give them a more accurate pronunciation. Case in point are the words *Hizb Allah* (Party of God), the Arabic-origin name for the political/militant/terrorist organization located in Lebanon. The Western press has long spelled the organization's name using the Iranian mistranscription and mispronunciation as though it were one word, *Hezbollah.* English readers who know the Arabic word for God, *Allah,* will readily see that the word *Hezbollah* does not contain the correct spelling of the word *Allah.* Therefore, since the Arabic word for political party is *Hizb,* not *Hezb,* and the word for God is *Allah,* not *ollah* or *bollah, Hezbollah* is an incorrect spelling resulting in an incorrect pronunciation. Other examples of unconventional yet more language-accurate spellings include Qur'an versus Koran, Ba'al versus Baal, Muhammad versus Mohammed, Muslim versus Moslem, and so on.

Most of the content of this manuscript, except for the first four pre-1950 historical chapters, is based on my firsthand, eyewitness account. I grew up in the Near East (1950–1967); was on active duty in the US Air Force as an intelligence and Near East area officer, with assignments to headquarters-level command Near East analyst positions in the Pentagon and the Defense Intelligence Agency (1973–1988); served as a military attaché in three Near Eastern countries, Israel, Saudi Arabia, and Qatar (1988–1999); and lived, traveled, and worked in the Near East both professionally and privately. As mentioned in the preface, this book is based on my being a lifelong eyewitness, participant, observer, and student of the cultures, societies, and geopolitical-military dynamics of the recent Near East.

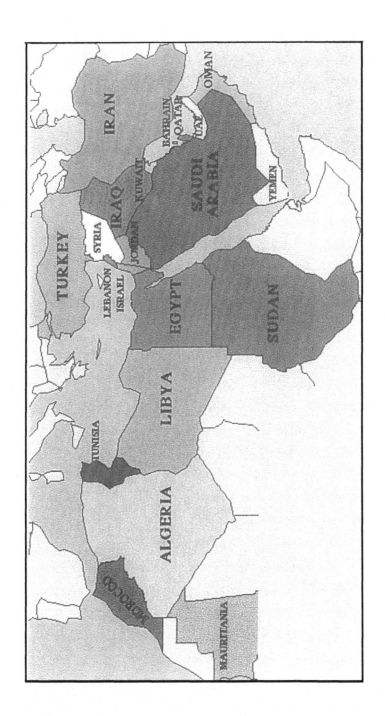

Chapter 1

The Promise—Religious and Historic Claims to the Land

Abraham and the Hebrew-Israelite Narrative

It is often difficult, if not impossible, to identify specific ancient events and personalities historically and archaeologically with definitive certainty. Such is the case with Judaism's legendary patriarch, Abraham. Identified only in the Tanakh, the Hebrew Bible (the Christian Old Testament), Abraham lived almost four thousand years ago, circa 1800 to 1700 BCE,[1] in the city of Ur of the Chaldeans, in Mesopotamia (present-day Iraq). Abraham postulated the unconventional notion that there existed only one universal God. Abraham's belief in a single God distinguished him from his Mesopotamian countrymen, who believed in a multiplicity of gods, a pantheon of deities (i.e., a sun god, a moon god, and gods of fertility, agriculture, harvest, rain, health, life, death,

---

[1] To assume a religiously neutral historical time designation, BCE, (Before the Common Era) has become the acceptable time designator in contemporary scholarship, replacing the traditional BC (Before Christ). Similarly, AD (Anno Domini, "the year of our Lord") has been replaced in scholarship with CE (Common Era).

and so on), an individual god for every human experience. This had been the prevailing belief for centuries before Abraham arrived at his enlightened understanding and remained so in much of the known world for most of the next two millennia. To Abraham, his God possessed the combined powers of all known gods in one. Furthermore, Abraham's God had power over all nature and was, in fact, the creator of the universe and all things on earth and in the heavens. To Abraham, God was the embodiment of all the Mesopotamian and ancient Near Eastern world's singular gods in one plurally named God, called Elohim (אלוהים, pronounced "eh-lo-heem").[2] The name *Elohim* included the primary Phoenician and Canaanite god El (אל), who was also the god commonly worshipped by people who lived in the region from western Mesopotamia to the eastern Mediterranean. *El* was the Semitic name used to designate the entire region's primary god. To Abraham, Elohim [plural of *El*] manifested the plurality of all the known gods in one. To paraphrase the biblical scholar Joel Burnett, in the ancient Near East the use of the plural form [Elohim] indicated the multiplicity of gods and equated the individual deity so identified as encompassing the pantheon.[3] The Hebrew Bible records in the book of Genesis that to reward Abraham for acknowledging and worshiping the one true God, Abraham was commanded to "leave your country, your people and your father's household and go to the land I will show you." The historical account states that Abraham, together with some of his extended family, migrated on a journey of faith to an unknown land.

---

[2]   When the Semitic prefix *El* is added to the suffix *im* (pronounced "eem"), designating the Semitic masculine plural, the combination appears to take the meaning "God in the plural." The linguistic root of the word/name *El* is the pan-Semitic name for the commonly worshiped deities of all regions speaking Semitic language, including Aramaic, Hebrew, and Phoenician. Abraham was making a bold new revelation and assertion that there is only one God, who is the singular unity and plurality of all the gods in one, Elohim. More than four hundred years later, the Hebrews adopted the name *YHWH* (יהוה, spelled out in English as *Yahweh* and pronounced *Yah-way*) as the personal name for their God. Some scholars believe that the Hebrew *YHWH* is an acronym based on the Hebrew verb meaning "to be," which in Hebrew grammar moves through the tenses to mean "I Am (my nature is) in the present, what it was in the past, what it will be in the future"—that is, "I am what I am (I am eternal)." *Yahweh* was later mispronounced and mistranscribed into English from the German as *Jehovah.*

[3]   Burnett's thesis explores other linguistic semantic and cultural traditions, showing that the singular and plural forms of the name of a deity were often interchangeable in the ancient Near East.

Abraham is said to have traveled in a direction and to a land he had never been to before and about which he knew nothing, from Mesopotamia to Canaan. Bible scholars believe that Abraham most likely took a northerly route out of Mesopotamia, following the Tigris-Euphrates River Valley, and then turned westward into today's Syria and finally southward into Canaan. Abraham, in effect, first followed the northeastern and then the southwestern branches of the Fertile Crescent. When Abraham arrived with his clan in the land of Canaan on the eastern shores of the Mediterranean Sea, the Hebrew scripture records, God told Abraham to stop his journey because he had arrived at the land that God had promised to give him and his descendants as an inheritance.[4] The Bible does not specify how God would give this land to Abraham, since there were already people sporadically inhabiting the land of Canaan—namely the various non-confederated tribes of what we collectively call Canaanites.

It is important to note that in the second millennium BCE and extending into relatively recent times, borders between various lands, peoples, empires, and nation-states were not surveyed, rigidly delineated, militarily guarded, or internationally recognized as they are today. In antiquity, a country's boundaries were vague at best, undefined and porous, and a portion of its population routinely migrated back and forth across fluid borders. People lived more in regions than within fixed, internationally recognized borders. Various people in the ancient Near East often migrated from one region to another, settling among different ethnographic and ethnolinguistic groups in open, uncontested areas, with no great concern or thought that they were invading or illegally occupying someone else's land, nor that they needed to get permission to settle in the location they had chosen. This is not to say that there were no military conquests and campaigns wherein

---

[4] The specific place in Canaan where God told Abraham to stop traveling and make camp was the town of Hebron. The Bible records that Abraham bought property in Hebron for the site of what later became his burial place and that of his wife, Sarah, and his sons, Isaac and Jacob. A shrine was built over these burial plots in 1000 BCE, and to this day, the site is revered by Jews, Christian, and Muslims as The Tomb of the Patriarchs. The structure today is divided into a Muslim mosque and a separate Jewish synagogue/yeshiva (seminary).

great empires and their armies were pitted against one another and the victors subjugated the conquered peoples, as was the case with the Babylonian, Persian, Assyrian, Greek, Roman, Byzantine, Arab and Crusaders empires and kingdoms. People also often migrated for various other reasons: sometimes to escape natural catastrophes, as may have happened with the "Sea Peoples," and sometimes for man-made reasons, such as conquests and wars. The Philistines (believed to be from the Peleset tribe) are one of several tribes of these Sea Peoples who migrated to the eastern Mediterranean shores from the Aegean Sea region in the mid to late second millennium BCE (1700 to 1400 BCE), for reasons not entirely clear to scholars—possibly earthquakes, volcanic eruptions, famine, or warfare.

Since the end of the last ice age, a rugged, nomadic, tribal people have roamed the Near East and North Africa in search of water and vegetation for themselves and their grazing animals.[5] Over time, the descendants of these migrants assimilated into the populations of their adopted lands and were absorbed into the indigenous cultures of their adopted homes. Scholars also believe that the opposite sometimes occurred—that is, that the new immigrants who arrived in an area in large numbers with strong, dominant cultural identities and traits, such as language, religion, customs, and advanced technologies, would eventually overwhelm the local populations, who would over time adopt, absorb, and replace their native cultures with those of the new immigrants. It is therefore not difficult to see how this scenario may have occurred in the dry desert climate of the Near East, where

---

[5] Near Eastern Arabic nomadic wanderers are known as Bedouins (Arabic: al-Badu [البدو]). Today, Badu numbers are dwindling, and they will soon disappear from the Middle Eastern landscape altogether as they settle in towns and villages, where local governments provide them with water and electricity, and in some cases build them complete, new settlements with walled-in homes and animal corrals to encourage them to become sedentary. Badu, like all people, are looking for the good life, and it is not unusual today to see air-conditioner units and a dish antenna attached to a goat-skin tent throughout the Middle East. A major reason that governments are eager to settle their Badu populations is that today's Near Eastern borders are often militarized because many countries have contested borders, are at war with their neighbors, and/or are fearful that cross-border migrating populations could be gun running, sharing information/intelligence on neighboring militaries and weapons dispositions, trafficking in narcotics, or doing all the above.

indigenous desert-culture people lived a nomadic lifestyle, wandering seasonally from one region to another in search of water and vegetation to sustain themselves and their herds. Thus, to have Abraham and some of his extended family members nearly four thousand years ago suddenly arrive in the Land of Canaan, pitch their tents, and graze their animals was by no means an unusual occurrence, nor was it seen as an alarming or threatening event to the indigenous Canaanite population.

Ethnogenesis and Nationhood

Modern archaeological discoveries and thinking may help explain how this land became transformed from one of predominantly Canaanite civilization and culture to one where Hebrew and Israelite culture dominated. Today, archaeological and biblical scholarship both point to a period of approximately three to five hundred years of initial integration and cohabitation in the land of Canaan between two distinct populations. The first comprised two groups of Hebrew tribes: one, which lived in the northern highlands of Canaan (in today's West Bank), whose population and culture would later be identified as Israelite, and the other, which lived in the southern Judean hills region, whose population and culture would later be identified as Judahite. The other ethnolinguistic group living side by side the Hebrew tribes in Canaan were various indigenous, non-confederated Canaanite tribes. This period lasted roughly from a high chronology of 1800 to 1700 BCE, or about the time Abraham and his clansmen first arrived in Canaan, to a more conservative low chronology of around 1400 to 1300 BCE, or about the time that the Hebrew tribes began returning to Canaan from Egypt and Canaan began to be recognized ethnolinguistically as a Hebrew-dominated land. Archaeologists refer to the earliest Hebrews who settled Canaan as proto-Israelites (see the note about the Habiru/Apiru below).

Between the fourteenth and the thirteenth centuries BCE (1300 to 1200 BCE), toward the end of the Bronze Age, the various Hebrew tribes had sufficiently integrated in the Land of Canaan to have

5

coalesced into a recognizable ethnolinguistic group and to have begun thinking of themselves as a unified people with three of the primary elements of any culture: a common language, a common religion, and a shared history. For certain, by at least 1200 BCE, the Hebrews, who had earlier been divided into twelve self-ruled tribes similar to the various loosely affiliated Canaanite tribes, banded together to form the two separate kingdoms, Israel and Judah, mentioned above. The larger kingdom, consisting of ten Hebrew tribes, was located in the northern Canaanite highlands, west of the Jordan River, and was called the Kingdom of Israel. The southern kingdom, with two Hebrew tribes, was called the Kingdom of Judah and was located in the southern region of Canaan, south of the Kingdom of Israel, in the Judean hill region and southward toward the Negev Desert. The southern Kingdom of Judah had a series of kings culminating with Saul, David, and his son Solomon. David ruled the Kingdom of Judah with its capital in Jerusalem from 1009 to 970 BCE, and Solomon from around 970 to 930 BCE (plus or minus five years, depending on the source). David made Jerusalem his capital in 1000 BCE and began what became the Davidic-Solomonic dynasty of the House of David. The northern ten tribes, united under the Kingdom of Israel, had capitals successively in the cities of Shechem (Hebrew: Shkhem [שכם], also known today by its Arabic name Nablis/Nablus),[6] Tirzah, and Samaria. Most of the lands ruled by the Hebrews/Israelites, both individually as the Kingdoms of Israel and Judah and later collectively under the United Monarchy of Israel (see "Davidic-Solomonic Dynasties and the United Monarchy" below), were located in what is known today as the geopolitical region of Israel-Palestine. This area includes the West Bank (of the Jordan River) but excludes the Negev Desert and the Gaza Strip, roughly the geographic area from the eastern Mediterranean Sea to the

---

[6] *Shechem* today is known to Arabs as "Nablus/Nablis," an Arabic mispronunciation of the Greek name given to the city by the Romans, *Neapolis,* meaning "New City." The mispronunciation is due in part to the absence of the letter *p* in the Arabic language. The mispronunciation took hold as Arabic began replacing Aramaic as the lingua franca (common language) in the region following the Arab-Islamic invasion and conquest of the Near East in the seventh century. The name change by the Romans was an attempt to erase any Jewish/Hebrew connection to the Land of Israel following the second Jewish uprising/war against Rome in 135 CE.

Jordan River. The geopolitical region known today as the Gaza Strip includes much of the ancient land of the Philistines, Philistia. Hebrews and their descendant Israelites, Judahites, and Jews ruled and called this land home off and on for more than 1,400 years, until their eventual eviction by the Romans in 135 CE These lands collectively called the Land of Israel were known for centuries by their Hebrew-Israelite-Judahite names of Judea and Samaria, names Jews use to this day.

Evolutionary versus Revolutionary Conquest

There are today two biblical-archaeological-scholarly debates regarding the ethnogenesis, or ethnic beginnings/origins, of the Hebrews/Israelites. The debate is over whether the Hebrew/Israelite conquest of the land of Canaan was revolutionary (i.e., a military conquest as detailed in the Hebrew Bible) or evolutionary (a gradual absorption of the Canaanites by the Israelites). The evolutionary-versus-revolutionary debate is a result of there being an absence of any extrabiblical evidence (evidence other than or outside of the Hebrew Bible/Old Testament) of a military conquest of the land of Canaan, such as archaeological evidence of collapsed walls of the city of Jericho or any written documentation of the event. Many archaeologists believe that the two cultures simply merged over time after the return of the Hebrews from Egypt to Canaan. This reasoning states that the returning migrants, and later all Israelites,[7] were at least in part transformed Canaanites who had over time dropped various ritual aspects of their religion, such as human sacrifice and worship of a pantheon of gods headed by their storm god, Ba'al (בעל, often spelled Baal).[8] These converted proto-Israelites also later accepted and worshiped the Israelite God, Yahweh. Scholars today

---

[7] Hebrews became known as Israelites during the Egyptian exile narrative, when they began thinking of themselves as a distinct people, sometime in the mid to late second millennium BCE, between 1500 to 1300 BCE.

[8] The name for the Canaanite god Ba'al (pronounced *Ba-al*) is a Semitic word that in Hebrew means "Lord" or "Master." In modern Hebrew, the word means someone of wealth or substance, such as someone who owns property, a business, or a home. Ba'al is also the commonly used Hebrew word in Israel today for husband.

also do not believe that *all* Hebrew tribes were enslaved in Egypt; rather it is more likely that one Hebrew tribe (possibly the Levites, based on Hebrew names found in Egypt) that had traveled to Egypt in time of famine was forcefully indentured or enslaved by the Egyptians and later was freed or escaped and returned to Canaan. Ancient Near East scholars are of the opinion that as the returning exiles told and retold their tribal story and passed it down by word of mouth from generation to generation, the narrative became accepted by all Israelites as their collective history. Additionally, scholars unanimously agree that there is no extrabiblical record or any archeological evidence to support the exodus of between 600,000 and 2,000,000 people from Egypt to Canaan.[9]

The latest consensus in biblical scholarship on the subject is that historical, physical, anthropological, and archaeological evidence tells us that for about five centuries, from around 1700 BCE to sometime before 1200 BCE, Hebrew culture gradually absorbed and replaced Canaanite culture in the land of Canaan. It is certain that between 1400 to 1200 BCE, the period between the Berlin Granite and the Merneptah Stele (see "Extrabiblical Evidence" section below), a people called Israel who lived predominantly in the Judean highlands, today's West Bank, were established, integrated, and recognized in Canaan by the regional superpower, Egypt. Therefore, the most likely scenario for the Hebrew-Israelite takeover of Canaan is a combination of both an evolutionary cohabitation and an eventual absorption of the Canaanites into the Hebrew culture, complete with Canaanite acceptance of the

---

[9] Some Near East scholars have linked the early Hebrews with the Habiru (aka Hapiru or Apiru), a people identified in numerous Egyptian writings from the second millennium BCE. Most scholars today agree that the term refers to a social class of people and not an ethnic group. However, the linguistic similarities between the words *Habiru* and *Hebrew* are obvious. The Habiru, who lived in Egypt and elsewhere in the Near East, are often identified as mercenaries, armed bandits, robbers, or laborers. The name *Habiru* may be linked etymologically to the Hebrew-Semitic word *aviru/abiru*, meaning "to cross over" (i.e., "those who crossed over"). This could have a regional or local reference to a people who migrated (crossed over) to Egypt, descriptive of Hebrews who came from Canaan in search of food during a time of severe famine, as documented in the Hebrew Bible book of Genesis. One scholar (Professor Anson Rainey) claims that the earliest Hebrews were the Shasu, known from Egyptian texts as a pastoral people who immigrated to Canaan from the east, which accords with the Hebrew Bible narrative.

Hebrew-Israelite culture (including language and religion), as well as some military conquests of various Canaanite city-states and strongholds by the Hebrews (see Jebusites below under Davidic-Solomonic Dynasties and the United Monarchy). In support of an evolutionary absorption theory, there are many admonitions in the Bible issued to the Israelites by their prophets directing them to stop worshiping false gods as their cohabitants, the Canaanites, were doing. Undoubtedly, during five hundred years of cohabitation, there was much cross-cultural exchange between Canaanites and Israelites. Otherwise, there would not have been the need for such admonitions from the Hebrew prophets. New archaeological findings and contemporary scholarly thinking appear to show more evidence of a gradual evolutionary takeover of Canaan by the Hebrews versus a revolutionary/military conquest with limited military engagement. This new thinking appears to be the position supported by the preponderance of archaeological and documentary evidence and is therefore the most likely scenario for Hebrew/Israelite establishment and eventual rule in Canaan.

Extrabiblical Evidence: Minimalists versus Maximalists

In the twentieth century, a group of archaeologists, mainly Europeans, began to strongly challenge the Jewish narrative of the origins and ethnogenesis of the Israelites in Canaan. They went so far as to also deny the existence of the Davidic and Solomonic dynasties of the tenth and ninth centuries BCE. These scholars became known as biblical minimalists. Other archaeologists and biblical scholars who accepted and defended the early Hebrew narrative were called biblical maximalists. Biblical minimalists argued that there is not a shred of extrabiblical evidence that corroborates anything written in the Hebrew Bible about the existence and the history of the Jewish people and that the Hebrew, Israelite, Jewish, and, by extension, modern Israeli claim to any historical reality and ownership of the Land of Israel/Canaan/Palestine is mythical and invalid. As the minimalists defended their position, there surfaced three extrabiblical archaeological artifacts with proof-positive to the contrary. The first was the Merneptah or Israel

Stele (pronounced "ste-leh" or in the plural *Stelae* pronounced "ste-lah"). The Merneptah Stele is an Egyptian hieroglyphic inscription carved into a granite slab that was first discovered in Egypt in 1896 and dated to 1200 BCE, during the reign of the Egyptian Pharaoh Merneptah (1230 to 1208 BCE). The inscription extolled the victories of Pharaoh Merneptah over several regional city-states, including Israel. The hieroglyphic specifically stated, "Israel is laid waste, its seed is not." Pharaoh Merneptah's claim to have totally annihilated Israel was an obvious exaggeration and incorrect. Pharaohs often exaggerated their military victories and downplayed their defeats. The specific hieroglyphic word used to describe Israel in the Merneptah Stele was not a proper noun, as in one's name, but a noun depicting Israel as a people, a nation, a polity.

The second artifact identifying Israel as a people, known as the Berlin University Egyptian Granite, is an Egyptian gray granite slab found in 1913 and dating to 1400 BCE; it identifies "Israel in Canaan." This inscription also uses the same nonproper noun to identify Israel as a people. Significantly for the biblical maximalist position, this archaeological find establishes Israel in Canaan a full two hundred years earlier than did the Merneptah Stele. It also backed up archaeologists and scholars who supported a high (earlier) chronology for the establishment of Israel in Canaan, as opposed to those who advocated a low chronology.

The third piece of extrabiblical archaeological evidence of the existence of a nation-state of Israel in Canaan is known as the Tel Dan Inscription, fragments of which were found in 1993 and 1995 during archaeological excavations at a ninth century-BCE Israelite city called Dan in northern Israel. The inscription is written on a black basalt stele in Old Aramaic and is believed to be the boastings of the king of Damascus, Hazael, who reigned in the ninth century BCE. In it, the king touts his victories over various regional kings, including "The King of the House of Israel." This artifact dates to approximately 1000 BCE and factually identifies the ninth century-BCE dynastic monarchy of the Judahite King David.

The significance of these findings as proof of the existence of an ancient Israel cannot be overstated. These findings confirm that major regional powers in the ancient Near East, in particular Egypt, the great superpower of its time, recognized and acknowledged the existence of Israel as an established polity with a national identity, territory, and self-rule. Following these three revelations, the biblical minimalists attempted to put a negative spin on these archaeological finds to discredit them as being wrongly translated and interpreted and therefore invalid. However, the ancient Near Eastern world scholarship community soon acknowledged and accepted the validity of these extrabiblical findings, and the argument was gradually put to rest.

Ethnogenesis does not happen overnight; a people do not emerge out of thin air on a specific calendar date. For a people to come together and coalesce with like traits that identify them as a unique, singular ethnicity with a common language and religion and common mores, customs, pottery styles, and architectural construction styles, it would most likely take not decades but centuries, especially when communication and transportation were extremely slow and primitive. Therefore, if Israel was a known ethnopolitical entity by the time of the Berlin University (Egyptian) Granite in 1400 BCE (fifteenth century BCE), it must have been inhabiting, coalescing, integrating, and becoming a singular distinct people in the Land of Israel for some time before this date.

Davidic-Solomonic Dynasties and the United Monarchy

In 1000 BCE, King David conquered the Canaanite Jebusite tribal stronghold city of Jebus and established it as his capital. The city, later called the City of David, has been known ever since as Jerusalem and has been considered by Jews to be the eternal Jewish capital for the past three thousand years.[10] David ruled the southern Hebrew kingdom of Judah from 1009 to 970 BCE, and David's son Solomon, who succeeded him, ruled from 970 to 930 BCE.[11] Solomon is credited with having built the first temple to Yahweh in Jerusalem, which housed the Ten Commandments and the Ark of the Covenant. For approximately one hundred years, from 1030 to 930 BCE (some sources say from 1047 to 931 BCE), the northern Kingdom of Israel and southern Kingdom of Judah attempted a union known as the United Hebrew Monarchy of Judah and Israel. The union did not last, and they eventually separated. The northern kingdom's capital moved to several different locations including Shechem, as mentioned above, and the southern kingdom's capital was first established in Hebron and later moved by King David to Jerusalem.

---

[10] The Jebusites were a Canaanite tribe who inhabited the area in and around what is known today as Jerusalem in the Judean hills. In addition to being known as Jebus, some sources record its name as "Rusalimum," "Urusalim," or "Salim/Salem," hence *Jerusalem*.

[11] These dates vary plus or minus three years depending on the source.

Notes

Joel Burnett, *A Reassessment of Biblical Elohim* (Society of Biblical Literature, Dissertation Series 183 2001).

Avraham Faust, "How Did Israel Become A People? The Genesis of Israelite Identity," *Biblical Archaeology Review* (November/December 2009).

Aaron Miller, *The Much Too Promised Land: America's Elusive Search for Arab Israeli Peace* (Bantam Books, Random House Publishing, 2007).

Igor P. Lipovsky, *Early Israelites: Two People, One History, Rediscovery of the Origins of Biblical Israel* (Lipovsky, 2012).

Igor P. Lipovsky, *Israel and Judah: How Two People Became One* (Cambridge Publishing Inc., 2014).

Anson Rainey, "Inside Outside: There Did the Early Israelites Come From?" *Biblical Archaeology Review* (November/December 2008).

Anson Rainey, "Shasu or Habiru: Who Were the Early Israelites?" *Biblical Archaeology Review* (November/December 2008).

Hershel Shanks, *Ancient Israel: From Abraham to the Roman Destruction of the Temple* (Prentice Hall and Biblical Archaeology Society, 1999).

Yosef Garfinkel, "The Birth & Death of Biblical Minimalism" *Biblical Archaeology Review* (May/June 2011).

Hershel Shanks, "When Did Ancient Israel Begin" *Biblical Archaeology Review* (January/ February 2012).

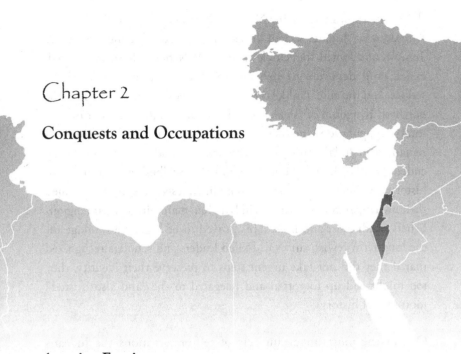

Chapter 2

Conquests and Occupations

Assyrian Empire

In 733 BCE, the new regional Near Eastern superpower was Assyria, whose king, Tiglath-Pileser, conquered the northern Kingdom of Israel. His forces invaded, captured, enslaved, and deported to Assyria all ten tribes that made up the northern kingdom. These enslaved and exiled northern tribes never returned or reconstituted themselves in Israel. As it was Assyria's custom to ethnically cleanse captured lands, following the deportation of all Israelites, Assyria repopulated the northern kingdom with other Assyrian captives, including Babylonians, Persians, and Arabs. The northern Hebrew tribes of Israel are among those peoples who have been forever lost to history.

Babylonian Empire

The next superpower to conquer the Near East was the Babylonian Empire. In 586 BCE, as part of his conquest from the Persian Gulf to the Mediterranean Sea, King Nebuchadnezzar conquered the southern Kingdom of Judah, sacked Jerusalem, destroyed King Solomon's Temple, and looted the temple treasures.[12] Nebuchadnezzar enslaved, exiled, and deported to Babylon the Judean ruling class, priests, scribes, and the elite. Unlike the Assyrian conquest and the exile of the northern Kingdom of Israel, the Babylonian conquest did not involve total depopulation and deportation. Many thousands of Judeans remained in Judah, though Judean self-rule and political autonomy ended. Unlike the northern exile and those tribes' eradication from history, the Judeans were able to remain cohesive in exile and formed their own separate communities in Babylon, maintaining their religious beliefs, traditions, and laws. This proved to be a great advantage for the long-term Jewish survival. Exiled leaders and scholars recognized that if they did not take urgent steps to preserve their identity, they too might end up forgotten and relegated to the "and also existed" footnotes of history.

One of the most important acts of self-preservations the Judeans undertook was to compile their scriptures into what later became the basis of the Tanakh, the Hebrew Bible. Because the Judeans were separated from their countrymen in Judea, Aramaic, the language of their Babylonian captors, began replacing Hebrew as the exiled Judeans' spoken language. This was a slow process that took several centuries, because Hebrew continued to be spoken in the Land of Israel by Judeans who had not been deported to Babylon. It was also during the period of the Babylonian exile that the word *Jew* saw increased usage to designate Judeans. Eventually, the term became the collective name for all descendants of the Hebrew tribes and all who identified with the Hebrew/Judahite/Israelite religion and narrative.

---

[12] Some historians have postulated that the temple treasures, including possibly the Ark of the Covenant, were spirited away and hidden as the Babylonian armies approached, not too unlike what future generations five hundred years later did with the Dead Sea Scrolls.

Persian Empire

The final Near Eastern regional superpower was the Persian Empire. In 538 BCE, almost fifty years after the start of the Babylonian captivity, the Persian Empire, under the rule of King Cyrus, conquered Mesopotamia, including the neo-Babylonian Empire. Cyrus allowed captives enslaved by Babylon, which included Judeans (Jews), to return to their ancestral homelands. Many Judeans did in fact endure the arduous journey some four hundred miles west to the Land of Israel and upon arrival rebuilt—or some would argue, refurbished—the Babylonian-destroyed First Temple of King Solomon. However, there were many Judeans who had by now been in Babylon for over a generation and who were too old or too infirm or had young families and could not physically endure the journey back to the Land of Israel. These Judeans opted to remain in Jewish-Babylonian communities, the only home many of them had ever known. Those who remained will become significant later in our study as we investigate the geopolitics of the Near East in the twentieth century.

Greek Empire

Following the invasion and occupation of the three regional Near Eastern empires—Assyrian, Babylonian, and Persian—the Near East was invaded and occupied by a series of foreign superpowers for a period of more than a thousand years, from the fourth century BCE to the seventh century CE. The first of these outside conquerors were the Greeks, who occupied the Near East from 333 to 64 BCE. The Greeks brought with them the Greek language and an enlightened culture—which included religion, medicine, athletic competition, the concepts of democracy and law, styles of architecture, art, and sculpture, and so on—known as Hellenism. Significantly for written history, the Greek language became the literary and learned language of the Near East. Greek enlightenment extended to the next foreign superpower to conquer the region, the Romans, and the sophisticated Hellenistic culture extended through the Greco-Roman civilizations.

Upon the death of the young Greek conqueror Alexander the Great in 323 BCE at the age of thirty-three, his empire was divided among his generals. The Seleucids ruled in Syria and Mesopotamia, and the Ptolemy dynasty ruled Egypt; these were known as the Seleucid and Ptolemaic Empires, respectively.

Hasmonean Dynasty

For parts of the first and second centuries BCE, Jews in the Land of Israel rebelled against and gained independent self-rule from the oppressive Seleucid Greek Empire. The revolt ushered in the Hasmonean dynasty that lasted from 166 to 37 BCE (129 years). The Hasmonean dynasty began as the Maccabean Revolt, named for its leader, Judas Maccabaeus. Hasmonean self-rule not only survived but thrived, and for the last twenty-six years of its existence, it overlapped and coexisted with the next foreign empire and regional superpower to invade and rule the Near East, the Roman Empire.[13]

Roman Empire

The Roman Empire controlled the Near East from 63 BCE to 313 CE. Rome was both a ruthless occupier and the Western world's most technologically advanced civilization to date. During Roman rule, Aramaic remained the lingua franca and Greek the educated written language. In 37 BCE, Rome appointed Herod the Great king over its Syrian province of Judea. Herod had been an ally of Rome and was rewarded for his loyalty and conquests. Although he claimed to be a Jew, the Jewish leadership rejected him because his mother was an Arab (Nabatean) princess. He was so eager to please Rome and his Jewish

---

[13] Many of Israel's professional athletic city teams today honor their Maccabean ancestors by naming their sports teams Maccabee Tel Aviv, Maccabee Jerusalem, Maccabee Haifa, and so on. An Israeli brewery also celebrates and commemorates this successful revolt and period of independent Jewish self-rule in the Land of Israel by honoring the Maccabees with an Israeli national beer called Maccabee Beer.

subjects that he embarked on a massive building campaign.[14] In an attempt to win over the Jews as their king, he rebuilt the Babylonian-destroyed First Temple of Solomon. He built it more splendidly and more opulently than the original, but the Jews still refused to accept his pedigree and continued to view him as a puppet of Rome.

In 66 CE, the Jewish leadership had enough of Roman oppression and began the First Jewish War/Revolt against Rome, which lasted four years until 70 CE Jewish rebels overran the Roman garrison in Jerusalem and slaughtered all its soldiers. When Rome heard of the revolt, it summoned its legions, headed by General Titus (later to become emperor), which descended on Judea and mercilessly slaughtered the Jewish rebels by the thousands. To show their ire over the revolt, Roman soldiers looted, tore down, and then torched Herod's Second Temple in Jerusalem. Temple treasures and Jewish prisoners were taken to Rome and paraded as a demonstration of total victory and the utter humiliation of the Jews.[15]

During the First Jewish War against Rome, an apocalyptic, messianic, monastic sect was living east of Jerusalem and south of Jericho in the Judean Hills, in the community of Qumran. Scholars believe that this monastic order transcribed and preserved hundreds of Jewish sacred texts and scriptures, which they hid in clay jars and placed in caves

---

[14] Herod's building campaign included the construction of a port city on the eastern Mediterranean called Caesarea Marittima, which had a population of forty thousand. He built it to honor Caesar Augustus, who appointed him king of Judea. The city was complete with a walled harbor, an amphitheater, a hippodrome, palaces, statues, and tributes to Roman gods and to Caesar. He also constructed palaces and fortresses throughout the province, including Masada on the site of an earlier Hasmonean fortress, Sebaste/Sebastia (the rebuilt and renamed city of Samaria), and Herodium, believed to be his resting place. Herod built a massive infrastructure of aqueducts, cisterns, and roads worthy of the Roman Empire that crisscrossed the province. Herod the Great should be identified historically as "Herod the Builder" or "Herod the Great Builder."

[15] Rome's victory over the Jews in the First Jewish Revolt is memorialized by a victory arch, the Arch of Titus, built at the entrance to the Forum in Rome. The Arch of Titus is like other empires' victory arches, such as the Arc de Triomphe in Paris. Carved at the top of the arch are depictions of artifacts looted from the temple in Jerusalem. Especially prominent is a large golden candelabra, which for centuries was the symbol of Judaism.

in the surrounding hills to protect them from the attacking Romans, who were killing, destroying, and burning everything in their path.[16]

Sicarii rebels, who had earlier overrun the Roman garrison at Masada and now controlled it, fled there with their families, numbering 960 people. Fearing the Roman onslaught, the rebels barricaded themselves into King Herod's desert mountain retreat of Masada, located due west of the southwestern shores of the Dead Sea in the Judean Desert. Herod the Great had built his Masada fortress and escape garrison/winter resort on the ruins of an earlier Hasmonean stronghold. It included a mosaic-floored palace, rainwater collection aqueducts, cisterns, and hot baths—all the amenities a king could want. The Sicarii rebels, who had fled with their families to Masada, held ten thousand Roman legionnaires at bay for three years, from 70 to 73 CE, until the Romans were able to retake the garrison. The Romans breached Masada's walls by spanning the valley between the Masada plateau and the neighboring hill by mounding earth and rocks, one bucketful at a time, and constructing an earthen ramp bridge. The Masada plateau rises to a height of 1,300 feet above the Dead Sea basin floor and was virtually impenetrable with its high, fortified walls. Before the construction of the earthen ramp, Masada was only accessible by a narrow, snaking path that could only accommodate single file.

The first century-CE Roman historian Flavius Josephus (37 to 100 CE), a Jew who was born Yosef Ben Mattityahu, provides the following account to the Masada narrative. Seeing that they were about to be overrun, the Sicarii rebels burned, destroyed, or threw out all valuables and food supplies, and the heads of households then killed everyone in their respective families. The remaining heads of households were

---

[16] Collectively, these earliest Jewish scriptures are known as the Dead Sea Scrolls. At the time of their discovery, the scrolls predated the earliest known Hebrew Bible (Old Testament) texts by one thousand years. They first of them was accidentally found in 1947 by a Bedouin shepherd boy looking for his stray goats when he threw a stone into one of the caves and accidentally broke a clay jar containing scrolls. Most of the scrolls were written on parchment, some were written on papyrus, and one was written on copper. The extreme aridity of the Judean Hills where the scrolls were hidden, plus the remoteness of the area, contributed to the scrolls' preservation and survival for nearly two thousand years.

killed by one, lone zealot, who was then to take his own life. This was preferable to being captured, tortured, and killed, their women being abused, and the survivors being taken as slaves and paraded in Rome. Critics of this theory charge that Josephus is the only source of this story, which does not receive even a passing mention in other Jewish writings of the day, and that Josephus wrote about it long after the event occurred. Some hypothesize that Josephus was that one, lone zealot who survived Masada and thus in his account revealed this plan, sometimes referred to as a mass suicide. There is another version of the story that claims ten rebels were chosen by lot to kill the 960, and then one of the ten was to kill the remaining nine and take his own life. In both scenarios, as narrator of this story, Josephus would have been the presumed sole survivor. Suicide is prohibited and considered sinful in Judaism, which is likely why only one person would have been expected to commit suicide in either case. If Josephus was in fact the remaining survivor in either scenario, he obviously did not take his life, and therefore no sin was committed. The victory was a hollow one for Rome, because Rome had nothing to show for its three-year-long effort—no prisoners, no loot, nothing. The fall of Masada in 73 CE signified the final chapter in the First Jewish Revolt against Rome. Today, units in the Israel Defense Forces (IDF) take their oath of service in a solemn ceremony on Masada and swear to defend the Jewish people to the death so that a Masada tragedy is never repeated. Their battle cry is "Remember Masada."

Jews and Romans always maintained an uneasy coexistence, which culminated in all-out warfare fifty-nine years after the end of the First Jewish War. In 132 CE, following years of guerrilla warfare between Jewish rebels and Roman soldiers, Jews launched the Second Jewish Revolt/War against Rome (132 to 135 CE) in response to severe religious restrictions placed upon them by Rome. This war, known as the Bar Kokhba Revolt, was named for its leader, Simon Bar Kokhba (Hebrew: Shim'on Bar-Khokhba שמעון בר כוכבא).

Early in this second revolt, Jewish rebels enjoyed initial success over Rome and controlled large areas of Israel and beyond. When news of this latest rebellion, defeat, and humiliation reached Rome, Emperor Hadrian's patience reached its limit, and he decided to put an end to the on-again-off-again Jewish uprisings. Hadrian dispatched his best generals from across the empire—which included Egypt, Britannia, and Germania—along with twelve legions (more than fifty thousand soldiers). They are said to have slaughtered six hundred thousand Jews and decreed that Jews would no longer be allowed to live in or even enter Jerusalem. Although most Jews who survived the Roman onslaught either were evicted or fled, there remained a scattered Jewish presence in the Land of Israel, but there was no longer Jewish political self-rule. This defeat and eviction of the Jews by the Romans formalized the nearly twenty-five-hundred-year Jewish Diaspora, the dispersion of Jews from the Land of Israel, which began with the Babylonian conquest of Judea in 586 BCE.

In an action not unlike those of some Egyptian Pharaohs who, wishing to erase all historical records of their rivals, chiseled their names off of monuments, statues, and stelae, Rome in 135 CE renamed the Land of Israel Palestina (Palestine) in an attempt to completely eradicate Jewish history from the Land of Israel and accentuate total Roman victory over the Jews. The new name was derived from that of Israel's ancient archenemy and nemesis, the Philistines. In addition to renaming the city of Shechem "Neapolis" (New City), commonly known today by its Arabic name, Nablis/Nablus, as discussed in chapter 1, Hadrian also destroyed Jerusalem, built a new city on its ashes, and renamed it "Aelia Capitolina." Obviously, the name *Jerusalem* survived even superpower Rome's attempt to eradicate it.

Notes

Abba Ebban, *Heritage: Civilization and the Jews* (Summit Books, 1984).

Abba Ebban, *My People: The Story of the Jews* (Berman and Random House Inc., 1984).

Hershel Shanks, *Ancient Israel: From Abraham to the Roman Destruction of the Temple* (Prentice Hall and Biblical Archaeology Society, 1999).

Orit Avnery, "How did the word "Jew" become the name most identified with the Jewish people," *Shalom Hartman Institute* (January 1, 2010).

Fergus Miller, *The Roman Near East, 31 B.C.-A.D. 337* (Harvard University Press, 1993).

G.A. Williamson, *Josephus-The Jewish War* (Hunt, Barnard & Co, Ltd, 1959).

G. J. Goldberg, "The Life of Josephus," *Josephus.org* (2012).

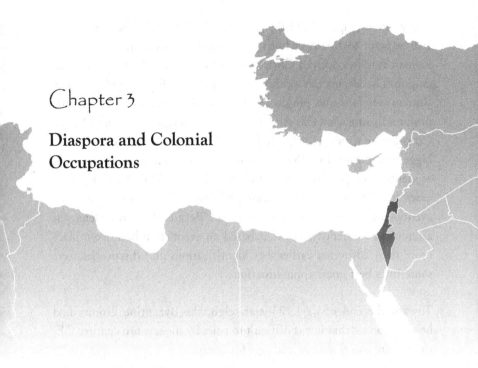

Chapter 3

Diaspora and Colonial Occupations

Byzantine Empire

The Byzantine Empire (Eastern Roman Empire) lasted from 330 to 1453 CE (1,123 years), making it the longest lasting Middle Eastern empire. Four events transpired in the fourth century CE that are credited with the rapid expansion of Christianity and the decline of the pagan old world. First, in 313 CE, Emperor Constantine embraced Christianity and decreed that Christianity was no longer illegal.[17] By so doing, he ended Christian persecution in the Roman Empire. Secondly, in 330 CE, Constantine moved his capital to Constantinople—present-day Istanbul, Turkey—from where he ruled the Eastern Roman Empire (Byzantium) following the split of the Roman Empire into eastern

---

[17] The fourth-century-CE church historian Eusebius (Pamphilus) detailed Constantine's conversion to Christianity. Eusebius writes that before a critical battle with a rival emperor, Constantine saw a vision of the cross, and he saw the same vision again that night in a dream. The cross bore the inscription "in this sign you will be victorious." The next day, Constantine's army went to war under the banner of the cross and was victorious. Constantine immediately converted to Christianity.

and western empires. Thirdly, in 380 CE, Emperor Theodosius, the last emperor to rule over both the eastern and western halves of the Roman Empire, decreed Christianity to be the official religion of the empire. Theodosius was most instrumental in eradicating the old pagan Roman religions and promoting Christianity. The fourth event that profoundly impacted Christianity's presence and growth occurred when Constantine's mother, Queen Helena, became his first convert and biggest supporter. In 326 CE, Constantine commissioned his mother to identify and preserve Christian holy sites in the Holy Land. In many cases, her identifications were most probably the actual locations of the events, but this is not true in every case. Because Queen Helena was attempting to identify locations based on events that had taken place more than 250 years earlier, her identifications and discoveries were sometimes best-guess approximations.[18]

Toward the end of its 1,123-year reign, the Byzantine Empire had become so vast that it was difficult to rule. By the seventh century CE, the empire was fractured and ripe for conquest.

Arab-Muslim Empires

Islam, the third monotheistic religion to come out of the Near East, began as a belief system promoted by its founder and prophet, Muhammad, but quickly developed into a militant movement and embarked on a military conquest. Muhammad's armies charged out of the Arabian Peninsula and began a three-phased regional and world conquest in the seventh century CE. The first phase was to capture, convert, and secure control over the Arabian Peninsula's numerous polytheistic Arab tribes and its Jewish population. This conquest

---

[18] Queen Helena is credited with identifying and enshrining Christian holy sites, including Golgotha, the location of Christ's crucifixion and burial, whereupon the Church of the Holy Sepulcher is built, the Mount of Olives, and the Garden of Gethsemane in Jerusalem; and Christ's birthplace in Bethlehem, now marked by the Church of the Nativity. By building shrines over Christianity's holy sites, Queen Helena not only identified these locations for the first time but preserved them for all time.

occurred during Muhammad's lifetime and continued after his death in 632 CE. Tribal warfare was a cottage industry in the Arabian Peninsula, where tribes fought one another for territory, power, control, and booty and competed for the desert's scarce resources. The second phase of the Islamic conquest was to attack the decaying Byzantine Empire and take control of the Near East, from Persia (Iran) in the east, to Egypt and Libya in the west. Jerusalem and Palestine fell to Muslim (Moslem) armies in 637 CE, and Cairo was conquered in 639 CE.

The third phase of the Muslim conquest extended the empire's frontiers to China in the east and to the Iberian Peninsula (Spain and Portugal) in the west, with battles taking place as far north as the middle of modern-day France. All this was accomplished within one hundred years of the death of Islam's prophet, Muhammad (632 to 732 CE), an impressive military conquest by any empire, previous or since. Islamic dynasties and power centers shifted from Arabia to Syria to Iraq to Spain and finally to Egypt and ruled from 632 to 1516 CE, 884 years. Although the Turkish Ottoman Empire was the last nominal Islamic empire/caliphate to rule and controlled much of the Near East for four hundred years, from 1516 to 1918, its rule was primarily political in nature. Unlike previous Islamic Near Eastern caliphates, the Ottoman Empire was not a religious caliphate, and the ruling dynasty was not Arab.

Crusader Kingdoms

The Crusades were initiated in France by Pope Urban II, who called for Christian European armies to liberate the Holy Lands from Islamic Saracen domination.[19] By 1099, Crusader armies had conquered Jerusalem. Crusader kingdoms ruled and controlled parts of the Near East for almost two hundred years from 1099 to 1291, when they were finally defeated by Muslim armies. Crusader kingdoms were established

---

[19] *Saracen* was a generic term for Muslims used by the Crusaders; it derives from the Latin and Greek terms for people who lived in Arabia. Similarly, Arabs referred to all Crusaders as "Franks." The Crusades began in France, and most of the first Crusaders were French.

in Turkey, Lebanon, Syria, and Israel-Palestine. Although Byzantine Christians and Jews were not the original targets of the Crusades, many thousands of Eastern Orthodox Christians and Jews were slaughtered along the way as Western European armies traveled to the Near East. Jews were labeled "Christ killers" by Crusaders, and entire Jewish communities were wiped out. Jerusalem finally fell to Islamic armies headed by one of the most famous Muslim leaders, the Kurdish-Muslim general Saladin (Arabic: Salah ad-Deen al-Aiyoubi صلاح الدين الايوبي). Although Saladin was a strong and ruthless military commander, he was also known for his fairness and compassion. In addition to being a commander and a warrior, he was an administrator. When Saladin saw priests and monks from various Christian orders physically fighting over control of the key to the Church of the Holy Sepulcher in Jerusalem, the shrine built over the site of Jesus Christ's crucifixion and burial, he took the key away and gave it to the Nusseibeh family, a local Muslim family. For the past eight hundred years, control of the key that daily opens and closes the doors to the holiest shrine in Christianity has been passed down from generation to generation by this same Arab-Muslim family, which still controls it today.

At the end of the two hundred years of Crusader rule, many thousands of Western Europeans remained in the Near East, intermarrying with the local population and mixing their European DNA with the local gene pool. Generations of Crusaders and their descendants only knew the Near East as home. Their genetic markers can be seen today in the Arab populations of Lebanon, Syria, and Israel-Palestine, whose people often have light skin, blond or red hair, and blue or green eyes.

European Persecutions

Jews had been peacefully settled in European communities for centuries before they were subjected to discrimination and persecution, beginning with the Crusades. It is unclear what event triggered the collective hatred and persecution of European Jews, but it is possible that it began with the Crusader charge that Jews were "Christ killers."

28

Some believe that anti-Semitism began when Christian communities in Europe were prohibited from lending money for profit because of biblical usury law, after which Jews became more involved in banking.[20]

The persecution of Jews in Spain came to a head in 1492 during the Spanish Inquisition. The Inquisition began with Spanish church leaders giving Jewish citizens three options: First, Jews could confess their sins, convert to Christianity, and be baptized. If they refused to convert, the second option was for them to leave Spain with only the clothes on their backs and no compensation for their homes, property, businesses, wealth, and so on. The third option, if Jews refused either to convert or leave, was for them to be arrested and tortured (possibly killed) until they confessed to false charges and converted under duress. History records that some Jews converted, many fled to other European countries farther east—such as Italy, Germany, Austria, Turkey, Poland, and Russia—while others stayed, were robbed of all their wealth and possessions, and then were infamously tortured and often killed by the church/state.[21]

The next collective persecutions of Jews in Europe were the Russian and Eastern European pogroms (persecutions) of the late nineteenth and early twentieth centuries. These persecutions spread to parts of today's Russia, Ukraine, Poland, Belarus, Lithuania, and Moldova. The pogroms began with attacks on Jewish communities by peasants.[22]

---

[20] Because some European communities prohibited Christians from lending money for profit, they relegated banking transactions to their Jewish populations. It was therefore easy to treat Jews as scapegoats when loans could not be paid or when national and regional economies experienced downturns or failed. Ironically, biblical usury laws are all found in the Old Testament, the Hebrew Bible, and were originally directed as Jewish prohibitions.

[21] Historians believe that Queen Isabella and King Ferdinand's financing of Christopher Columbus's voyage to the New World was paid for in part with Jewish wealth confiscated during the Spanish Inquisition.

[22] Russian and Eastern European pogroms began with the anti-Semitic charge of "Christ killers" and grew to encompass horrific rumors of Jews kidnapping Christian babies and then boiling and eating them. The pogroms included the burning of Jewish businesses and homes, murder, rape, and the wholesale, random killing of entire Jewish communities. The largest single mass murder of Jews during the pogroms is believed to have taken place in the city of Odessa in 1905 when 2,500 Jews were killed.

Although it is still denied, there was often state-sponsored collusion or at least tacit government support for the pogroms. Governments enacted anti-Jewish laws restricting the movement, residency, and business dealings of their Jewish populations. The persecutions were part of the greater European anti-Semitic fervor of the time. While exact numbers were never recorded and are not available today, it is believed that Jewish murders during the Eastern European and Russian pogroms numbered in the tens of thousands. The Russian pogroms were significant in that they began the first modern-day immigration of European Jews to Palestine. The pogroms began a serious geopolitical discussion of Jewish self-rule, where Jews would be responsible for their own security and safe from the pervasive and growing European anti-Semitism and attacks. Jews migrating to Palestine initially established communal agricultural settlements and became the first modern-day Zionists.

Dreyfus, Herzl, and the Birth of Zionism

As seen above, anti-Semitism was pervasive throughout Europe in the late eighteenth and early nineteenth centuries. In 1894, a young Jewish artillery officer in the French Army, Captain Alfred Dreyfus, was patriotically serving his country when senior officers became aware that he was Jewish. They devised a plan to have him removed from the army by falsely charging him with giving French military secrets to Germany and accusing him of treason. He was arrested, imprisoned, quickly tried, and found guilty of all charges. Captain Dreyfus was stripped of his military rank and sent to prison. Press coverage of the trial revealed the sham of the baseless charges, and public outcry demanded his release. In 1899, he was retried, and the guilty judgment was upheld. The second guilty judgment brought even greater public condemnation in both France and abroad. Eventually, world outcry over this clear case of state-sponsored anti-Semitism forced France, in 1906, to overturn his two previous wrongful convictions and completely exonerate him. He was subsequently promoted to the rank of major, and his military career was restored. Dreyfus later served in World War I and retired with the rank of lieutenant colonel.

Attending the first Dreyfus trial was a Hungarian-Jewish journalist named Theodore Herzl (pronounced *hurt-zul*). Seeing the absurdity of the false charges against Captain Dreyfus and reacting to the growing anti-Semitism in Europe, Herzl wrote a book in 1896 titled *Der Judenstaat* (*The Jewish State*) in which he called for the creation of an autonomous, independent Jewish state. Herzl pointed out that ever since the defeat and eviction of the Jewish people from the Land of Israel by the Romans in 135 CE, Jews had been persecuted and killed simply for being Jews. He argued that Jews would only be safe when they became solely responsible for, and in control of, their own safety and destiny in their own country. He called for a Jewish country to be established in the Jewish ancestral home, Palestine. The publication of Herzl's book and his call for the creation of a Jewish state are credited with giving birth to modern political Zionism, and Herzl is recognized as the father of modern Zionism. The word *Zionism* is derived from Mount Zion, a mountain on which Jerusalem is built.

To move forward with the idea of creating a Jewish state, the Jewish Agency for Israel was created to collect money, purchase land in Palestine, and promote Jewish immigration. During this period, Palestine was controlled and ruled by the Ottoman Empire, which would soon be defeated by Great Britain and its allies in World War I. Jews now began immigrating to Palestine by the thousands, initially from Eastern and Western Europe. They established Jewish agricultural settlements on newly purchased land on the same model begun earlier by Russian and Eastern European Jews fleeing the pogroms. The land was purchased from local Arab landowners as well as absentee Turkish-Ottoman landowners. As these new immigrants began settling, it quickly became evident that, coming from numerous countries and speaking a multitude of different languages, they needed a single unifying language if they were to establish a successful, cohesive nation. After some discussion as to whether to choose German, Hebrew, or

Yiddish, Hebrew was chosen as the new lingua franca of the resurrected Jewish state.[23]

The problem with Hebrew was that it was an ancient language that had not been spoken for more than two thousand years and was only read in synagogues as a liturgical language by rabbis and Hebrew scholars. For the revival of the Hebrew language to succeed, new words had to be invented, and an educational system had to be developed to teach the new (old) language. A Jewish linguist and scholar by the name of Eliezer Ben-Yehuda is credited with establishing the basis for reviving ancient Hebrew and is honored as being the father of modern spoken Hebrew. Committees of Hebrew-language scholars were established to develop and articulate the new resurrected language from the ancient and long unspoken tongue. Hebrew-language schools were established throughout the Diaspora as well as in Palestine as Hebrew began to be taught to young children in Jewish Sabbath schools, similar to Christian Sunday schools.

---

[23] Yiddish is a hybrid language—a mix of Hebrew, German, Aramaic, and Slavic languages. It was developed and spoken by Eastern European Jews during the Diaspora. Sometimes today the term *Yiddish* is confused with and used as a synonym for modern spoken Hebrew. Ladino, also a hybrid language spoken by Sephardic/Spanish Diaspora Jews, was another language considered as the new spoken language for modern Israel.

Notes

Abba Ebban, *Heritage: Civilization and the Jews* (Summit Books, 1984).

Abba Ebban, *My People: The Story of the Jews* (Berman House Inc., and Random House Inc., 1984).

Sydney N. Fisher, *The Middle East: A History* (Knopf, 1960).

Arthur Goldschmidt Jr., *A Concise History of the Middle East* (Westview Press, 1983).

Corrie Ferguson and Amy Grupp, "Constantine and Christianity," *The Web Chronology Project* (2016).

Thomas Nelson, "Constantine and the Helena Churches," *The Bible Journey, New Century Version, Thomas Nelson Publishers* (2018).

Bernard Lewis, *What Went Wrong? Western Impact and Middle Eastern Response* (Oxford University Press, 2002).

"Timeline of Islam." *Religion Facts, Wikipedia* (November 22, 2016).

Chapter 4

World War I—British Mandate and Partition

World War I

During World War I, the Ottoman Empire, which had ruled much of the Near East, including Israel-Palestine, for the previous four hundred years (since 1516), sided with Germany and the Central Powers. The Central Powers lost to the Allied Western powers, which included the United States. The Ottoman Turks were routed from the Near East and created a new Turkish country in Western Anatolia from the ashes of their shrunken Ottoman Empire. The largely British-driven victory over the Ottoman Turks in the Near East is in part credited to a junior British Army intelligence officer, Lieutenant Thomas Edward Lawrence (usually written as T. E. Lawrence).[24]

---

[24] T. E. Lawrence is credited with organizing warring Arab tribes and convincing them to join British forces to evict the Ottoman-Turks from the Near East. Lawrence would later be immortalized by an American journalist, Lowell Thomas, as "Lawrence of Arabia." Before World War I, Lawrence had spent time in the Near East as an archaeologist and had become fluent in Arabic. During this time, he is said to have made the best maps of the region available to Great Britain at the outbreak of the war and to have been Britain's preeminent Near East

During World War I, Great Britain became either a signatory or a party to three conflicting agreements. These three agreements (technically two agreements and one understanding) have to this day had a profound impact on the map of the Near East as we know it and have been the cause of many of the conflicts that have plagued the region ever since. The agreements reflect Great Britain and France's desires to maintain their prewar strategic and economic foothold in the Near East and to remain players on the world scene.[25]

The 1915 McMahon-Hussein Correspondence

In 1915, during the British-Arab campaign to rid the Near East of the Ottoman Turks, the British high commissioner in Cairo (the senior political representative of England), Sir Henry McMahon, engaged in an exchange of letters with Sharif Hussein Ibin Ali, the emir of Mecca. These letters, later known collectively as the McMahon-Hussein Correspondence, involved a request made by Sharif Hussein (and agreed to by Sir McMahon speaking for the British Crown) that the Arabs be allowed to rule themselves in Arab lands once the Ottoman Turks were defeated and evicted. Great Britain, eager to enlist the help of the Arab armies to defeat the Turks, willingly agreed to Hussein's requests without detailing exactly how Arab rule would occur or which Arabs would rule which lands. While there was no formal agreement, statement, or declaration to come out of London, nor a signed document by either party formalizing the promises made in this correspondence, the understanding between the two men was clear and unimpeachable. In fact, most Arab-British dealings during the campaign over such things as weapons supplies, money payments,

expert. His biggest accomplishments were unifying the Arab armies and taking the Red Sea port of Aqaba from the Turks in an attack launched from the vast, empty Nafud Desert, a feat not believed tactically possible from that direction. Lawrence was an eccentric, a loner, and a showman.

[25] In the early twenty-first century, the Islamic State (ISIL/ISIS/IS) that was attempting to establish itself in Iraq and Syria called out France and Great Britain for creating Israel and artificial Arab states throughout the Near East in the Sykes-Picot Agreement, which is discussed later in this chapter.

gold transfers, training, and battlefield tactics, were conducted without a formal written agreement. All was done with a handshake, verbally, informally, and expediently.

The 1916 Sykes-Picot Agreement

As allies and world powers in World War I, France and Great Britain were interested in maintaining strategic and economic control over the Near East after the war ended. Contrary to the promises made by Great Britain to the Arabs in the McMahon-Hussein Correspondence, Great Britain and France secretly signed an agreement to carve up and rule the Near East after the war. The agreement was signed by the British foreign service officer and diplomat Mark Sykes and his French diplomat counterpart, Francois Picot (pronounced *pee-co*). The Sykes-Picot Agreement, known formally as the Asia Minor Agreement, called for France and Great Britain to carve up the Near East into separate French and British spheres of influence with full political and military control over what we know today as Lebanon, Syria, Israel-Palestine, Trans-Jordan (the area between the east bank of the Jordan River and Iraq), Iraq, and all lands to the Persian (Arabian) Gulf. The agreement was a formal (yet secretly signed) document drawn up with the full knowledge, backing, and understanding of the two governments. Sharif Hussein suspected the existence of a secret pact between France and Great Britain concerning the Near East but had no proof and received only denials when he questioned British officials. It is believed that T. E. Lawrence was also not read in on the agreement and was deliberately left out so that he could in good conscious deny any knowledge of a secret plan that contradicted the McMahon-Hussein Correspondence.

The 1917 Balfour Declaration

While speaking out of both sides of its mouth with the McMahon-Hussein Correspondence and the Sykes-Picot Agreement, Great Britain agreed to another earth-shaking, conflicting promise that would change the geopolitical direction of the region for the next hundred years. This third agreement produced at least five major wars and numerous minor ones that continue to plague the region to this day.

Zionist leaders were looking for a way to formalize and gain world support for their dream of creating a national Jewish homeland in Palestine after nearly two thousand years of the Diaspora. They approached numerous European leaders in hopes of receiving support for the establishment of a Jewish state in Palestine but were initially unsuccessful. However, when they approached the British government through the foreign secretary (secretary of state), Sir Arthur James Balfour, they received a receptive ear. After pleading their case, European Jewish leaders agreed to encourage Jews to enlist in Allied armies and join the fight against the Central Powers, and in exchange, Lord Balfour agreed that the British government would view with favor the establishment of a Jewish state in Palestine after the Ottoman Turks were evicted from the region at the end of World War I. This formal, written, and publicly announced British government document, which was to become official British foreign policy for the region, is known as the Balfour Declaration and was signed November 2, 1917.[26] Jewish leaders and Zionists the world over could not have hoped for a better outcome than the spirit and the letter of the Balfour Declaration. Jews throughout Europe and the United States began to enlist in Allied armies to fulfill their end of the bargain. The Jewish Agency began immediately collecting money from world Jewry and to plan worldwide Jewish immigration to Palestine, at first primarily from Europe. World War I ended with the defeat of Germany and the other Central Powers, including the Ottoman Turkish Empire, which was routed and evicted from the Near East.

---

[26] The exact text of the Balfour Declaration reads, "His Majesty's Government view with favour the establishment in Palestine of a national home for the Jewish people, and will use their best endeavours to facilitate the achievement of this object, it being clearly understood that nothing shall be done which may prejudice the religious and civil rights of existing non-Jewish communities in Palestine, or the rights and political status enjoyed by Jews in any other country."

In their excitement over their success in having obtained the promises contained within the Balfour Declaration, Jewish leaders and Zionists only focused on the first part of the declaration (see full text in the footnote above) and treated the declaration as though it ended at the first comma. It was not so much that they ignored the rest of the declaration as that they chose not to concern themselves with the details of the entire declaration. This is best seen in a slogan promulgated by the Jewish Agency which said that Palestine was "a land without a people for a people [the Jews] without a land." This statement was obviously only partially true, for at the end of World War I, there were approximately 740,000 non-Jews, primarily Arabs, living in Palestine. These Arabs were the "non-Jewish communities in Palestine" specifically addressed in the Balfour Declaration whose religious and civil liberties were not to be prejudiced. Jewish and British leaders minimized the significance of these indigenous Arabs and had no real plan for addressing the potential seriousness of what would happen to this "non-Jewish community" with the implementation of the Balfour Declaration.[27]

League of Nations and Mandates

At the conclusion of World War I, after seeing the horrors of modern warfare—brought about by the invention of new technologies like the machine gun, tanks, air power, and higher-yield explosives, all of which produced millions of casualties in a relatively short period of time—world leaders established the League of Nations to promote peace and reduce conflict. One of the first acts of the newly formed League of Nations was to recognize the Sykes-Picot Agreement by giving France and Great Britain a mandate to govern the region. This mandate was only to last until the newly freed Arab people in the former Ottoman Empire could govern themselves, at which time they would be granted independence. France and Great Britain quickly

---

[27] Of the 740,000 Arabs, 657,000 were Moslem, and 81,000 were Christian. There were at the time 59,000 Jews also living in Palestine, bringing the total Palestinian population to 797,000 people.

concluded that the Arab populations in these newly liberated lands were not ready for self-rule and that they would require time to mature and develop governmental institutions and governing skills. Self-governing skills had not been practiced by Arabs for four hundred years, since the Sultanates had last ruled in 1516, when the Turks conquered the Levant, Egypt, and the Hijaz, incorporating them into the Ottoman Empire. France was given a mandate over Syria-Lebanon, and Great Britain was given a mandate over the area from Palestine on the eastern Mediterranean to Iraq on the Persian Gulf. The League of Nations specifically stipulated that France and Great Britain would only have temporary custody of these regions and would not indefinitely possess them as colonies. These mandates were not time limited, however; they deliberately declined to stipulate end dates. France and Great Britain sent military forces to their respective mandated territories to establish authority and extend de facto colonial control over the area.

British Mandate and Arab Nationalism

Arab populations and leaders were understandably unhappy with the British promises contained within the Balfour Declaration, which would allow Jews to establish a Jewish state in majority-Arab Palestine. As Jewish immigration increased and the Jewish population of Palestine grew in the thirty years of the British mandate rule of Palestine from 1918 to 1948, Arab militias began attacking and killing Jewish settlers in hopes of discouraging continued immigration and preventing the eventual establishment of a Jewish state. Numerous massacres of Jews occurred in Jerusalem, Jaffa, Hebron, and elsewhere, only to be answered with counterattacks by Jewish militias, who began organizing armed defenses around Jewish settlements. These militias later became the basis of the Israel Defense Forces (IDF) that were established after Israel attained statehood. In addition to buying weapons on the international market whenever and wherever available, the militias began producing their own weapons and ammunition, a practice that led to today's huge and highly successful and profitable Israeli defense industries.

Arabs insisted that Great Britain hear their concerns and curb Jewish immigration into Palestine. In response to Arab demands and increased violence between Arabs and Jews, Great Britain issued the 1922 White Paper on Palestine, which limited Jewish immigration to Palestine to what amounted to fifteen thousand persons per year. As anti-Semitism grew in Europe, Jews began fleeing to Palestine in increasing numbers. To enforce the new immigration limitations, British naval forces blockaded the Palestinian coastline and would board and turn around ships with Jewish refugees trying to enter. From the Jewish perspective, although Great Britain had promised Jews that they could establish a homeland in Palestine, the White Paper was partially walking back this promise, and Great Britain was in fact militarily and politically siding with the Arabs against the immigrating Jews. In response, Jewish militias developed an elaborate underground network to breach the blockade and continue bringing in Jewish immigrants fleeing the Nazi death camps in Europe. British forces in Palestine became targets of Jewish militias, and lethal armed clashes became the norm between the two groups.[28] Arab-Jewish armed engagements also continued during this period and increased in lethality and frequency. Many uninformed Near East observers mistakenly characterize the Arab-Israeli conflict as one that has been raging for centuries with its roots in antiquity. The accurate historical reality is that this period in history, between the two world wars, is the genesis of today's Arab-Israeli conflict.[29]

During this period, the Arab world was becoming nationalistic and eager for self-rule. Majority-Arab Palestine was no exception, and Palestinian Arabs raised their voices for independence and self-rule. Palestine had just come out of four hundred years of Ottoman Turkish rule, was now under de facto British colonial rule, and faced a future

---

[28] Jewish-British violence reached its height in 1946 when the more militant Jewish militia, Irgun, blew up a wing of the King David Hotel in Jerusalem, which housed the British military headquarters, killing ninety-one people.

[29] Some wrongfully believe that the Arabs and Jews have been at war with one another for thousands of years. This is simply not supported by history. True, Arab-Muslim armies attacked Jews of the Arabian Peninsula who refused to convert to Islam and join Muhammad's army, just as they also attacked other tribes who refused to join Muhammad's cause. Arabs and Jews only began warfare in Palestine after the beginning of the British mandate period in 1918.

of being ruled yet again by foreigners emigrating, for the most part, from Europe. Palestinians were asking themselves and the world, When would they (Palestinians) get to rule themselves in Palestine, their home?

Modern Palestinian nationalism needs to be accurately identified in its historical reality. The reality is that there has never been Arab self-rule in Palestine, nor has there ever been a country called Palestine. Palestine was the name imposed by the Romans on the former Land of Israel and the name of the Roman province of Syria-Palestine. The last indigenous people to have had self- rule in Palestine were the Jews, who were exiled by the Romans in 135 CE. This notwithstanding, Arabs in Palestine, who later identified themselves as Palestinians or Palestinian Arabs, were now demanding that their national aspiration be heard. Arabs argued that the fact that a people, or their ancestors, lived in a land nineteen hundred years earlier does not today give them the right of ownership and the right to rule the current majority ethnic group living in that land. They argued that if this were to become accepted as new international canon (law), then world populations would be required to play musical chairs, as the descendants of former inhabitants would immigrate to take over their rightful inheritance and displace centuries-old established communities. Habitation, hegemony, and control of Palestine, both by local powers and by outside superpowers, had changed many times in the previous two thousand years.[30]

Nazism and the Urgency for Statehood

As clashes between Arabs, Jews, and the British continued to become the new normal with no solution to the British-created nightmare in Palestine in sight, Hitler and Nazism were coming to power in Germany, and persecution of Jews intensified as Hitler's armies conquered large

---

[30] Ironically, it was Jews living in Palestine during the British mandate years, 1918 to 1948, who identified themselves as Palestinians, not the local Arabs, who usually identified themselves as either Arabs, Syrians, or Syrian Arabs.

sections of Europe. Jewish escape from Europe had now become a matter of life and death as Nazism implemented its Final Solution to the Jewish Problem, extermination and genocide. Jewish underground militias were now more determined than ever to extricate as many Jews as possible from the clutches of the Nazi death camps and bring them to Palestine. Consequently, these Jewish militias became increasingly aggressive and more militantly confrontational against British forces in Palestine in their opposition to British immigration quotas and the blockade of Palestine's shores.

At the end of World War II, Great Britain, finding itself in a self-created, endless downward spiral that was getting worse with an ever increasing death toll on all sides, presented the United Nations with the "Palestine Problem." The United Nations, the successor to the failed League of Nations created after World War I, was formed at the end of World War II to resolve world conflicts peacefully and prevent war. Great Britain relinquished the Palestinian problem to the United Nations, saying that it (Great Britain) would honor whatever recommendation and solution the UN came to for Palestine. In 1947, the United Nations sent a commission of inquiry to investigate and assess the problem in Palestine and issue its findings. After investigating all aspects of the growing problem, the United Nations recommended the partition of Palestine into separate Arab and Jewish states. The demarcation lines would be drawn based on demographic concentrations of each population. The UN Commission on Palestine, as it was called, concluded that because of the deep Jewish, Christian, and Muslim connections to the city of Jerusalem, it would not be controlled by either Arabs or Jews after partition but would be "internationally administered" under a plan to be developed at a future date. The land of Palestine was to be divided with 54 percent going to the Jews and 46 percent going to the Arabs. Although over half of the area designated to become the Jewish state was situated in the barren Negev Desert, the Jews accepted the UN partition plan, reasoning that "something from nothing is something." The Arab state would encompass much of the north and the Galilee region; all of the fertile Jordan River Valley, including the West Bank;

the southern coastal area of the Gaza Strip; and a continuation of a strip of land south of the Gaza Strip between the Negev and Sinai Deserts. Arabs, both in and out of Palestine, resoundingly rejected the plan, demanding that all of Palestine be given exclusively to the local Arabs.

On November 29, 1947, the United Nations General Assembly passed resolution 181 approving the partition of Palestine into separate Arab and Jewish states (countries), to take effect in May 1948. Jews the world over were ecstatic, while Arabs condemned the vote and began arming themselves and calling for the annihilation of the Jewish state once it was established. On May 14, 1948, British forces in Palestine lowered the Union Jack, and the last British soldiers in Palestine set sail for England. On the same day, in a ceremony in Tel Aviv, David Ben-Gurion, executive head of the World Zionist Organization and chairman of the Jewish Agency for Palestine (and soon-to-be-elected first prime minister of Israel), declared the establishment of a national homeland for Jews in Palestine to be called the State of Israel. Immediately upon this declaration of statehood, Lebanon, Syria, Jordan, Egypt, Iraq, and later Saudi Arabia declared war on the new Jewish state.

Notes

Currivan, Gene. "Zionists Proclaim New State of Israel." https://www.nytimes.com/library/world/480515israeli-state-50. May 15, 1948.

"The Declaration of the Establishment of the State of Israel," *https://www.knesset.gov.il/ docs/eng/megilat-eng.htm* (May 14, 1948).

"1947: The International Community Says YES to the Establishment of the State of Israel,"

Israel Ministry of Foreign Affairs (2013).

Matti Friedman, *Spies of No Country: Secret Lives at the Birth of Israel* (Algonquin Books, 2019).

Alain Gresh and Dominique Vidal, "The New A-Z of The Middle East" (I. B. Tauris & Co. Ltd., 2004).

Held and Cummings, *Middle East Patterns: Places, People, and Politics* (Westview Press, 2014).

Bernard Lewis, *The Middle East: A Brief History of the last 2,000 Years* (Scribner, 1995).

Arthur Goldschmidt Jr., *A Concise History of the Middle East* (Westview Press, 1983).

Bernard Lewis, *The Arabs In History* (Oxford University Press, 1960).

Bernard Lewis, *Islam and the West* (Oxford University Press, 1993).

Bernard Lewis, *Islam and the Arab World* (Random House, 1976).

Phillip K. Hitti, *The Arabs: A Short History* (Princeton University Press, 1949).

Phillip K. Hitti, *History of the Arabs: From the Earliest Times to the Present* (MacMillan and Co. Ltd. 1953).

T.E. Lawrence, *Seven Pillars of Wisdom* (CSA Word Classic, 2009).

Bernard Lewis, *What Went Wrong? Western Impact and Middle Eastern Response* (Oxford University Press, 2002).

Chapter 5

Statehood, Nakbah, and Arab-Israeli Wars

Statehood and the Nakbah

Although the United Nations called for the creation of separate Arab and Jewish countries in Palestine more than seven decades ago, there has existed only a Jewish state in Palestine. The Palestinian Arab country never materialized because Arabs rejected the UN Partition Plan in favor of war to destroy Israel—"Drive the Jews into the [Mediterranean] Sea!" was the Arab call—and take all of Palestine for themselves. After nearly two thousand years of exile (Diaspora), Jews the world over were jubilant at the creation of a Jewish state in their ancestral homeland, the Land of Israel, while the Arab world referred to the creation of the State of Israel and loss of Palestine as the Nakbah, or catastrophe. Immediately upon Israel's creation and the outbreak of war between the Arabs and Israel, there occurred a virtual population exchange between Jews living in Arab lands and Arabs living in Israel. In anticipation of Israeli statehood, an estimated 30,000–50,000 Arabs fled areas designated for Israel, and over the next year, approximately 650,000 Arabs either were evicted or fled Israel to the surrounding Arab countries. Simultaneously, from 1948 to 1951, an estimated 800,000 Jews either fled or were evicted from Arab countries. After Israel's creation, descendants of generations of Jews who had lived in Muslim Arab lands for centuries and were for all practical purposes culturally Arabs (they spoke Arabic, ate Arabic food, sang and danced to Arabic music, and identified with the Arabic culture), were attacked by their Arab countrymen. Their homes, synagogues, and businesses were burned, women were raped, and many were murdered. Life was no longer safe for these Jews in Arab lands, as it was not safe for Jews in Nazi Europe. Similarly, many Arabs who were not evicted by Israeli forces fled willingly to the surrounding Arab countries, either because they did not want to live under Jewish-Israeli rule or out of fear for their and their families' lives. Some also fled because of encouragement from Arab leaders, who called for Palestine's Arabs to leave their homes and come to the surrounding Arab countries, promising that in a matter of weeks, the combined Arab armies would "drive the Jews into the sea" and Arabs would be able to return to their homes.[31]

Upon its creation, Israel was eager to welcome and absorb Jews from everywhere, especially Jews escaping persecution and death. Israel quickly absorbed 650,000 of the 800,000 refugees fleeing Arab countries. (The remaining 150,000 who fled Arab countries immigrated to Europe, the United States, and Canada). Absorption was not what waited Palestinian Arabs being evicted or fleeing from Israel. The creation of Israel and the aftermath of the first Arab-Israeli War produced an estimated 650,000 Palestinian refugees, a number equal to that of the Jews who fled Arab lands and came to Israel. However, unlike the Jewish refugees, the Palestinian refugees were

---

[31] Khalid al-Azm, the Syrian prime minister from 1948 to 1949, admitted in his memoirs that Arab leaders were partially to blame for the creation of Palestinian refugees because they (the Arab leaders) had encouraged Palestinian Arabs to leave their lands in Palestine that were designated for Israel.

not absorbed by the surrounding Arab countries but were confined to United Nations–run refugee camps.[32]

Israel's War of Independence

As noted above, when Israel declared independence on May 14, 1948, the surrounding Arab countries of Lebanon, Syria, Jordan, and Egypt, as well as Iraq and later Saudi Arabia, attacked Israel on all fronts. The combined population of these six Arab countries was over 30,000,000, while the Jewish population of Israel was 650,000. Arab armies were fighting to destroy Israel, while Israel was fighting for its very survival. Israel knew that if it lost the battle, all would be lost. After ten months of intense fighting and a series of failed cease-fires, the war ended with a final cease-fire/armistice that was signed in March 1949.[33] By the end of the war, Israel had increased the territory it controlled by 50 percent more than that granted to it by the UN Partition Plan. Jerusalem became a divided city, with Arab East Jerusalem held by Jordan and Jewish West Jerusalem held by Israel. After the war, Jordan annexed (made part of Jordan) all the territory allocated to the Palestinian state west of the Jordan River (the West Bank). This included East Jerusalem, which contained most of the holy sites of all three Abrahamic religions—Judaism, Christianity, and Islam—including the holiest site of Judaism, the Western Wall of King Herod's Temple (the Second Temple). Egypt controlled and annexed the Gaza Strip, which had also been designated to be part of the Palestinian Arab state. Palestinians

---

[32] One third of these refugees and their fourth-generation descendants continue to live in refugee camps in Arab countries surrounding Israel; others live in areas outside the camps, as well as in greater Damascus and Jerusalem. Their international status continues to be stateless refugees. Jordan is the only Arab country to provide a pathway to citizenship for Palestinian refugees. The United Nations estimates the total number of registered Palestinian refugees today to be five million.

[33] The five Arab countries' force contributions were as follows: Lebanon 2,000, Syria 5,000, Jordan 13,000, Egypt 20,000, and Iraq 15,000. Saudi Arabia, which had not formally declared war on Israel, also provided 3,000 fighters. By the end of the war, Arab armies and other militias fighting Israel totaled 64,000 soldiers.

ended the war with no land, no statehood, and nothing but promises from Arab leaders to resume the fight another day. Although they could have, after the war, Arab leaders chose not to create a Palestinian state out of Arab-held Palestinian territory. Palestinians who fled or were evicted before and during the war were not allowed by Israel to return to their homes after the war and became the original permanent Palestinian refugees discussed above.

Jordan's and Egypt's Heads of State

In 1951, Jordan's King Abdullah I was assassinated by a Jordanian national as he prayed in the al-Aqsa Mosque in Jerusalem because he was meeting secretly with Israeli government officials. He was succeeded by his son Talal (bin Abdullah), who served for only one year. Talal was discretely removed because of mental health issues and replaced by his nineteen-year-old son, Hussein (bin Talal), who reigned from 1951 until his death in 2000. Upon being crowned king, Hussein was the world's youngest monarch, and upon his death, he was the world's longest-reigning monarch. His youth and lack of experience notwithstanding, King Hussein proved to be a stabilizing force not only in Jordan but throughout the Near East. He was energetic and athletic, he raced cars and motorcycles, flew airplanes, and parachuted with his troops. King Hussein was much loved by his military and countrymen alike, all of whom were extremely loyal to his leadership. The king also had his enemies and survived numerous assassination attempts. Although it fought two major wars with Israel, through King Hussein's leadership, Jordan later became the second Arab country, after Egypt, to sign a peace treaty with Israel.

At the creation of the State of Israel, Egypt was ruled by King Farouk, the last of an Albanian dynasty that had ruled Egypt since 1800. In 1952, senior Egyptian military officers executed a bloodless military coup that overthrew King Farouk and ended the Egyptian monarchy. King Farouk was known by Egyptians as a playboy puppet of Great Britain who was only interested in the good life for himself and his close friends and not concerned with the welfare of Egypt and the Egyptian people. The senior Egyptian officers who effected the palace coup included Colonel Jamal (Egyptian pronunciation *Gamal*) Abdul al-Nasser. He became president of Egypt in 1955 and wasted no time in disrupting the status quo in this former colony of Great Britain and the no-war, no-peace stalemate between Israel and the Arab world. His charisma and persona would ignite newfound pride in people on the Arab streets, not only in Egypt but throughout the Arab world.

The 1956 Suez Crisis

In July of 1956, less than a year after ascending to the presidency, Nasser announced he was nationalizing the Suez Canal, declaring that it was the Egyptian Canal, not the British Canal. It had been built by the French in the 1800s and co-owned by France and Great Britain through the Suez Canal Company. Great Britain had military forces stationed on the canal not only to guard it but also to protect British monetary and strategic navigation interests. Until the end of World War II, Great Britain was a world colonial power and the world's maritime superpower. The Suez Canal was of utmost strategic importance for Great Britain, enabling it to quickly access its colonies in the Far East, as well as providing the Crown treasury with considerable revenue.

Nasser mobilized the Egyptian military to the canal and evicted British forces. Nasser then called on the Arab world to resume its fight with Israel, calling for the annihilation of the Jewish state and the restoration of Palestine to the Arab fold. He backed up his rhetoric and showed his resolve by mobilizing more than fifty thousand Egyptian troops in the Gaza Strip and on the Egyptian-Israeli border in the Sinai Peninsula, a force that included tanks, artillery, infantry, and aircraft. Additionally, he blockaded the Straits of Tiran, Israel's only southern water outlet from its port of Eilat. Nasser thrust himself into the Near East and world scene as a serious actor and instantly became the most popular Arab leader not only in Egypt but throughout the Arab world. He was charismatic, fearless, ambitious, and nationalistic, and he hit all the right chords in the Arab streets. Arabs were eager for bold new leadership after their humiliating defeat at the hands of Israel in 1948 and 1949 and the loss of Palestine. His speeches were electrifying, energetic, captivating, motivating, and unifying, and they sparked instant connection and enthusiasm throughout the Arab world. Overnight Nasser became the strongman of the Arab world.

In response to Nasser's nationalization of the Suez Canal, France and Great Britain secretly developed a military plan to retake the canal. The pact, which included Israel, called for the Israeli military to first attack Egyptian forces massed on and threatening its southern borders in Sinai, after which a joint Anglo-French airborne force would land on and retake the Suez Canal. On October 26, 1956, Israel began a full-border attack on the Egyptian forces poised to attack it in the Gaza Strip and on its southern border. Two days later, on October 28, France and Britain landed airborne troops north of the Suez Canal. In nine days, the Israeli military had defeated the massive Egyptian Army in the Sinai

Peninsula and the Gaza Strip, reopened the blockaded Straits of Tiran, and gained control of all the Sinai Peninsula to the Suez Canal. When US President Dwight Eisenhower heard of the Anglo-French landing, he was livid, because he had not been consulted or forewarned of the impending military action that threatened to destabilize the region. It was the middle of the Cold War, and Egypt was, at the time, a military client state of the Soviet Union. Russian president Nikita Khrushchev threatened to attack Europe with nuclear weapons if France, England, and Israel did not withdraw from the territory recently held by Egypt. It took a year, but eventually, Eisenhower persuaded the French and British to withdraw from Egypt, and the Suez Crisis/Sinai Campaign of 1956 was defused and resolved. Eisenhower was irate with the French and British for not informing him of their plans to land forces and retake the Suez, because during the Cold War, the world was one crisis away from nuclear apocalypse, with the Western powers led by the United States fighting against the Soviet Union and the Eastern Bloc nations. Eisenhower, who had been the supreme commander of Allied forces in World War II, was driven to defuse tensions and reduce the chances of a new world war.[34]

The issues between Israel and its Arab neighbors were more problematic. Israel's adversaries were poised on its borders, and Israel faced annihilation daily. With the capture of Sinai, Israel now had a peninsula-wide buffer zone between its population and the largest and most powerful Arab military force, Egypt. Understanding Israel's concern and wanting to defuse tensions, Eisenhower made Israel a historic and extremely attractive offer. Eisenhower told Israel that if it withdrew from the Sinai Peninsula, the United States would guarantee its security against its adversaries. The importance of this guarantee cannot be overstated, and it would have ramifications well into the future. With this promise, the United States, one of the world's two superpowers, had gone on record pledging to defend Israel against its enemies. Eisenhower had

---

[34] Before Nasser nationalized the Suez Canal and evicted British troops, Egypt was in the process of buying the canal. Eisenhower convinced Egypt to accelerate payments in exchange for a French and British withdrawal.

no intention of sending US troops, then or in the future, to fight on the battlefield alongside Israeli forces. He negotiated with the United Nations to establish the first ever international peacekeeping force, called the United Nations Truce Supervisory Organization (UNTSO). This UN peacekeeping force, armed only with small arms, binoculars, and radios, would monitor the situation and report on Egypt's and Israel's compliance with the disengagement agreement they had both signed. The disengagement agreement created a demilitarized zone, limiting the number of Egyptian and Israeli tanks, artillery, and troops that could be deployed within certain proximity of each other's border. The UNTSO was never intended to be a fighting force that would intervene militarily to prevent war. As a representative of the will of the international community, the UNTSO could at best only discourage war by its presence. It was nothing more than a truce observer, not a peacekeeper.

The 1967 Six-Day War

For the next ten years, there was no outbreak of major warfare between Israel and its Arab neighbors. On the surface, it appeared that the UNTSO was effective as a peacekeeping force and was in fact preventing war.[35] Conflict had not ceased, not because the Arabs and Israelis had decided against war or had signed a peace treaty but because they were not yet ready for war. All sides were arming, training, and planning for the next big engagement. Egypt and Syria, both on the forefront of the Arab confrontation states against Israel, were acquiring new state-of-the-art weapons and training from the Soviet Union, their arms benefactor. Jordan, which had been close to the British Crown since before it had achieved statehood, going back to the mandate years, was primarily armed and trained by Great Britain. However, being part

---

[35] Calling the UNTSO a peacekeeping force does not correctly describe its charter or capabilities. Its mission was only to stand guard between Israel and Egypt along their mutual border in the Sinai Peninsula and monitor the truce, not enforce the peace. The UNTSO did not have the manpower, weaponry, or legal authority to enforce the peace. It was only effective as a peacekeeper if both belligerent parties were willing for it to be so.

of the Arab world and one of the confrontation states that had fought Israel in 1948 and 1949, Jordan was very much in the pan-Arab camp and was committed to the Arab objective of warfare with Israel. The Israeli government purchased its arms from France and the United States, as well as from its own burgeoning arms-production industry.

From its strategic high ground in the Golan Heights, Syria for years routinely shelled Israeli farmers below as they plowed and worked their fields in the Galilee region of northern Israel. In response, Israeli farmers were forced to armor their tractors, leaving narrow observation cutouts/slits in the metal windshields and side metal panels. Israel is the only known country in history whose farmers were required to armor their tractors in order to safely work their fields.[36] Also, over the years, Syria had attempted to divert the waters of the Jordan River and its tributaries that flow south from Syria into Israel. These tributaries were the main water sources that fed the Sea of Galilee, Israel's primary and vital national freshwater reservoir. In response, the Israeli Air Force (IAF) attacked and halted the Syrian diversionary project.

In the spring of 1967, tensions escalated between Israel and its Arab neighbors. There were frequent cross-border skirmishes, and in May, the IAF shot down six Syrian Soviet-built MiG fighter aircraft in one engagement. In a bizarre move, and for reasons not altogether clear to this day—except perhaps that the Soviet Union wanted to agitate Israel, which was in the Western camp during the Cold War— Moscow falsely told Syria through the visiting speaker of the Egyptian Parliament, Anwar Sadat, that Israel was massing troops on its border. Syria investigated and reported to Moscow that it did not find any evidence of Israeli mobilization. The Soviets explained that Israel was mobilizing under the cover of night. When Moscow continued to promote this false scenario, Syria felt compelled to mobilize army units onto the Golan Heights on Israel's northern border. These events began an unstoppable march toward war that would soon ignite and engulf

---

[36] These tractors are on display today in northern Israel as reminders and monuments of this historic period and of the strategic importance of the Golan Heights to Israel's security.

the entire region and whose outcome and repercussions are felt to this day, over a half century later.

As tensions between Israel and Syria intensified, Egypt, Syria, and Jordan concluded that the time was right to renew active warfare against Israel. Arab political and military leaders believed their forces were ready to take on and defeat Israel and usher in a Palestinian Arab state. To this end, Egypt, Syria, and Jordan, signed a mutual defense agreement, which stated that if hostilities broke out between Israel and any one of the signatories to the pact, the other two countries' militaries would come to the defense of their Arab ally and join the fight against Israel.

Further escalating tensions, Egypt's President Nasser informed the United Nations that he was dismissing UNTSO from Egyptian territory, demanding their immediate departure. As he had done in the 1956 Sinai/Suez Crisis, Nasser again closed the Straits of Tiran to Israeli shipping by imposing a naval blockade. Israel warned Nasser that under international law, naval blockades were an act of war, and by imposing one, Egypt would in fact be firing the first salvo in a new war. Israel stated that any military action it would then take would be defensive and justifiable. Egypt's President Nasser scoffed at the Israeli charges and, in a broadcast, declared that he welcomed war with Israel. Finally, with no attempt to conceal their actions or intent and in full view of the international press, Egypt, Syria, and Jordan fully mobilized their militaries, which were several hundred thousand strong, and announced that a war to exterminate Israel would soon be launched.[37]

In response to Syria mobilizing forces on its northern border, Egypt's naval blockade of the Straits of Tiran, the signing of the joint Egyptian-Syrian-Jordanian Mutual Defense Pact, and total Arab force mobilization, Israel mobilized its reserves and prepared

---

[37] At the outbreak of hostilities in 1967, Israeli forces numbered 264,000, with 300 combat aircraft and 800 tanks. The Egyptian forces facing Israeli on its southern border comprised 100,000 troops, and the total Egyptian, Syrian, and Jordanian forces facing Israeli totaled 340,000 fighters, 950 combat aircraft, and 2,500 tanks.

for war with its neighbors.[38] Most of Israel's fighting force is made up by its reserve forces. Israel maintains a relatively small standing military and depends completely on the strength of its reserves when it goes to war. Since private citizens make up the backbone of Israel's economy, after mobilizing its reserves, the Israeli economy comes to a standstill. Economically, Israel cannot afford to have its reserves called up for an extended period and engage in a long, drawn-out war. It is a small country wedged between the Mediterranean Sea and Arab countries bent on its destruction and has no geographic depth into which it may strategically fall back to assume a new defensive or offensive warfighting position. Neither Israel nor any other country with similarly limited narrow geographical features could then or can today survive a prolonged conventional defensive war. In 1967, Israel was outnumbered by its adversaries by a margin of twenty to one. If it hoped to survive, Israel would have to wage a quick, hard-hitting offensive war aimed at taking away its enemies' ability to wage war against it. This was the stark reality of the third Arab-Israeli War.

Israel had known that a third war with its neighbors was inevitable and had been preparing for it for years. Although Israel's first line of defense, its air force, is not the biggest air force in the region in terms of numbers of aircraft, it proved itself in 1967 the most capable air force in the region, and it remains so today. Israeli pilots had practiced their tactics for years and knew their precise times over targets assigned to them at the outbreak of hostilities. Egypt, which had the largest and most powerful of the Arab militaries, was Israel's primary concern and would therefore be its first target. Israeli intelligence knew that Egypt's radars were pointed toward Israel both from Egyptian airbases in Egypt on the African continent and from Egyptian air bases in the Sinai Peninsula. Israel's intelligence also knew the schedules of all Egyptian squadrons, including when they rotated shifts, the times when radars

---

[38] At eighteen years old, I witnessed the events of the Six-Day War firsthand. As I walked the ghostlike streets of Tel Aviv and Haifa in the week prior to the war, the absence of military-age men and women was immediately obvious, eerie, and ominous. I had never seen Israel like this before. Although I daily heard and saw the country preparing for war, the reality of the drumbeat march to war now took on a more serious and imminent reality.

were shut down for maintenance, and even the details of when aircrews ate their meals and stood down for the call to prayer.

In the weeks leading up to war, Arab militaries could see Israel's defense forces wound like a spring with their fingers on the triggers, ready to strike. After Israel determined that war was inevitable, knowing it had to preempt and go on the offensive, it devised a deceptive plan to lull Arab leaders into believing that war was not imminent to lower its adversaries' guard. For weeks leading up to the war, the Israeli chief of staff, Yitzhak Rabin (pronounced *yits-Hak ra-been*) had not left the Ministry of Defense building in downtown Tel Aviv. To gain maximum surprise, Israel announced the weekend before its preemptive attack that its chief-of-staff had gone home for the night to be with his family and backed it up with press reporting showing his car parked at his residence for the first time in weeks. Israel's Defense Ministry also announced that it was releasing thousands of reservists to go home for the weekend. Thousands of military reservists were seen for the first time in weeks walking the streets of Tel Aviv and other cities, enjoying life as usual in restaurants, at theaters, and with their families. As discussed in a footnote above, until this time, Israeli city streets had been devoid of military-age men and women between the ages of eighteen and fifty-five.

On the morning of June 5, 1967, Israel launched a preemptive defensive military action to free itself from the encircling Arab armies, who were bent on its destruction. At 7:50 a.m., IAF jets began hitting Egyptian Air Force (EAF) targets in Egypt and the Sinai Peninsula. The first wave of Israeli fighters cratered Egyptian runways so that planes could not take off, after which fighter-bombers attacked Egypt's aircraft on the ground. The timing of this attack was chosen because Israeli military intelligence had been observing EAF operations for years and knew that at this precise time, there would be a major shift change on Egyptian bases, Egyptian aircrews would be having breakfast, and Egyptian radars would be down for maintenance. The IAF tactic was to attack Egyptian airfields out of the west, not the east—the direction from which they were expected to attack and toward which Egyptian radars were oriented. To do so, IAF pilots headed west out of Israel over the Mediterranean Sea, flying approximately one hundred feet above the waves to evade Egyptian radar, turned south into Egypt, and then finally turned east and attacked Egyptian airfields from the west, the Egyptian radars' blind side. By so doing, the IAF destroyed 90 percent of Egypt's Air Force on the ground before it could react and be a threat. After eliminating the main threat, the IAF concentrated on the Syrian Air Force (SAF), using the same tactics of first cratering the runways and then attacking aircraft on the ground. As a signatory to the tripartite defense pact, and in reaction to the outbreak of hostilities, the Jordanian Air Force (JAF) attempted to engage the IAF, but it too was quickly destroyed. Within the first two hours of the first day of the war, the IAF had virtually neutralized the EAF, and by midday, Israel had taken out virtually all the Egyptian, Syrian, and Jordanian air forces. There were some Arab fighter aircraft that took off to engage the attacking Israeli fighters, but with their much-diminished numbers, they proved no match for the IAF, which by this time enjoyed air supremacy over the skies of the Near East.

With the IAF in total command of the skies, the Israeli Army could now begin an all-out, protected ground attack against Arab forces. Because Egypt was Israel's biggest threat, Israel concentrated first on attacking the Egyptian Army massed on its borders in Gaza and Sinai. The Israeli Army, with tanks and artillery and now supported by air power, began a relentless, dismantling assault on the Egyptian Army. From the outset, the assault was very much one-sided, and the Egyptian Army began a hasty retreat westward toward the Suez Canal and Egypt. Over the next several days, as the Israelis routed the Egyptian Army and drove it across the Suez Canal, there was some attempted Egyptian tank and artillery resistance but nothing credible.

Having ensured that the Egyptian forces on the southern front were no longer a threat, Israel directed its energies to dismantling the Syrian Army on its northern front. Israel began an all-out assault on Syrian forces, who were well dug into hardened bunkers on the Golan Heights. Israeli tanks, artillery, and infantry, supported by total air supremacy, began a vicious attack on the Syrian Army. After some heavy fighting, the Israeli Army began to rout the Syrian military, as they had done in the south with the Egyptian Army. Eventually, Israeli forces totally defeated the Syrian Army, and the surviving Syrian forces fled east toward Damascus. By the time of the cease-fire on the sixth day of the war, Israel had taken all of the Golan Heights from Syria and had decimated Syria's army and air force.

Israel's fight against Jordanian forces was less of a straightforward military engagement. In compliance with its obligations under the Mutual Defense Pact, as soon as hostilities began between Israel and Egypt to the south and Syria to the north, Jordanian forces began indiscriminate tank and artillery shelling of Israel's West Jerusalem in the center of the country. Remember, Jerusalem was a divided city, with Israel holding the western half and Jordan holding East Jerusalem and all the West Bank, after having annexed these territories in 1949. During the first day of the war, the Israeli military was totally occupied with Egypt and Syria and did not have the manpower to open a third front in the center of the country with Jordan. Through diplomatic channels and repeated radio broadcasts, Israel admonished Jordan to stop its shelling of West Jerusalem, stating that Israel's fight was not with Jordan and that if Jordan stopped its attack on Israel, no harm would come to it. Unfortunately for Jordan and King Hussein, in accordance with the conditions of the Mutual Defense Pact, Jordanian forces were placed under the command of an Egyptian general, who insisted that Jordanian forces keep up the attack on Israel in hopes of diverting Israeli forces to the Jordanian front, thus relieving the pressure on the Egyptian forces, which were coming under heavy Israeli attack. Incredibly, even though he was in theory the commander of his country's military, the king was no longer in command of his military. In an interview after the war, King Hussein admitted that he knew early on that the fight against Israel was hopeless and that the Arabs would be defeated.

As the first day of fighting turned to night, Jordanian forces under Egyptian command continued shelling West Jerusalem. Because Jordan would not stop its attack, Israeli infantry, tanks, and artillery, supported by paratroopers redirected from the Egyptian front, began an assault on Jordanian forces, both in East Jerusalem and along the West Bank border with Jordan.

During the first day of the war, aside from broadcasting calls for Jordan to stop its assault on West Jerusalem, Israeli radio maintained total news silence on the progress of the war. Israeli radio only played marshal music. By contrast, Arab radio broadcasts were interrupting their steady stream of marshal music to claim great air and ground victories against Israeli forces. No one in Israel outside of the military was privy to the reality of what was happening on the battlefield. Egyptian radio was falsely claiming to have downed numerous Israeli aircraft and reporting that its forces had broken out of the Gaza Strip and were marching on Jerusalem. Egyptian radio warned the Israeli public that its leaders were taking it down the path of death and destruction and admonished Israelis to turn on their leaders while there was still time. It soon became evident to Arab leaders that their broadcasts were failing in their purpose, but they continued with the broadcasts for local Arab-street consumption and to keep from demoralizing their remaining fighting forces.

On the second day of the war, the world woke up to a vastly different and contradictory reality revealed by the Israeli government. Israeli radio broke its silence with reports of unimaginable battlefield victories that totally contradicted the previous day's Arab claims. To the ignorant public, these announcements initially appeared to be at a minimum an over exaggeration following the sweeping claims of Arab broadcasts the day before. Although there might have been cautious confidence in Israel's military leaders before the outbreak of hostilities, the world could not imagine tiny Israel achieving such a total victory over its overwhelming adversaries in such a short time.[39]

On the third day of the war, confident that the southern Egyptian front was under control, Israel diverted paratrooper units from Sinai to join the battle for Jerusalem. Because of the high concentration of religious sites revered by Judaism, Christianity, and Islam, Israel could not engage in an all-out, scorched-earth assault with heavy weapons on Jordanian positions in Jerusalem. Israeli forces fought house to house, street to street, and neighborhood to neighborhood in extremely fierce and bloody fighting during the battle for Jerusalem.

On June 8, 1967, the fourth day of the Six-Day War, an event occurred that has not yet been fully explained to the satisfaction of many. The United States was operating a signals intelligence collection ship, the USS Liberty, off the northern coast of Egypt's Sinai Peninsula, where Egyptian forces were coming under heavy Israeli air and ground attack as Israeli forces raced toward the Suez Canal. On this fateful day, Israeli fighter aircraft and naval torpedo boats began a merciless assault on this unarmed, noncombatant US naval ship that left 34 American sailors dead and 174 injured. The US and Israel subsequently conducted investigations into the incident, the details of which remain classified to this day. Israel claimed that the attack was a tragic case of mistaken identity due to the fog of war. One alternative explanation is that the error occurred during and after a shift change between two Israeli general officers and their staffs in Israel's war room command center. The incoming commander and his staff cleared the positions of the previous shift's maps, which had identified all known ships off the Sinai Peninsula, and incorrectly repositioned vessels on the new maps, identifying the USS Liberty as an Egyptian trawler. US naval personnel

[39] In an attempt to save face in the Arab world after he realized his military and that of Syria and Jordan were being decimated at the hands of a smaller number of Israelis, President Nasser of Egypt convinced King Hussein of Jordan in a secret telephone call to issue a joint statement accusing the United States and Britain of fighting with the Israelis against the Arabs. King Hussein balked at Nasser's insistence on implicating the British, with whom he had excellent ties, but eventually relented. Israeli intelligence intercepted this phone conversation and made it public to the international media.

who were on board the USS Liberty testified that the Liberty was flying the US flag and that the ship's name was clearly visible on its hull. US sailors claimed that before beginning their attack, Israeli fighter aircraft flew over the vessel and could easily identify it as a US Naval ship. The official US position is that it accepts Israel's explanation. Like the Israeli investigation, the US investigation remains unavailable for public examination. In addition, USS Liberty personnel are prohibited from discussing the incident.

Some have claimed that Israel understood that the ship was a US signals intelligence collection platform and deliberately attacked it because the US was intercepting communications that incriminated the Israeli military in killing Egyptian prisoners of war. But even if for the sake of argument, we were to assume that this unsubstantiated claim is true, what benefit would Israel derive from attacking the USS Liberty after the fact for collecting and transmitting this intelligence? This, together with the fact that the US is Israel's strongest ally and need not be provoked, leaves no rational explanation as to why Israel would deliberately attack a US Naval vessel. The US and Israeli governments, eager to put this dark chapter behind them, remain silent on the matter. Not so the surviving crew members of the USS Liberty. Every year on the anniversary of the attack, its surviving crew gathers to memorialize their fallen brothers.

After six days of fighting, the Arabs agreed to a cease-fire (armistice) but not before suffering an overwhelming, humiliating defeat.[40] Within six days, the small Jewish state had destroyed three large, well-equipped, and well-trained Arab armies and air forces. Although the actual fighting during the Six-Day War only involved the Arab armed forces of Egypt, Syria, and Jordan, the fight had pan-Arab support. In the weeks leading up to the war, hundreds of thousands of Arabs took

---

[40] War casualties for the Arabs included more than 23,000 killed, 35,000 wounded, and 5,400 captured, in addition to 600 tanks and 450 aircraft destroyed. Israeli casualties included 700 killed, 4,500 wounded, and 15 captured, as well as 45 aircraft and 20 tanks destroyed. During the war, ships were sunk in the Suez Canal, which closed the canal for years to come. As a result, a huge source of revenue for Egypt was now lost.

to the streets in Beirut, Damascus, Baghdad, Amman, Cairo, and other cities across the Arab and Islamic world to show solidarity and support and encourage Arab armies to annihilate Israel. Saudi Arabia pledged money toward this end, and Iraq was in the process of sending ground forces and equipment to the fight.[41]

Post Six-Day War Israel with the Sinai, the West Bank, and the Golan Heights.

---

[41] The duration of the war was so short that before Iraqi forces could reach the battlefield, the war had ended. The Iraqi Air Force had attempted to engage the Israeli Air Force with MiG fighter aircraft but were shot down over Jordan before reaching Israeli airspace and never posed a serious threat to Israel thereafter.

The war quadrupled the land area Israel controlled. Israel now had possession of all the Sinai Peninsula to the Suez Canal, including the Gaza Strip, which had been under the control of Egypt, and all of the West Bank (Judea and Samaria), which had belonged to Jordan. They had also wrested control of east Jerusalem from Jordan, giving them total control over the city, and all the Golan Heights from Syria. The new de facto boundaries would change the geopolitics of the region for the next half century and beyond. This latest war did not solve anything in the long term but only gave Israel a sense of short-term security. The Palestinian and now pan-Arab-Israeli problem continued to be a stalemate. Hatreds and animosities were only exasperated and perpetuated by this latest war and caused both sides to dig their heels in even deeper. After the war, Israel declared Jerusalem to be its reunited, eternal Jewish capital, never to be divided again. Israelis were as exuberant as Arabs were humiliated and deflated. There was in Israel a palpable, euphoric sense of invincibility, a new pride that was also felt by world Jewry. Comparisons were made following the war between young Israel and King David, who had slayed the mighty Goliath of biblical legend. For the first time in nearly two thousand years, all of Jerusalem was in Jewish hands. Jews could now pray on the Temple Mount, Judaism's most sacred site, which was the location of the Western Wall of King Herod's Second Temple and the site of King Solomon's First Temple. Access to these sites had been denied to Jews for nineteen years, ever since Israel had attained statehood in 1948 and East Jerusalem fell into Jordanian hands. This was Israel's finest hour.

For Arabs, it was the total opposite. There was a realization on the Arab street with this latest humiliation that Israel, which had achieved an overwhelming victory in six days, was here to stay. It was obvious that while Arab states had been building up their militaries and threatening Israel with total annihilation, the Israeli government and military had been taking Arab threats seriously. Israeli generals had been planning the only strategy with which Israel could survive a multifront war against overwhelming odds—one based on good intelligence, strategic deception, surprise, and a crushing, hard-hitting, preemptive first-strike offensive that would take away its adversaries' offensive capabilities.

Arabs were once again humbled by yet a third and more total defeat at the hands of the tiny Jewish state. The first, which began the Nakbah, was the 1947 United Nations vote that created the Jewish state, the defeat in 1949 of the combined Arab armies, and the creation of Palestinian refugees during Israel's War of Independence. The second was the crushing defeat of the Egyptian Army in 1956 during the Suez Crisis in which Israel captured all the Sinai Peninsula. The third was the defeat they had suffered during their recent attempt to annihilate Israel during the Six-Day War, which had resulted in the complete destruction of three of the Arab world's most powerful militaries. The Nakbah had now become a pan-Arab, head-bowing dishonor and shame, which in the Arab psyche could only be avenged by yet another war.[42]

For a short time immediately after the war, Israel was receptive to the idea of returning all the lands it had captured—Sinai from Egypt, the Golan Heights from Syria, and the West Bank (minus reunited Jerusalem) from Jordan—in exchange for peace treaties declaring nonbelligerency and an end to the Arab call for Israel's destruction. Sadly, this was not to be. The twenty-two nations of the Arab League met in Khartoum, Sudan, in August 1967 with three pressing items on their agenda: Israel, the recent defeat, and a unified next course of action. At the conclusion of its conference, the Arab League issued its famous (infamous) "Three Nos" declaration: no to Israel, no to negotiations, and no to peace.[43] The opportunity to end the cycle of

---

[42] Three years after the humiliation of the Six-Day War, on September 28, 1970, Egypt's President Nasser died of a heart attack. Some claim that he died of a broken heart because he could not regain the Sinai Peninsula and restore honor to his people. Nasser was replaced by his vice president, Muhammad Anwar Sadat.

[43] As previously mentioned, I witnessed the Six-Day War from central Israel about a mile from no-man's-land and the Jordanian border. I fully expected to see the Jordanian Army come across the border in an attempt to cut Israel in two and divide its strength at its narrowest point (only nine miles wide) where I lived. By the end of the war, I was idealistic and naive and thought that surely now there would be peace between Israel and its Arab adversaries. Seeing the total

war quickly vanished. This third war had only reinforced animosity and provided new reasons for hate and calls for revenge, retribution, and more war.

In an attempt to resolve the perpetual cycle of warfare in the Near East, the United Nations passed Resolution 242 calling on Israel to withdraw from Arab lands captured during the war in exchange for peace treaties by the Arabs and Arab recognition of Israel's right to exist—"Land for Peace," as it became known. With the Arab League's Declaration of the "Three Nos," this resolution was stillborn and today sits on the table of what could have been. Israel and the Arabs were no closer to coming to an understanding about how to live in peace as neighbors in the Near East, nor were they seriously working to resolve their conflict and their deep-rooted mutual animosity. The Arab world and Israel were now further than ever from reconciliation. New borders and new regional geopolitics had created new conditions and new "facts on the ground." If the warring parties did not quickly take advantage of the new realities, conditions for peace would become even further out of grasp and unattainable. Unfortunately, that is precisely what occurred.

Shortly after the 1967 War, Arab governments asked France to stop selling Israel the Mirage-3 fighter aircraft. Arabs partially blamed their defeat in the Six-Day War on this French-built, state-of-the-art, supersonic, delta-winged aircraft, built by the French Dassault Aircraft Company. Arab governments threatened to boycott French goods if France continued selling the Mirage to Israel. Recognizing the economic benefits of selling to fifty million Arabs versus two million Israelis, the French government of Charles de Gaulle capitulated and agreed to stop the sale of the Mirage to Israel.[44]

Arab humiliation and the incredible strength of the IDF, I could not imagine that Arabs would want to continue the fight with Israel and risk yet another future humiliation. I was wrong.

[44] France also announced that it would stop the sale of fifty more advanced Mirage-5 fighter aircraft to Israel, even though Israel had already completed payment for this new contract. The French government announced it would reimburse Israel for the cancelled aircraft sale. A conflicting rumor stated that France had secretly shipped the fifty contracted and paid-for Mirages in inconspicuous crates to Israel. The Mirage-5s were currently in production and Israeli pilots were undergoing predelivery flight training. In a scenario worthy of a Cold War

Israel needed to make up for the loss of a source of advanced fighter aircraft and looked to the United States. Although the Mirage-5 was a new-generation, supersonic, state-of-the-art fighter aircraft, the Johnson administration, after much debate in the US Congress about introducing such an advanced aircraft into the Middle East, agreed to sell Israel the McDonnell Douglas F-4 Phantom aircraft, which had only recently been delivered to US and NATO air forces. Many argued that the F-4 and Mirage-5 fighter aircraft were in fact comparable next-generation aircraft and that the sale of the F-4 to Israel would not tip the balance of power in the region. In a turn of events, the French later sold the Mirage-5 to numerous Near Eastern countries, including Egypt.

As a footnote to the new regional geopolitics, ever since Israel took the West Bank and the Gaza Strip from its Arab adversaries in the Six-Day War, Arabs have insisted that Israel give these territories to the Palestinians for the creation of a Palestinian Arab state. Ironically, every day for the nineteen years before the war, from 1948 to 1967, when Arabs held all these territories, they could have given them to the Palestinians for the creation of an independent self-ruled Palestinian county but chose not to. Instead, Arab governments had annexed these territories that they were now insisting Israel give to the Palestinians (Jordan had annexed the West Bank, including East Jerusalem, and Egypt had annexed the Gaza Strip), while for nineteen years daily threatening to annihilate the Jewish State.[45]

Since Israel's new de facto boundary with Egypt was now the Suez Canal, Israel built massive defenses on the east bank of the canal. These

---

novel, Israeli pilots plotted to fly some Mirages out of France to Israel, but the French became suspicious when the Israelis requested additional long-range fuel tanks for winter "training" and thwarted the plot. More importantly, the Mossad, Israel's preeminent spy agency, was able to steal blueprints for the advanced Mirage-5, and by 1971, Israel was producing indigenous fighter aircraft that looked suspiciously like the Mirage-5: first the Nesher (Eagle) and then the Kfir (Lion Cub).

[45] Although accurate figures are difficult to find and vary widely depending on the source, the Six-Day War added between 280,000 and 325,000 new Palestinian refugees, according to the United Nations Relief and Works Agency for Palestine (UNRWA).

defenses included bunker fortifications every three miles on top of sixty-five-to-eighty-foot high sand embankments/berms that spanned the ninety-three-mile length of the east bank of the Suez Canal. These defenses were called the Bar-Lev Line, named for their architect, Israel's then chief of staff, Haim Bar-Lev. The IDF believed this impressive defensive system to be impenetrable to Egyptian attack and believed it would give Israel two to four days' advanced warning should the Egyptians attempt an assault. This advanced warning time would allow Israel to bring its military force to bear and defeat an Egyptian attack before it could succeed.

In addition to the usual conventional threats from its Arab neighbors, Israel faced a growing new random threat. During the late 1960s, 1970s, and 1980s, the Palestine Liberation Organization (Arabic: Harakat Tahrir Falasteen حركه تحرير فلسطين) stepped up its cross-border hit-and-retreat guerrilla attacks on Israel from Lebanon, Syria, and Jordan. The Palestine Liberation Organization (PLO) also attacked Israeli targets of opportunity throughout the world and hijacked international air carriers with Israeli passengers in hopes of negotiating the release of PLO operatives held in Israeli prisons.

The PLO was founded in 1964 by Yasser Arafat with the chartered goal of annihilating Israel and replacing it with a Palestinian Arab country. Arafat believed that the Arab countries were not always acting in the best interests of the Palestinians, and he had grown impatient with the fact that Arab militaries had not yet defeated the Jewish state, as was their promised goal. The PLO began a guerrilla warfare campaign to attack Israel and Israeli interests worldwide.[46]

---

[46] The PLO and a splinter group, the Popular Front for the Liberation of Palestine (PFLP), conducted numerous airplane hijackings and attempted hijackings, including, with the participation of the far-left German terrorist organization known as Baader-Meinhof, the hijacking of an Air France plane bound for Israel, which they diverted to Entebbe, Uganda. The hijackers were successfully attacked by Israeli commandos, and all but three hostages survived. In another operation, the PLO hijacked an Italian cruise ship, the Achille Lauro, and killed a Jewish passenger. The most murderous of the PLO attacks occurred in 1972 during the Olympic Games in Munich, Germany, when the Black September Brigade kidnaped and murdered eleven Israeli athletes from their apartments in the Olympic Village.

The 1973 Yom Kippur/Ramadan/October War[47]

Immediately following the 1967 Six-Day War, the Soviet Union, Egypt and Syria's weapons supplier and supporter on the world stage, began massively resupplying them with military arms to make up for those lost to Israel during the war. The resupply included upgrades to the state-of-the-art MiG 21 fighter aircraft; new surface-to-air missiles (SAMs), SA-2/3/6/7s; artillery; and T-55 and T-62 tanks. The Russian military assistance package included military advisors, who at their height numbered close to six thousand technicians plus their families.

As early as 1972, Israeli military and Mossad intelligence sources were receiving credible information that the Egyptians and Syrians were planning the next war and that it was imminent. Although Israel had good intelligence on its Arab adversaries, it was receiving mixed signals, which caused it to prematurely call up reservists, anticipating an imminent attack, only to have them stand down at great cost, both to the IDF and the Israeli economy. The information was both false and likely deliberately deceptive. In 1972, Egypt gave confusing signals by cutting military ties with its longtime benefactor, the Soviet Union, and evicting most of the six thousand Soviet advisors, technicians, trainers, and their families. In 1973, after receiving what it thought to be credible reports, Israeli military intelligence assessed that the Egyptian military lacked sufficient spare parts (most likely an Egyptian deception) and would be unable to wage full-scale war without the recently ousted Russian advisors. Israel also understood from intelligence sources that Egypt would not risk another war until it received a more advanced variant of the MiG-23 fighter aircraft from the Soviet Union. Another factor affecting Israel's political decision-making was a US warning to Israel not to preemptively attack as it had done in the 1956 Suez Crisis and the 1967 Six-Day War. World public opinion would not be sympathetic, and Israel would be portrayed as the aggressor.

---

[47] Israelis refer to the War as the Yom Kippur War because it began on Yom Kippur, the Jewish High Holy Day of Atonement. Egyptians and Arabs generally call it the October 6 War, the October 1973 War, or the Ramadan War, because it began on October 6, 1973, the tenth day of the Muslim holy month of Ramadan.

Twice in 1973, in May and August, the Egyptian Army conducted large-scale exercises, which included water-crossing equipment, that brought Egyptian forces to the edge of the west bank of the Suez Canal, as though rehearsing a canal crossing and an attack on Israeli forces on the Bar-Lev Line. In addition to being rehearsals for a future attack, the exercises were viewed by Israeli military intelligence as muscle-flexing bluster by Egypt meant for public and pan-Arab consumption to give credibility to Sadat's continuous call for war against Israel. Then, in the weeks leading up to the outbreak of the fourth Arab-Israeli war, the Egyptian military dismissed up to twenty thousand reservists and encouraged soldiers who were taking college courses to register for the upcoming semester to feign that war was not imminent and give the appearance of normalcy. Sadat appeared to have taken this chapter on strategic deception out of Israel's 1967 Six-Day War playbook. The stage was now set for Egypt's final deception, which would catch Israel off guard and ill prepared for a quick and credible response.

On the morning of October 6, 1973, the tenth day of the holy month of Ramadan during which Muslims the world over do little in the way of physical activity during daylight hours but fast and pray, hundreds of thousands of Egyptian ground forces raced to the east bank of the Suez Canal as they had done twice before that year in what looked like a third exercise. Like the two previous exercises that year, as soon as they reached the canal, they turned around as though returning to garrisons. By the time Israeli military and Mossad intelligence were convinced this was not a third exercise, it was too late. At 2:00 p.m. that day, Egyptian forces turned back east and began their all-out assault on the woefully unprepared Israeli defenses on the Bar-Lev Line. Egyptian units first attacked the Bar-Lev Line with massive aircraft and artillery fire as their engineers and ground forces assembled pontoon bridges that spanned the canal. Simultaneously, the EAF took out Israeli airfields in Sinai. Expecting the IAF to launch fighter aircraft against their ground forces, the Egyptians were ready for Israel's standard first line of defense. Egypt had received state-of-the-art, advanced SAMs from the Soviet Union that Israel had not yet encountered and for which it had not yet

71

developed effective countermeasures. Egyptian air defenses lined the length of the canal with overlapping SAM coverage, which in effect created a SAM "umbrella," under which its ground forces could engage the Israelis without fear of being attacked by the highly vaunted and war-tested IAF. To ensure a successful assault of the Bar-Lev Line, the Egyptians had devised a fail-safe method to breach the eighty-foot-high sand embankments: high-pressure water cannons.[48]

In a coordinated attack, the Egyptians began their assault on Israeli defenses on the Suez Canal in the south simultaneously with Syria's massive bombardment of Israeli positions in the Golan Heights to the north. Syrian forces initially overwhelmed the inadequately defended Israelis in the Golan Heights. In the first day of fighting, the Syrians routed and destroyed most Israeli defenses in the Heights, and Syrian tanks, armor, and infantry units began advancing into Israel's northern Galilee. However, by war's end, Israeli forces had mobilized and regrouped in the north and successfully neutralized Syrian air power. They were then able to provide air cover for Israeli armored ground forces and take the fight to the Syrians, who had experienced early battlefield successes. By the signing of the cease-fire three weeks later, the IDF had not only defeated the Syrian forces in the Golan Heights but had advanced to within thirty miles of Damascus, close enough to be within range of Israeli long-range artillery.

The first day of fighting in this fourth major Arab-Israeli war was unlike that of any previous war the IDF had experienced in its twenty-five-year history. Previous wars had been fought with much planning by Israel and fought on Israel's terms; this one was different. In addition to receiving conflicting intelligence signals as to whether and when the war would take place, what complicated this war was the fact that the Egyptians and Syrians had deliberately initiated it on Yom Kippur,

---

[48] While attempting to find a solution to the eighty-foot-high berms of the Bar-Lev Line, a young engineer lieutenant approached his commander and said he knew of a guaranteed method to breach the seemingly impenetrable Israeli sand embankments. The young lieutenant told his commander that when he took his family to the beach and they built sandcastles, the easiest and quickest way to destroy them was with water. The rest is history.

when they knew Israel would be virtually shut down for Judaism's holiest day.[49] Because there were no operating telecommunications or modes of public transportation in Israel on this day, the IDF could not call up reservists in the traditional manner. Soldiers drove their personal vehicles to fellow soldiers' homes, picked them up, and raced to their posts and the front lines. Because Israel's forces were always vastly outnumbered by Arab armies, for it to have any chance of a military victory on the battlefield, Israeli military planners had always depended on Israel striking first, as it had done in 1956 and 1967. However, this time, an Israeli preemptive first strike was not an option, and for the first time in Israel's military history, its generals were forced to fight reactive and defensive battles before they could go on the offense and execute the fight on their terms.[50]

Within twenty-four hours, most Israeli active and reserve forces were with their units and either in the fight or on their way to the battlefronts. The IAF had never encountered such a formidable barrier as that the Egyptians had put up with the SAM umbrella. Attributed primarily to the new advanced SAMs, first- and second-day IAF aircraft losses were like nothing they had experienced before, reported to be as high as 20 percent, a figure unsustainable and unacceptable to the IAF. As IDF units attained full strength, they divided their forces between the northern and southern fronts and slowly began to stop Arab advances and begin their counterattack. The fighting was fierce and historic in its dimension, the likes of which the world had not seen since World War II. Attrition rates of armor, artillery, ammunition, and aircraft were high on both sides. The United States and the Soviet Union began resupplying their respective client states' militaries as the war raged.

---

[49] On Yom Kippur in Israel, nothing moves. All vehicular traffic is forbidden from operating except for fire trucks, ambulances, and police and military vehicles. Israeli children ride their bikes and skateboards on transnational highways. Israeli radio and television stations are off the air, and no noncritical activity takes place from sundown on Yom Kippur eve until sundown on Yom Kippur. The timing of the Arab attack was well calculated and not coincidental.

[50] Depending on the source, it is believed that at the outbreak of war, the combined Arab armies facing Israel totaled between 500,000 and 800,000 personnel, 2,900 tanks, and 600 combat aircraft, while the Israeli military comprised over 400,000 soldiers, 1,700 tanks, and 440 combat aircraft.

The US and the USSR warned each other not to intervene with fighting forces for their respective allies. Early in the war, the situation was so bleak for Israel that Israeli leaders, it was later revealed, contemplated using battlefield nuclear weapons if its situation became dire. History also shows that the US and USSR put their respective nuclear forces on high alert, and the world came the closest it had come since the Cuban Missile Crises of 1962 to a nuclear confrontation.

Egyptian military planners had not intended to go beyond crossing the Suez Canal, defeating the Bar-Lev Line, and holding a fifteen-mile-deep position in the Sinai Peninsula. The SAM umbrella only protected Egyptian ground forces for about fifteen miles from the Suez Canal east into Sinai. To advance any farther would put the Egyptian forces outside the umbrella's protection and make them vulnerable to Israeli air attack. However, something happened that went against the Egyptian military war planning that called for Egyptian forces to only hold a defensible fifteen-mile footprint in Sinai and not break out from under the security of the SAM umbrella. It involved the fighting in the north on the Syrian front.

What changed the dynamics in Sinai was the need to take pressure off Syrian forces that were now under a heavy Israeli counteroffensive. Syria's president, Hafez al-Assad, asked Egypt's president, Sadat, to have the Egyptian army break out from under its fifteen-mile secure SAM umbrella and take the fight to the Israelis so that Israel would redirect forces from Syria to Sinai. Sadat eventually agreed to Syria's request despite the strong objections of his chief of staff. Egyptian generals knew they were safe under the umbrella and would be vulnerable to the IAF and antitank fire if they pressed forward. As Egyptian forces advanced in Sinai out from under the SAM protection, Israeli air power and armor predictably decimated them. What ensued was one of the largest tank battles the world had seen since those in the European theater in World War II. The Israeli Army eventually counter-crossed the Suez Canal, attacked Egyptian military and supply lines on the west bank of the canal on the African continent, and inflicted heavy casualties on the Egyptians in Sinai, encircling and threatening to destroy Egypt's Third Army.

On October 22, 1973, three weeks after the war began, Egypt, Syria, and Israel agreed to a US-brokered United Nations cease-fire. The US secretary of state, Henry Kissinger, had spent weeks during the war flying between world capitals to bring an end to hostilities. His efforts, eventually successful, ushered in the term *shuttle diplomacy*. Although all parties agreed to the 22 October Cease-Fire, fighting continued sporadically, with most of the heavy fighting ending by October 28.

After yet a fourth war, the Arab-Israeli conflict was again no closer to a resolution than it had been before the war. Although it had enjoyed initial battlefield success, Syria had gained absolutely nothing for its efforts and had lost more territory by the time the cease-fire was signed. Egypt had also only enjoyed initial battlefield success and now had a fifteen-mile foothold on the east bank of the Suez Canal in the Sinai Peninsula. Egypt primarily gained national and military pride by crossing the Suez Canal and defeating Israeli forces on the ostensibly impenetrable Bar-Lev Line. Israel lost its prewar swagger and the sense of invincibility that it had enjoyed for six years following the Six-Day War of 1967. Some observers claim that part of the reason Israel was not as prepared for this fourth war was that it had become overconfident and thought that Arab countries would not risk or attempt an attack on Israel because of its formidable, proven strength and reputation. The mood this time was reversed on the Arab and Israeli streets. Arabs were jubilant that they could inflict such punishment on Israel, while Israel lost its confidence and felt vulnerable. Given Israel's small population, it is estimated that due to the heavy casualties of this war, every family in Israeli experienced a loss, with relatives either killed or wounded in action.[51]

---

[51] The following is one estimate of the Yom Kippur/Ramadan War losses: Total Arab casualties included 18,000 dead, 35,000 wounded, 8,800 captured, 500 aircraft destroyed, 2,300 tanks destroyed, and 19 ships sunk. Israeli casualties included 2,800 dead, 8,800 wounded, 290 captured, 380 aircraft destroyed, and 1,060 tanks destroyed, damaged, or captured,.

The Camp David Accords and the
Egyptian-Israeli Peace Treaty

It would not be wrong to say that Israel and Egypt were war-weary after the last war. Having fought four wars and after losing thousands of young men, Israel and the Arabs were no closer to a resolution. War had cost their collective economies billions of dollars. The toll was especially high for Egypt, the most populous Arab country with the biggest and strongest Arab military. When the Arab world went to war with Israel, it was Egypt who paid the heaviest price, not only in terms of expense and manpower but also in terms of real estate, having repeatedly lost the largest piece of real estate of any Arab country to Israel: the Sinai Peninsula. With its military defeat also came the loss of its pride and honor. After this last war, President Anwar Sadat was convinced that there must be a better way to regain lost national dignity. In 1977, he approached other Arab heads of state and proposed direct talks with the Jewish state. They all categorically refused to even consider the proposal. President Sadat argued that the Arabs had tried everything else, including numerous wars, and had nothing to show for it but repeated defeat and humiliation. Arab countries had always maintained the position that they would not only deny Israel's right to exist but also not attend any international meetings, conferences, or sporting events that also had an Israeli representation. Most Arabs refused to even utter the word *Israel*; rather, they would refer to Israel as "Occupied Palestine" or the "Zionist Entity." Arabs subscribed to the position that Israel must be militarily defeated, wiped off the map, and replaced with an Arab-Palestinian state. The often-heard slogan beginning in 1948 was "drive the Jews into the sea." A face-to-face dialogue was totally off the table, and Sadat proposing it was even treasonous to the pan-Arab cause and the Ummah al-Arabiyyah (greater Arab Nation).

During a press interview in 1977, President Sadat casually threw out the notion of direct talks with Israel. The proposal was initially interpreted by the Israelis as a public relations stunt. Sadat suggested that he would even travel to Jerusalem, Israel's capital, to move the perpetual state of war off dead center. Sadat's offer was dismissed by most as not sincere or even unrealistic. However, within a few days, Israel's prime minister, Menachem Begin (pronounced "bay-gin"), not wanting to dismiss the opportunity if it were indeed genuine, accepted Sadat's initiative and extended a formal invitation through the US ambassador to Israel. The invitation was delivered, and Sadat and Israel quickly made plans to host the visit. On November 20, 1977, to the surprise of the world, Anwar Sadat became the first Arab head of state to make an official state visit to Israel. To characterize the event as surreal would not come close to describing the electrified atmosphere. The head of state of the most populous Arab nation, which had not only been at war with Israel ever since Israel's founding twenty-nine years earlier but which had led the Arab world in its call for Israel's destruction, was now landing in an Egyptian airplane with senior Egyptian military officers as official members of the visiting party and being received in a red-carpet ceremony at Israel's Ben-Gurion Airport by the Israeli prime minister. The next day, President Sadat prayed at the al-Aqsa Mosque in Jerusalem, laid a wreath at the Holocaust Memorial, and addressed the Israeli Parliament. Most Near East watchers had never imagined they would see this day in their lifetime.

The Arab world did not share the rest of the world's euphoria over Sadat's visit. The Arab League of Nations, a consortium of the twenty-two Arab nations, shuttered the doors to its Cairo headquarters and moved to Tunis, Tunisia. Most Arab countries condemned Sadat's initiative and broke off diplomatic relations with Egypt. The Egyptian Moslem Brotherhood (Arabic: Jama'at al-Ikhwan al-Muslimin جماعه الاخوان المسلمين), also known as the Freedom and Justice Party, which had a long history of opposing Egyptian governments—many of its members, including its leadership, had even been arrested and imprisoned for antigovernment activities—also strongly came out in opposition to Sadat's Israel initiative.

Jimmy Carter, the US president, recognizing the potentially historic opportunity, invited Sadat and Begin to the US in 1978 for serious negotiations to see if they could indeed arrive at something that resembled peace. The US-brokered talks between Sadat and Begin took place at the US presidential retreat in Camp David, Maryland, from where it received its name, "The Camp David Peace Talks." After nine days of difficult negotiations, which nearly ended several times, Egypt and Israel came to an understanding and a framework for peace that became known as the Egyptian-Israeli Camp David Accords. The agreement was formalized at a White House garden signing ceremony in March 1979 and became the first Arab-Israeli peace treaty. It called for Egypt and Israel to disengage their forces that were entangled on both sides of the Suez Canal and for the creation of a United Nations international monitoring organization, the Multinational Observer Force (MFO). Most significantly, the agreement called for Egypt to recognize Israel's right to exist and pledge nonbelligerency in exchange for Israel's phased withdrawal from the Sinai Peninsula (minus the Gaza Strip, which Egypt was not interested in retaining). In addition, the US under President Carter pledged billions of dollars in annual economic and military aid to both countries and agreed to build a new airbase in the Negev Desert in southern Israel to compensate Israel for the airfields it would lose by vacating Sinai. Egypt and Israel agreed to full normalization of diplomatic relations, including the establishment of embassies in each country and ambassadorial exchanges.

The agreement was a win-win for both countries. Egypt could now raise its head high because it had secured Sinai and avenged the national shame. Sadat could claim he had restored honor to the Egyptian and Arab camps. He could boast that through direct, face-to-face negotiations with the Arabs' once sworn enemy, he had regained what others could not in warfare. With this agreement, Israel received a peace treaty from its primary adversary and the recognized leader of the Arab world, a request it had been making since its creation in 1948. Israelis could now sleep easier knowing that their strongest adversary was out of the equation in any future war. As the unquestioned Near

Eastern superpower, Israel had proven time and time again that it could engage the combined Arab armies and be victorious. Now Israel was more certain than before that it could win any future war with its Arab adversaries, because Egypt, the Arab world's most populous nation with the largest and most capable military, was no longer a threat.

The agreement had its critics both in the Arab world and in Israel. Israeli critics argued that the peace treaty was only as good as any future Egyptian government wanted it to be, and Israel could possibly find itself once again in a state of war with Egypt if a future Egyptian leader decided to shred the agreement. If this were to happen, not only would Israel no longer have a peace treaty with Egypt, but it would have forfeited the buffer of the Sinai Peninsula at a high cost and would be back to square one, facing the strongest Arab military on its southern doorstep. Supporters of the agreement, however, argued that this was a risk Israel would have to take. As with statehood, "something from nothing is something." It would be an understatement to say that the agreement was politically costly for President Sadat. It was stillborn in the entire Arab world. It would prove to be even more costly to Anwar Sadat personally.

In October 1981, two and a half years after the signing the Camp David Accord, President Anwar Sadat and his military leaders were celebrating the anniversary of crossing to the east bank of the Suez Canal during the 1973 Ramadan War and defeating Israel's Bar-Lev Line. Members of the Moslem Brotherhood, armed with automatic weapons, jumped out of their trucks as they reached the presidential reviewing stand and sprayed it with machine-gun fire, killing Sadat and others and injuring his vice president, Hosni Mubarak. With his bold initiative to reach out to Israel and bring peace to the troubled Near East, Muhammad Anwar Sadat had stepped out from under the "Arab consensus umbrella" and become personally vulnerable. Although he had secured his place in history as a visionary who put Egypt and Egyptians first, he had done so at the highest personal cost.

Mubarak succeeded Sadat as the president of Egypt and served thirty years from 1981 to 2011, when he was forced to resign under massive protests. After the wave of uprisings that swept the Near East during the so-called Arab Spring of 2011, Egyptians narrowly elected Muhammad Morsi of the Moslem Brotherhood as their president in 2012.[52]

---

[52] I do not like the term "Arab Spring" for the movement because "spring" normally has a positive connotation and outcome. Except for Tunisia, where the movement was started, the outcome for the average person in the Arab street has not been a positive one. I prefer "Twenty-First-Century Arab Revolt" or "Twenty-First-Century Arab Awakening." Ironically, after a series of power-grabbing decrees and legislation to Islamize the historically secular Egyptian government, Morsi was deposed by his appointed military chief, Abdul Fattah al-Sisi, in a bloodless military coup in July 2013. Morsi died in prison in June 2019.

Notes

"Timeline of Jewish History: Modern Israel & the Diaspora (1970–1979 & 1980–1989)." *Jewish Virtual Library*. 1998–2018 (American-Israeli Cooperative Enterprise.2018).

"Israel Declares Independence," *New York Times* (May 15, 1948).

"The Declaration of the Establishment of the State of Israel," *https://www.knesset.gov.il/ docs/eng/megilat-eng.htm* (May 14,1948).

Alain Gresh and Dominique Vidal, *The New A-Z of The Middle East* (I. B. Tauris & Co. Ltd., 2004).

"1947: The International Community Says YES to the Establishment of the State of Israel. Israel," *Ministry of Foreign Affairs* (2013).

Howard A. Schack, *A Spy in Canaan* (Birch Lane Press 1993).

Joseph E. Katz. "Memoirs of Khalid al-Azm, 3 Volumes, Beirut, 1973. "A Collection of Historical Quotations Relating to the Arab Refugees." *Eretz Yisroel.org.* https://www.eretzyisroel.org.

Joseph E. Katz. "1948 Khaled al-Azm on Palestinian Refugees." *Center for Online Judaic Studies.* https://www/cojs.org/1948-palestinian-refugees-khaled-al-azm/.

Martin Gilbert, *The Rutledge Atlas of the Arab Israeli Conflict* (Taylor & Francis Publisher, 2012).

Jeremy Bowen, "1967 War: Six Days That Changed the Middle East," *BBC* (June 5, 2017).

Shlomo Aloni, *Six-Day War 1967: Operation Focus and the 12 Hours that Changed the Middle East* (Ospry Publishing, 2019).

Shabtai Tevet, *The Tanks of Tammuz: An Eye Witness Account* (Lume Books Publisher, 2018).

Jeffry St. Clair, "Israel's Attack on the USS Liberty: A Half Century Later, Still No Justice," *Counter Punch* (June 8, 2018).

Miriam Pensak, "Fifty Years Later, NSA Keeps Details of USS Liberty's Attack Secret," *The Intercept* (2017).

Niyazi Gunay, "Arab League Summit Conference, 1964–2000," *The Washington Institute* (2000).

Simon Dunstan, *The Yom Kippur War: The Arab Israeli War of 1973* (Osprey Publishing, 2007).

"Profile: Hosni Mubarak," *BBC* (March 24 2017).

Chapter 6

Modern Israeli Society and Culture

Demographics and Cultural Character

In 2020, Israel's population was 9.25 million. Of this, 6.7 million people were Jewish, 2.1 million were Muslim Arabs (Palestinians), 400,000 were Christian Arabs (Palestinian), and 136,000 were Druze or members of others ethnoreligious groups. These figures do not include the 2.9 million Palestinian Arabs in the West Bank or the 1.9 million Palestinian Arabs in the Gaza Strip who were granted semiautonomous self-rule by the 1993 and 1995 Israeli-Palestinian Oslo (Norway) Peace Conferences.

Israeli society is a diverse multiethnic, multicultural, multilingual melting pot of human contradictions. As discussed earlier, the first modern-day Jewish settlers fleeing persecution were Russian Jews in the late 1800s. Following World War I, the Balfour Declaration, and the fall of the Ottoman Empire, Eastern European Jews became the primary Jewish immigrants to Palestine. During and immediately following

World War II, the need to escape the Nazi Holocaust accelerated the European Jewish flight and immigration to the promised safe haven in Palestine.

The Jewish population of Israel is composed of four primary ethnolinguistic regional groups: Ashkenazi Jews,[53] primarily from Eastern Europe and Russia; Sephardic Jews from the Iberian Peninsula (Portugal and Spain); Eastern or Oriental Jews from Arab, Near Eastern, Islamic, and north African countries (Oriental Near Eastern as opposed to the Occidental Western); and Ethiopian sub-Saharan African Jews. The total number of Jewish immigrants to Palestine-Israel is estimated to have been 3.6 million. At statehood in 1948, the total Jewish population of Palestine-Israel was only 650,000.[54]

Religion

Israel enjoys freedom of religion, as seen in its religious diversity. Jerusalem is home to Judaism's holiest site, the Temple Mount, built on Mount Mariah. The Temple Mount is the location of King Solomon's First Temple and King Herod's Second Temple and today includes the last surviving remnant of the outer wall of Herod's Second Temple, the Western Wall. The wall is known to Jews as ha-Kotel ha-Ma'ravi (הכותל המערבי) and is sometimes referred to by non-Jews as the Wailing Wall. Jerusalem contains two of Christianity's most sacred sites, both located within the Church of the Holy Sepulcher: the shrine over Golgotha, the site of the crucifixion, and the tomb of Jesus Christ. Jerusalem also contains other Christian holy sites, such as the Mount of Olives and the Via Dolorosa (the Way of the Cross). Finally, Jerusalem

[53] The word *Ashkenazi* comes from the name *Ashkenaz*, a grandson of biblical Noah's son Japheth.
[54] From 1900 to 1948, 375,000 Jews immigrated to British-mandate Palestine, primarily from Europe. From 1948 to 1955, 650,000 Jews immigrated to Israel from the Arab world, and an additional 250,000 had immigrated by the 1970s for a total of 900,000. From 1990 to 1991, after the collapse of the Soviet Union, 900,000 Jews and non-Jews immigrated to Israel from Russia. In 1984, 1990, and 1991, there were several airlifts to Israel of Ethiopian Jews, totaling 92,000. Smaller airlifts continued from 2018 and 2020.

is the third most holy site in Islam after Mecca and Medina. Muslims believe that their Prophet Muhammad was transported in a dream to Jerusalem and from Jerusalem to heaven. Muslims built the al-Aqsa Mosque and the Dome of the Rock on the Temple Mount, the site of the two previous Jewish temples, to commemorate this event. Because of its deep significance to the world's three monotheistic religions, Jerusalem is referred to as the Holy City, and Israel is known as the Holy Land.[55] Unfortunately, the Holy Land has been the cause of numerous wars and hundreds of thousands of deaths during the past three thousand years, all in the name of religion and control.

Jews make up 76 percent of Israel's population, Muslims 17 percent, Christian 2.8 percent, Druze 2 percent, and Bahais and others 2.2 percent. The Druze, Israel's most successful ethnic minority, are an ethnoreligious group whose secretive beliefs are Abrahamic but not Muslim. They are an Arabized population of the Near East who are found in Lebanon, Syria, Jordan, and Israel. Bahaism is a faith that celebrates the goodness in all religions and is known for its beautiful gardens and world-famous architecture. Bahaism was established in Iran in the 1800s, but Baha'is were forced to flee Persian/Iranian persecution. Today, the Baha'i Faith has its center in Israel's northern port city of Haifa. Of Israel's non-Jewish religious minorities, 80 percent are Muslim, 10 percent Christian, and 10 percent Druze. Judaism is divided into three primary denominations or sects: Orthodox, Conservative, and Reform (see Social Character below).[56]

---

[55]   Arabs and Muslims call Jerusalem "al-Quds" (القدس, [The Holy]).

[56] Populations and religious/secular percentages of major cities: Jerusalem 1.2 million, (60 percent Jewish Orthodox); Tel Aviv 440,000 (95 percent secular); Haifa 280,000 (90 percent secular); Beersheba 500,000 (no figures, considered to be majority secular); Tiberias 41,000 (70 percent secular); Eilat 48,000 (98 percent secular); Nazareth 75,000, predominantly Arab (70 percent Muslim and 30 percent Christian). Although Tel Aviv's population is 440,000, Israel's central costal region around greater Tel Aviv is a large, metropolitan megalopolis where over a third of all Israelis live—a total population of 3.95 million.

Language

Until July 2018, Hebrew and Arabic were coequal official languages of Israel. Since 2015, the Israeli Parliament (Knesset) has been passing laws to "maintain the Jewish character of Israel." On July 19, 2018, Israel's Parliament passed the most controversial of these laws, called the "nation-state law," which restates Israel as "the nation-state of the Jewish people." The law declared Hebrew to be the only official language of Israel, into which laws and government documents are translated, with Arabic having a "special status."

Education

One of the most highly esteemed qualities among world Jewry is unarguably education. Scholars have long pondered why this might be and have concluded that it was, ironically, most likely forced on Diaspora Jews by anti-Semitic gentiles. Because Jews were treated as outcasts, shunned, and often not allowed in many professions and occupations while living in foreign lands during the Diaspora, they were forced to depend on their own initiative to survive. Education was their upward-mobility ticket out of poverty and toward social acceptance. The importance of education to the Jewish people has always been an ethnocultural-religious characteristic, which is manifested and made obvious in the disproportionately high percentage of Jewish Nobel Prize winners today, especially in the sciences.[57]

Israeli law mandates that all its citizens receive eleven years of education. Not surprisingly, Israel has one of the highest world literacy rates—as high as 97 percent for men and 93 percent for women. This figure should be viewed against the backdrop of earlier and often older

---

[57] As of 2018, of the 902 total Nobel Prizes awarded, 203 (22.5 percent) were awarded to Jews. Jews make up only 0.2 percent of the world population, making Jewish Nobel Prize winners 11.25 percent above average. Jews represent 26 percent of Nobel Prize winners in science and medicine and 39 percent in physiology. Despite accounting for only 1/1000 of the world's population, Israel ranks a disproportionate fifth place in the world in terms of Nobel Prizes won.

immigrants, who had much lower literacy rates. Beginning in the ninth grade, students must choose a path in the two-track educational system: college preparatory or technical/vocational. Students wanting to pursue a college education spend their high school years studying their chosen field. Starting in the eleventh grade, these students begin taking Bagroot (pronounced *bug-root*) academic proficiency (matriculation) exams, which are used by Israeli colleges and universities for admissions evaluations. In addition to the Bagroot exams, Israeli universities require a psychometric exam. Like the US SATs and ACTs, this exam measures general academic knowledge. High school students opting for technical careers earn certifications in carpentry, plumbing, electricity, medical technology, and so on.

Because military service is compulsory for most Israelis when they reach the age of eighteen, college entrance is usually delayed until they leave the military between the age of twenty-one and twenty-three. Following military service, it is customary for most Israeli young people to take a gap year to travel and decompress before beginning their college education. It is therefore not unusual to find beginning undergraduate Israeli students between the ages of twenty-six and thirty, as they also may have opted to work for a few years after their military service to save money for college. The median age of Israeli college students is reported to be twenty-seven. As a result of their military service and real-world experience, beginning Israeli college students tend to be more certain of the direction of their studies, more goal oriented, and more mature than their Western counterparts, who often enter college immediately after high school at age eighteen.[58]

This emphasis on education can be quantified in real-world accomplishments and innovation: Israel produces the most scientific papers per capita; has the highest rate of patents per capita; has the

---

[58] Israelis can boast of having the second-highest ratio in the world of people with tertiary degrees (US college degree equivalent); 46 percent of Israelis have a college degree, and 12 percent have a graduate degree (same as the US). By comparison, 43 percent of US citizens have college degrees versus 31 percent worldwide. Russia claims to have the highest rate of tertiary degrees at 53 percent.

most start-up per capita; has the second-highest number of books published per capita; Motorola-Israel developed the first cell phone; and Israeli companies have designed early chip technology. Israel has the highest concentration of hi-tech companies outside of Silicon Valley; the Pentium MMX was developed by Intel-Israel; most of the Windows NT operating system was developed by Microsoft-Israel; the flash drive was developed in Israel; and an Israeli medical technology company has developed a noninvasive bariatric camera, called Pillcam, which when swallowed produces a live image display for diagnosing gastrointestinal tract disorders. Israeli military industries have produced some of the world's most sophisticated and advanced weaponry, which is bought by militaries across the globe, including by Western powers, who recognize Israeli hi-tech weaponry to be the cutting edge.

Social Character

Israel's first prime minister, David Ben-Gurion, said it most accurately: "Israel is in but not of the Middle East." What he meant was that although Israel is geographically located in the Near East, at the time he made the statement, Israel's society was not majority Near Eastern, since most of Israel's early immigrants came from Europe. Although more than one million Jews immigrated to Israel from Arab countries, Israel is not Arab in character. Eastern/Oriental Jews emigrating from Arab-Islamic countries were generally less educated than their European counterparts and were viewed as less sophisticated and less advanced. Consequently, Eastern/Oriental Jews often suppressed their identities and attempted to blend into the European Jewish immigrant community. They did this by sometimes changing their names from Eastern/Arabic names to European/Hebrew names and by deliberately speaking with a modern Hebrew European pronunciation and dropping their Eastern/Arabic native pronunciation.

There is, however, much today that is Near Eastern and Arab-like in Israeli society. Many Israeli foods were brought to Israel by

Arabized Jewish immigrants. Foods the world identifies as Israeli, such as pita bread, hummus, falafel, and shawarma, are in fact Arab in origin. There are distinct Ethiopian, Yemeni, Moroccan, Iraqi, and other neighborhoods in Israeli cities that have maintained cultural characteristics unique to the Arab countries from where they emigrated, such as language, dialect, accent, music, food, and dress.

Israelis and Jews coined the term *Ingathering of the Exiles* for the return of the Jews to the Land of Israel after nearly two thousand years of exile in the Diaspora. One of the first laws the new State of Israel enacted in 1948 was the Law of Return. This law states that anyone who can prove his or her Jewishness has the right to live in Israel and will be granted immediate citizenship upon arrival. The Law of Return requires any prospective Jewish immigrant to show proof of his or her bona fides as a Jew. One cannot simply claim to be Jewish and be granted immediate Israeli citizenship. One's Jewishness has historically been determined matrilineally (i.e., someone is considered Jewish because his or her mother is Jewish) or by orthodox Jewish conversion. Before the advent of DNA testing, one usually knew the identity of one's mother but was not always 100 percent sure as to one's father's identity. Now that lineage can be determined by genetic testing, Israeli rabbinical courts have ruled that Jewishness can be legally established either matrilineally or patrilineally.

Israel's population is largely secular. When Israelis today claim to be Jewish, it is not necessarily a religious designation. Jewishness has taken on the additional connotations of ethnicity, citizenship, and nationality. An estimated 67 percent of Israeli Jews claim to be secular (i.e., nonpracticing) but celebrate and observe Jewish holidays. Twenty percent of Israelis fall in the category of Orthodox Jews (12 percent Ultra-Orthodox and 8 percent Orthodox observant). Another 13 percent of Israelis are said to be "lightly religious"—that is, they observe the Sabbath; males wear a *Kippah*, the skullcap head covering (Yiddish: *Yarmulka*), prayer shawls, and tassels; and women wear long sleeves and long dresses going past the knees, often to the ankles. There are varying degrees of religious observance and expression in Israel, including several Orthodox Jewish orders (denominations). Interestingly, there are some Ultra-Orthodox Jews who reject completely the notion of the Jewish state of Israel, claiming that modern Israel is illegitimate. They believe that the legitimate Jewish state will only be ushered in with the coming of the Messiah.

Coming from one hundred different countries, there is constant friction between Orthodox Jews who want to mandate strict Sabbath laws and the secular majority. Sabbath laws prohibit public, and sometimes private, transportation, commerce, and leisure entertainment (such as going to the beach or theater) on the Sabbath. Israel's majority secular population does not want the religious minority telling them how to conduct their lives or practice their religion on the Sabbath or any other day. There has also been racial tension between European (Ashkenazi) Jews and African Jews from Ethiopia. Sometimes their collective Jewishness and common language are insufficient glues to hold Israelis together against deep-seated, universal racial prejudices.

Modern Israeli society rose out of the ashes of state-sponsored genocide of the Nazi Final Solution, the Holocaust, and was born as the Jewish state, a safe haven for Jews. As a result, Israelis today have a strong self-preservation instinct, even an obsession. First and foremost, Israelis are driven by an innate need for security. To paraphrase Theodor Roosevelt, when it comes to security, Israelis live by a motto of "speak *loudly* and carry a big stick."[59] Born with an instinct for survival, Israelis are aggressive, impatient, confrontational, confident, and self-assured. Israelis are opinionated, speak their mind, have *khutspah* (moxie; brash, unapologetic, in-your-face daring; and aggressive boldness), stand their ground, and do not back down from a fight. Conversely, on a one-on-one personal basis, Israelis are generous, compassionate, warm, and loving. As with other Mediterranean and Near Eastern societies, Israelis

---

[59] The director general of Israel's Defense Ministry in the early 1990s, David Ivry (retired lieutenant general and former commander of the IAF), had a sign in his office above his desk that read, "I too look for the day when the lion shall lie down with the lamb, but on that day, I want to be the lion."

dote on their children and maintain a short personal space when facing one another. Israel values life to the extent that it does not have a death penalty. This was an outgrowth of the fact that Jews decided they had seen too much state-sponsored murder and killing during World War II and the Holocaust and were therefore not interested in passing laws that allowed the Jewish state to legally take Jewish or any other life. It had nothing to do with the fifth Mosaic Law of the Ten Commandments, "Do not murder" ("Thou shall not murder").[60]

Finally, Israelis fight each battle and war like there is no tomorrow, because both tactically and strategically speaking, there *is* no tomorrow. With a geography that provides no strategic depth, given that it is only nine miles wide at its narrowest, if Israel's military loses the fight and is forced to retreat, it has nowhere from which to regroup and establish new defensive fighting positions; ergo, there is no tomorrow. Historically, Israel has been wedged between the Mediterranean Sea on the west and a hard place on the east, surrounded by enemies vowing to destroy it. The fighting spirit of the Israeli soldier has been the critical difference in Israel's many victories over its more numerous adversaries. Israeli soldiers fight for their homes and families; they are not deployed to distant lands. They fight in both their front yards and backyards.

Physical Features

Located on the eastern shores of the Mediterranean Sea, Israel's total land mass is 8,630 square miles, about the size of New Jersey. Israel is 290 miles long. At its widest, it is 85 miles across, and at its narrowest, going by Israel's internationally recognized pre-1967 borders, there are only nine miles between the Mediterranean Sea, its western boundary, and the west bank of the Jordan River, its eastern boundary.

---

[60] The (original) Hebrew Bible (the Old Testament) uses the specific Hebrew wording *do not murder*, not *do not kill*, as it has been mistranslated into English and other languages. Killing, not murder, was condoned in time of war and for specific crimes that were punishable by death in ancient Hebrew/Israelite belief.

Israel is located on the Asian continent at the tricontinental junction of Europe, Asia, and Africa. It is bordered on the north by Lebanon and Syria, on the east by Jordan, and on the south by the Gaza Strip, Egypt, and the Red Sea. Saudi Arabia is only twelve miles down the Red Sea coast from Israel's southern border. Israel's geography, topography, and climate are diverse, from the temperate coastal Mediterranean plains to the arid Negev Desert in the south, the snowy seven-thousand-plus-foot-high Mount Hermon in the north, and the fertile Jordan River Valley in the east. The Jordan River Valley is an extension of the Great Rift Valley, which plunges from seven hundred feet below mean sea level at the Sea of Galilee to nearly fourteen hundred feet below mean sea level at the Dead Sea, the lowest point on the earth's surface. Israel has hot, dry summers and cool, wet winters, with snow limited to the higher elevations in the north, the Golan Heights, Jerusalem, Tzfat (Safed), and occasionally Nazareth. Israel receives an average annual rainfall of four inches and it only rains during the rainy season from November to March. Northern Israel receives the most precipitation, forty-three inches of combined rain and snow; the coastal area receives twelve inches; and the southern Negev Desert and Judean hills only receive negligible precipitation from seasonal flash flooding. Israel's major cities are Tel Aviv, Jerusalem, Haifa, Tiberias, Beersheba, Eilat, and Nazareth.

Water Concerns

Israel's naturally available water resources are inadequate for its needs, and the problem will only become more acute as its population grows and its agriculture expands. Its major natural water sources are the Sea of Galilee, the Jordan River, springs, and wells. To make up the shortfall, Israel has two desalination plants—and a third under construction—that draw water from the Mediterranean Sea. Some Near East watchers predict that there will be a future war fought over water. However, as seen in chapter 5, the 1967 Six-Day War was fought in part over Syrian diversion of the Jordan River.

Israel's longest shoreline runs along the Mediterranean Sea, which has historically connected Mediterranean people in trade, culture, and warfare, while Israel's short shoreline along the Red Sea, which connects Israel to Africa and Asia, provides its only southern water outlet. The Jordan River connects Israel's two internal bodies of water, the Sea of Galilee and the Dead Sea.[61] At seven hundred feet below sea level, the Sea of Galilee is both Israel's largest single source of fresh water and its largest freshwater lake. The Sea of Galilee is the world's lowest freshwater lake and Israel's second-lowest lake after the Dead Sea. Its waters flow south via the Jordan River and drop from seven hundred to almost fourteen hundred feet below sea level, where it empties into the Dead Sea. As a conduit between the lowest and second-lowest points on the earth's surface, the Jordan River is technically tied with these two bodies of water for being both the lowest and second-lowest points on earth. As the population has grown over the past seventy years and has placed greater water demands for agricultural and other human consumption, the Sea of Galilee has dropped by more than fifteen feet, and its shoreline has receded by twenty feet; 95 percent of its waters that would have emptied into the Dead Sea have been diverted.[62] With no outlet and a high evaporation rate, the Dead Sea has become the saltiest body of water in the world and the one with the highest concentration of minerals. Dead Sea water is 25 percent solid material. Over the decades, Israel and Jordan have taken advantage of this rare body of water and have commercially extracted from it fertilizer, potash, potassium, and other minerals. The Dead Sea's rich muds are also believed to have health benefits, which draw people from all over the world to come

---

[61] Applying the term *sea* to both the Galilee and the Dead Seas is somewhat misleading. In antiquity, while standing on their respective shorelines, they may have appeared as vast seas, but in reality, they are only good-sized lakes. Nevertheless, the names stuck. In Arabic, the Sea of Galilee is called Buhairat Tabaryyah (Lake Tiberias), and in the New Testament book of Luke, it is referred to as Lake Gennesaret. The Sea of Galilee measures eight by thirteen miles, and the Dead Sea eleven by forty-two miles.

[62] The level of the Sea of Galilee had dropped so low in 1986 that the hull of a first-century-CE fishing boat was exposed and removed. It took several years to restore its nearly two-thousand-year-old water-logged, wooden hull with a preservative resin. Because of its early date of origin, it was originally dubbed the "Jesus Boat" but has since been called the first-century fishing boat. The boat is today on display in a museum specifically built to house it at Kibbutz Ginosar, near where it was found on the northwestern shores of the Sea of Galilee.

and pack their bodies in its healing minerals. The extraction of water from the Sea of Galilee and Jordan River before it reaches the Dead Sea has reduced the latter sea's level to a point where the southern third is virtually dry and cut off from the upper two-thirds by a land bridge that now connects Jordan and Israel. Over the past sixty years, the Dead Sea has dropped by more than 265 feet, and its shoreline has receded by more than 150 feet. Today, along both its Jordanian and Israeli shores where its waters used to be, are several hundred sixty-foot-deep sinkholes. If this trend continues unchecked, there may not be a Dead Sea in the future. Time will tell if a desalination project to restore water to the Sea of Galilee will provide enough water to raise its level and in turn increase the outflow into the Jordan River, which will then flow into the Dead Sea and eventually allow it to slowly recover the water volume that has been removed over the past fifty-plus years. This process will take several years to complete, and its goals will most likely not be realized for another decade or more.[63]

Social Concerns

Israeli society is by no means a utopia; nor is it always a "light unto the world." Like all countries and societies, Israel has its share of problems, such as crime, corruption, and racial, ethnic, and religious

---

[63] To reverse this potentially catastrophic water shortage, in 2018, Israel approved a project to bring desalinated water to the Sea of Galilee from the Mediterranean Sea via an underground pipeline. It will take years before the benefits of this project will be felt.

There is another project, also approved by the Israeli government in 2018 after having been on the table for more than a decade, aimed at restoring the depleted waters of the Dead Sea. The proposal, known as the Red Sea–Dead Sea Canal Project, is a joint Jordanian-Israeli canal to be dug from the Red Sea's Gulf of Aqaba (Eilat) connecting the Red Sea to the Dead Sea. Since the Dead Sea has only historically been fed by fresh waters from the Jordan River, in order not to change and destroy the salinity and mineral balance of the Dead Sea, the water would have to first go through desalination before it would be allowed to pour into the Dead Sea. The proposal also includes harnessing the seven-hundred-foot drop between the level of the Red Sea and that of the Dead Sea with hydroelectric plants, which would benefit both Jordan and Israel. Additional proposals include the construction of resorts along the length of the canal to attract tourism and further benefit the Jordanian and Israeli economies. This proposal is a win-win proposition that shows what is possible when nations choose peace and cooperation over hatred and war.

discrimination. Israel's crime rate is reported to be ninety-second in the world out of 123 countries. By comparison, the United States is reported to be forty-ninth, and the United Kingdom fifty-ninth. This lower ranking of ninety-second may be related to the fact that Israel is a country where many citizens obtain permits to openly carry handguns and where warfighters are required to have their combat-issued small arms on their person at all times. In Israel's case, availability of and access to lethal weapons does not translate into higher gun-crime rates. Not only must Israelis with gun permits register their handguns, but also all ammunition they purchase is cataloged and accounted for.

Not unlike many other countries, Israeli society suffers from corruption, seemingly at all levels of society, from the highest officers of government to the average man and woman on the street. Israeli corruption specifically and Near Eastern corruption in general are most likely an outgrowth of a regional tradition of monetary payments (some might say bribes) to facilitate transactions at the street level—a tradition known by its Arabic name, *Baksheesh*, a practice of greasing the palm. Examples of past high-level Israeli corruption cases include a former prime minister, former mayors of major cities, and senior IDF general officers who all served prison sentences for bribery and corruption. As of the writing of this manuscript, Israel's former prime minister, Benjamin Netanyahu, was under indictment in four cases of corruption and bribery. Israelis are masters of finding the loophole in the law. Even at the level of the common man and woman, Israelis are notorious for underclaiming income, so much so that they have an ironic term for unreported revenue: *kesef nakee* (clean money).

As mentioned above, Israelis are not exempt from ethnic and racial discrimination. Although Israel was founded as a haven for Jews worldwide, there are constant complaints by Ethiopian and other African Jews of racial and ethnic discrimination. In 1996, some Israeli blood-donation centers were discovered throwing out blood collected from Ethiopian Jews even before their blood could be tested, fearing their blood might be contaminated with HIV. There are today persistent examples of Ashkenazi (white European) Jews not wanting non-Ashkenazi Jewish children attending schools with their children. Many but not all communities and settlements restrict home ownership and residency to various ethnic and religious groups. Orthodox—especially Haredi (Ultra-Orthodox)—Jews prefer to live in all-Orthodox communities and neighborhoods, just as non-Orthodox Jews prefer to live in non-Orthodox, secular communities.

Although Jews from Muslim countries (Oriental/Eastern Jews) make up half of Israel's population, a persistent complaint is heard that they are marginalized and underrepresented in the country's halls of power and government. As discussed earlier, political Zionism began as a movement among European Jews in the nineteenth century. The first Zionist immigrants who came to Palestine with the goal of establishing a haven for the world Jewry were predominantly secular Eastern European Jews. However, immediately after attaining statehood, the floodgates burst wide open, and hundreds of thousands of culturally Arabized Eastern Jews from Arab-Muslim lands came to Israel as refugees. These Jews tended to be more religious than their European counterparts and brought with them Near Eastern mentalities, the result of centuries of acculturation.

In the early 1950s as the new Jewish state began to take form, its powerbrokers and leaders in government, industry, the military, entertainment, and communications were almost exclusively European Jews, even though at the time, Jews from Arab and Muslim countries made up the majority of new immigrants. Oriental/Eastern Jews were less educated and were viewed by European Israelis as unsophisticated and incapable of leading a modern, twentieth-century country. One place this manifested itself was in the dominant pronunciation of the newly revived Hebrew language, which took on a unique new European/French-German pronunciation as opposed to a more correct Near Eastern Semitic pronunciation.[64] In the 1950s and 1960s, educated

---

[64] The European-influenced pronunciation gives English-speaking Israelis a French-European accent (see footnote below).

Israeli journalists with a correct, original Eastern/Oriental/Semitic pronunciation were chosen to read the news over the radio, and that carried over into television in the late 1960s. However, by the 1970s, these Eastern journalists were gradually replaced by Hebrew speakers with a more modern, European-sounding pronunciation. This is today the accepted Israeli Hebrew pronunciation, which is taught as the correct Hebrew pronunciation in elementary schools and in new-immigrant language academies across Israel. Ironically, it is Arabs and native Arabic speakers who today pronounce Hebrew more phonetically true to its original pronunciation than do most Israelis.[65]

Interestingly, in the twenty-first century, there has been a shift in the visibility and acceptance of the Eastern/Oriental Jewish voice, especially in the cultural footprint of modern Israel. Today's Israeli music is reaching a widespread audience and gaining broader acceptance, and it is seeing a revival of the use of Near Eastern and Mediterranean syncopated beats common to music from the Aegean to Southwest Asia. As mentioned earlier, there is no such thing as typical Israeli food since Israelis come from more than one hundred different countries. Although many European Jews brought with them traditional East European (Ashkenazi) foods, most Israeli foods today have a Near Eastern/Arabic flavor. Israelis today are embracing their Oriental/Near Eastern cultural roots and are giving a new voice to a segment of their population that had for the first decades been ignored, sidestepped, and regarded as unsophisticated but is now celebrated and mainstreamed.

---

[65] The following examples show how modern Hebrew dropped its original Semitic sound and adopted a more European pronunciation. The pronunciation of the eighth letter of the Hebrew alphabet, the unaspirated, guttural/throaty sound of *h* (*Het* ח) has been replaced in modern Hebrew by the "kh" sound found in Dutch and German and similar to the pronunciation of the eleventh letter of the Hebrew alphabet, *Khaf* כ. The sixteenth letter of the Hebrew alphabet, the iconic Semitic *Ayin* ע, is a letter not found in any European or Latin language and is extremely hard for Westerners to pronounce. It has been replaced in modern Hebrew by the "a" sound (*Alef* א pronunciation). More and more modern Hebrew speakers are pronouncing the fifth letter of the Hebrew alphabet, the traditional, aspirated *h* (*Hey* ה), as an *a* (*Alef* א), especially if it appears as the first letter of a word. Finally, the Semitic *r* (*Resh* ר), traditionally pronounced like the Spanish trilled *r*, has been replaced in modern Hebrew by the guttural French pronunciation of *r*.

Perhaps the loudest and oldest discrimination complaint heard in Israel today is that from Arabs, both Israeli citizens and noncitizen Arabs, who claim that the Jewish state has an unwritten, institutional policy of not providing equal benefits to them as it does to Israel's Jewish communities. They often complain that if Sephardic or Oriental Jews feel like they are second-class citizens, then they (Arabs) are third-class citizens.

Notes

"Israel," *The Central Intelligence Factbook* (2019).

Israel Ministry of Foreign Affairs. *"The Land: Geography and Climate,"* (2013).

"Total Population by Country," *World Population Review* (2018).

"The Demographics of the Arab World and the Middle East from the 1950 to the 2000s," *I.N.E.D.* (2005).

"Population of Cities in Israel (2018)," *World Population Review* (2017).

Thomas C. Frohlich, "The Most Educated Countries in the World," *USA Today* (2014).

"Jewish Biographies: Nobel Prize Laureates." *Jewish Virtual Library. 1901–2020. American-Israeli Cooperative Enterprise.* https://www. jewishvirtuallibrary.org/nobel-prize-laureates. 2020.

"Jewish Nobel Prize Winners." *Jinfo.org.* https://www.jinfo.org/Nobel_ Prizes. 2002–2018.

Neil Patrick, "The Sea of Galilee or "Jesus Boat," *The Vinage News* (2016).

Kevin Connolly, "Dead Sea Drying: A New Low-Point on Earth," *BBC* (2016).

Hanson R. Hosein, "The Dying Dead Sea: Levels Falling Precipitously as Rivers are Diverted" *NBC News* (1999).

"Crime Index for Country 2019 Mid-Year," *Serbia 2009–2019* (2019).

Chapter 7

Government, Infrastructure, and the Military

Government

On November 29, 1947, the world's nations, through the United Nations General Assembly, voted to partition Palestine into two separate countries.[66] On May 15, 1948, Israel declared independence. Following a war of extermination, Israel's War of Independence, which was waged upon Israel by six Arab countries—Lebanon, Syria, Jordan, Iraq, Egypt, and Saudi Arabia—Israel's de facto borders were set within what is internationally known as the Green Line. Today, this Green Line is recognized as Israel's legal boundary by the United Nations and much of the world community. As noted in chapter 5, because of Jerusalem's importance to Judaism, Christianity, and Islam, the 1947

---

[66] United Nations General Assembly Resolution 181, which established separate Arab and Jewish countries in Palestine, was passed on November 29, 1947, by a vote of thirty-three for to thirteen against, with ten abstentions. Ten of the thirteen no votes were from the Arab and Muslim-majority countries of Afghanistan, Egypt, Iran, Iraq, Lebanon, Pakistan, Saudi Arabia, Syria, Yemen, and Turkey, while the remaining three no votes came from the non-Muslim and non–Near Eastern countries of Greece, Cuba, and India.

United Nations Palestine Partition Plan decreed that it should become an internationally administered city, a *corpus separatum*. However, since Jerusalem became a divided city after the war, with Jordan in possession of East Jerusalem and Israel in possession of West Jerusalem, Israel declared and established the western half as its capital. Like all sovereign nations, Israel exercised its right to locate its nation's capital in a city under its jurisdiction.

Following Palestine's partition, the Hashemite Kingdom of Jordan annexed the West Bank, which included East Jerusalem, denying Jews access to their most sacred sites. West Jerusalem became known as its own entity, "Jewish Jerusalem," or "Israeli West Jerusalem." Since Israel attained statehood, all Israeli government ministries—executive, legislative, and judicial—except for the Ministry of Defense (MOD) have been located in West Jerusalem. The MOD was and remains located today in Tel Aviv in a secure, walled "village" (*kiryah*), where it can better direct military operations in times of war, far from and more secure than the much-fought-over city of Jerusalem.

Although Israel has had its capital in West Jerusalem since 1949, to reaffirm this fact, the Israeli legislature passed the "Jerusalem Law" in 1980, declaring Jerusalem to be its "Eternal and Indivisible Capital." For Jews, no other city could be considered as a capital, since Jerusalem had been the Jewish capital going back to the year 1000 BCE, when King David made it his capital. Jews that had been in Babylonian captivity since 586 BCE prayed daily for their return to Jerusalem and longed to rebuild the temple. Their daily prayer, beginning during this time in Babylon and continuing throughout the almost 2,500-year Diaspora was "next year in Jerusalem." To Arabs, for the most part, Israel's historical connection to this land is ancient history, not current reality.

Israel is a parliamentary democracy with universal suffrage at age eighteen that boasts of being the only liberal democracy with an independent free press in the Near East. Its branches of government are the executive (office of the prime minister, head of state), the legislative Parliament (Knesset), the judicial (Supreme Court), and the largely ceremonial office of the president. Israel is a multiparty democracy that allows any legally registered party to participate in elections and present candidates. Unlike in the United States, Israelis vote for a specific party, and the winning party's head becomes the presumptive prime minister (head of state). Following an election, which is held every four years, the president of Israel gives the party with the largest percentage of the votes twenty-eight days to form a majority government by coalition with other parties in order to achieve a majority of 61 of 120 parliamentary seats. Although there have been more than two hundred political parties since Israel's founding, many have come and gone, and today there are about twenty registered parties. Interestingly, Israel was governed by liberal labor-coalition governments during the first half of its seventy-three-year history and conservative-coalition governments in the second half. Israel's political system allows for Ultra-Orthodox Jewish parties; conservative and liberal parties; center, center-right, center-left, exclusive Arab political parties, and the Communist Party.

Jerusalem: Beyond the Rhetoric

In December 2017, United States President Donald Trump announced that the US would be transferring its embassy from Tel Aviv to Jerusalem. On May 14, 2018, the US embassy in Israel took up official residency in Jerusalem, the former location of the US consulate in West Jerusalem. The date was no accident; it was the exact date of Israel's declaration of independence seventy years earlier, May 14, 1948. In 1995, exactly twenty-three years earlier, the US Congress, in a bipartisan and unanimous vote, had passed the Jerusalem Embassy Act, authorizing the US to move its embassy to Jerusalem. Until this date, the United States and most other countries with diplomatic and ambassadorial-level relations with Israel maintained their embassies in Tel Aviv. The reason most countries today keep their embassies in Tel Aviv is political.

103

It is diplomatically customary for nations with ambassadorial-level relations to place their respective embassies in their host country's capital. Since the United Nations had declared that Jerusalem should be governed by an international body as a *corpus separatum*—a plan that was never realized—rather than making a politically controversial statement and placing their embassies in Israel's declared capital, Jerusalem, most countries with diplomatic relations with Israel opted to place their embassies in Tel Aviv, Israel's largest city and commercial capital. Countries with diplomatic relations with Israel adopted the position that they would wait to move their embassies to Jerusalem until a final, negotiated settlement of the Arab-Israeli conflict, which would also address the ultimate disposition of Jerusalem, following future direct negotiations between Israel and the Arab nations. Countries simply did not want to appear to take political sides in the Arab-Israeli conflict but rather sidestepped the question of Jerusalem's ownership. However, all this changed when the US moved its embassy to Jerusalem in 2018. Several countries now felt emboldened and unrestrained to act on their desires to have their embassies moved to Israel's capital, Jerusalem. In May 2018, immediately after the Trump administration moved the US embassy to Jerusalem, Guatemala moved its embassy from Tel Aviv to Jerusalem, and that opened the door for other countries to follow.[67]

To further complicate the Jerusalem question, since Israel attained statehood and Arab and Palestinian nationalism began to rise, Palestinians have made clear their hope of having Jerusalem as their capital if and when a Palestinian state is established. Jerusalem has never been the capital of an independent Palestine—not under today's Arabized population, not during the Arab-Islamic rule of the Near East, nor at any time in the pre-Islamic-Arab Near East. There has

---

[67] Brazil, Hungary, and Bulgaria have opened diplomatic missions in Jerusalem. The Czech Republic, Romania, Australia, Moldova, Serbia, Honduras, and Uruguay have announced plans to move their embassies to Jerusalem, and Italy is said to be considering moving its embassy there as well. In February 2021, Kosovo, a Muslim-majority country, announced that it would not only be establishing diplomatic relations with Israel but that it would be locating its embassy in Jerusalem, making it the first Muslim country to do so.

never in history been a self-ruled country of Palestine. Palestine has only been a geographic region, originally the Syria-Palestine province of the Roman Near East. That is not to say that Palestinian Arabs do not desire an independent Palestinian country or that there may well be at some point in the future an independent Arab-Palestinian country. Arab claims to Jerusalem are through Islam.[68] Jerusalem is regarded by Muslims as Islam's third most holy site, but never has it been a capital to any Arab-Islamic state or caliphate. In its three-thousand-year history since its capture by King David from the Jebusites, Jerusalem has only been the capital of Judea, the United Jewish Monarchy of Israel and Judea, and now the modern State of Israel.

Economy

With a fraction of the Near East's population, Israel's gross domestic product (GDP) is larger than the economies of all the non-oil-producing countries of the Near East combined. Israel accomplished this feat, often called an economic miracle, in the past seven decades while absorbing more than three million refugees and funding and fighting four major wars and smaller subwars. Israel's dynamo economy flourished while enduring an Arab-led international political and economic boycott known as Boycott, Divestment, and Sanctions (BDS). Israel has one of the highest tax rates in the world, with a graduated income tax ranging from 10 to 50 percent. Israelis pay an additional 17 percent value-added sales tax on most products. Israel does not produce cars domestically, and Israelis pay a 110 percent tax on imported vehicles (taxed by weight and engine size). The government regulates prices on staples such as dairy, bread, eggs, flour, and salt. Because of its need to maintain a strong military, Israel spends 5.5 percent of its GDP, or $23 billion, annually on defense. By comparison, the US spends $571 billion on defense (3.5 percent of its GDP), and Egypt an estimated $50 billion (reported to be up to 40 percent of its GDP).

---

[68] The name *Jerusalem* does not appear in the Qur'an, but the Qur'an speaks of a "northern city" from which Muhammad ascended to heaven on his horse in a vision and in a dream. Muslims interpret this city to be Jerusalem.

Agriculture was the primary economic activity for immigrating Jews in pre-statehood Palestine when much of the Jewish population lived and worked on collective farms called *kibbutzim*. During the past forty years, agriculture has given way to industry and manufacturing. Today, most Israelis are employed in hi-tech R & D, manufacturing, electronics, aviation, engineering, chemicals, communications, pharmaceuticals, tourism and hospitality, service and entertainment, food processing, diamond cutting and polishing, and armaments manufacturing. Israel still produces most of its required agricultural needs, including fruit, vegetables, beef, dairy, lamb, poultry, and pork. After Israel attained statehood, pork raising and processing was restricted to Arab Christian communities living in Galilee, because pork is prohibited in both Judaism and Islam. However, with the influx of Russian immigrants in the 1980s and early 1990s following the collapse of the Soviet Union, raising and processing pork has spread to other regions of the country. Although eating pork is prohibited in Judaism for being non-kosher (unclean), many European Jews who immigrated to Israel had eaten pork for generations in their native European lands. These immigrants brought with them not only a taste for the meat but a knowledge of processing and smoking it.[69] Israelis are credited with eating more turkey per capita than any other people in the world. Along with lamb and veal, turkey is often eaten as fast food in shawarma—meat grilled on a rotisserie and eaten in pita bread, like a Greek gyro.

Israel has few natural resources, and what little it has—including copper, phosphate, bromide, potash, clay, sand, and sulfur—comes from the Dead Sea and the southern Negev Desert area. In many ways, Israel's economic success is like that of other successful countries with few natural resources, such as Japan, South Korea, and Singapore. Israel's biggest natural resource is brain power, which drives its entrepreneurial spirit, energy, imagination, and innovation.

---

[69] Growing up in the all-Arab southern Galilee city of Nazareth, our next-door Christian Arab neighbors, who raised pigs on their property, leased part of their land to two Romanian Jews, who built a large, industrial meat smoker on the property and produced their smoked pork in the safety of the Christian Arab population.

The US has designated Israel a major non-NATO ally and often refers to Israel as a US ally in the political-military context. Both countries partner in numerous scientific, research, economic, and military cooperative ventures. As a result of the 1979 Camp David Accords, the US gives Israel $1.2 billion annually in economic aid together with $1.8 billion in military assistance and credit that Israel may use only to buy US-made military equipment, not weaponry from other countries. With this requirement, the dollars given to Israel for military assistance are in part returned to the US economy as Israel purchases weapons systems from US defense contractors, which employ Americans.

Trade

Israel maintains close ties and trading partnerships with numerous countries, none stronger or closer than its relationship with the United States. Historically, US-Israeli relations have been excellent, transcending each country's internal politics. This relationship is referred to as "special" (exceptional), with numerous agreements and cooperation on issues including trade, security, information-sharing, arms sales, and others. In September 2018, the US inaugurated the first permanent US military presence in Israel. Israel initially identified it as a US military base, but the US quickly corrected that it was a military facility. The facility is located on an Israeli air base in the southern Negev Desert at the home of Israel's air defense school. The facility is said to have a permanent cadre of dozens of soldiers, though officials have not disclosed the exact types of equipment present or the specific number of permanent US forces.[70] The lowest point in the US-Israeli relationship was during the eight-year Obama administration from 2009 to 2016. The highest point in US-Israeli relations began under the Trump administration in 2017. Since attaining statehood, Israel has maintained excellent relations with other countries, primarily the European nations

---

[70] The mission of the US presence is most likely to conduct joint air defense training and operate air defense systems in support of US forces in the region. The US has funded and cooperated with Israel's development of the world's first true anti–ballistic-missile missile, the Arrow, and the antirocket Iron Dome system.

of Germany, Great Britain, the Netherlands, and Belgium, as well as with South Africa and other sub-Saharan African countries. Germany and Israel have had a unique close relationship since Israel attained statehood in 1948.[71] Germany has paid Holocaust survivors billions of dollars in war reparations and has been a strong economic trading partner with Israel. Germany was one of the top purchasers of the Uzi assault submachine gun manufactured by Israel Military Industries (IMI), which was made famous during the 1967 Six-Day War and continues to buy Israeli-made weaponry today. Great Britain and Israel trade in pharmaceuticals, telecommunications, medical equipment, vegetables, fruit, and textiles. The Netherlands is one of Israel's biggest European trading partners and strongest European supporters. South Africa and Belgium trade with Israel in other products: South Africa sells Israel raw, uncut diamonds, and Belgium provides Israel with an outlet to the world for its cut and polished diamonds. Diamonds and armaments make up two of Israel's biggest sources of foreign revenue. Israel has long sold manufactured products and armaments to numerous Central and South American countries. For decades, Israel has maintained strong trade, economic, agricultural, military, and manufacturing relationships with many African countries. Its disaster recovery teams are among the first responders to natural disasters worldwide. Israeli humanitarian presence and trade can literally be found on every continent.

Not normally in the spotlight is Israel's long behind-the-scenes trade and contact with select Arab countries. Since 2018, Israel and several Arab countries have made public their private contacts and explicitly stated a desire for more normal relations. These include the Persian/Arabian Gulf countries of Bahrain, the United Arab Emirates (UAE), and Oman. Because Iran is expanding its influence and supporting proxy conflicts in Iraq, Syria, Lebanon, Yemen, and the Gaza Strip, Israel and Arab Gulf countries are finding mutual strategic interests

---

[71] While I served as an assistant air attaché to Israel in the 1990s, the German military attaché told me that his most important duty was to lay a wreath at the tomb of the unknown soldier in Jerusalem on Israel's War Remembrance Day. After the dark days of the Holocaust, Germany feels a special obligation to atone to the Jewish people.

that are drawing them closer. This came to a head in August and September 2020 when the UAE and Bahrain announced they would be normalizing relations with Israel, including ambassadorial and embassy exchanges.[72] In October, Sudan announced it would be normalizing relations with Israel, and in December, Morocco announced it would establish full diplomatic relations with Israel. Arab Gulf countries have for years warned against Iranian aspirations throughout the Near East, and today, old hatreds and alliances are giving way to new threats that are causing former adversaries to adopt a more pragmatic stance toward the Jewish state. Gulf state alliances with Israel may soon result in Israeli weapons, technology, forces, and military might on Iran's doorstep, a huge balance-of-power game changer that will keep Iranian expansionism in check. As the adage states, the enemy of my enemy is my friend.

The UAE, Bahrain, and Sudan normalizing diplomatic relations with Israel has opened the floodgates for other countries outside the Near East to also announce they would soon be establishing relations with Israel. Among these are Kosovo (a Muslim-majority country discussed in a footnote above under "Economy"), Serbia, and Malawi. Many developing countries are eager to benefit from Israel's advanced technologies and trade.

Social Services

Having first been settled by Jews fleeing Russian pogroms of the late 1800s, followed by other European Jews, Israel and its first-generation political leaders have long had a propensity for European-like socialism, specifically social welfare programs. Today, Israelis expect their government to be a generous provider of services. It's in their DNA. These services are provided to all Israeli citizens, Jew and Arab alike.

---

[72] The UAE stated that its embassy in Israel would be located in Tel Aviv, as will most likely those of other Arab countries. There are persistent rumors that Oman and possibly Saudi Arabia will soon normalize diplomatic relations with Israel.

Since its early years, Israel has had a national single-payer health care system and generous social security programs; these were created in response to pre-statehood and early-statehood economic conditions at a time when the population was relatively poor and few people had or could afford a private vehicle. Consequently, employers in Israel today are mandated by law to provide their employees with either a home-to-work transportation allowance in their paychecks or actual home-to-work transportation. Many career military officers are assigned a military vehicle, which is not only used to get the soldier to and from work but can also be used for personal family transportation needs; in certain conditions it can even be driven by a military member's spouse, a practice very foreign to Americans for which US service member would be charged with misuse of government property. The practice of giving designated career military officers a government vehicle to get to and from work grew out of Israel's security situation, which requires critical warfighters to be able at a moment's notice to quickly drive to their units or assembly points in order to immediately defend Israel in times of hostilities.

Maternity benefits are generous in Israel and more closely mirror those enjoyed by Europeans. Israeli women are given full-salary paid maternity leave for fifteen weeks (3.75 months) with guaranteed return reemployment for up to one year.[73] In addition to receiving eighteen days of annual paid sick leave, all Israelis enjoy annual, mandated paid vacations of ten days during their first four years of employment and fifteen days following employment of over seven years.

Military service, which is mandatory in Israel for all Jewish citizens and optional for non-Jewish citizens and permanent residents, provides its own incentives and monetary rewards. Upon separating from military

[73] Israeli woman can also be granted eleven additional weeks (three months) of unpaid maternity leave for a maximum of twenty-six weeks (6.5 months) of leave, which is generous and enviable by any country's standards. Israeli fathers receive seven days of maternity leave. In early 2019, a bill was presented in the Israeli Parliament to extend fathers' maternity leave to thirty days. Israel gives a childbirth cash-payment grant of $486 per child, up to $3,650 for triplets. Additionally, Israel provides a monthly childhood allowance from birth to age eighteen of $42 for the first child and a maximum of $250 for five children.

110

service, noncombat veterans receive a one-time cash award of $2,400, while warfighters receive $5,550. Separated soldiers also receive grants for education, housing, or business start-ups in the amount of $5,200 for noncombat-support veterans, $6,450 for combat-support veterans, and $7,500 for warfighters. Israelis value their defenders and reward them well following their service.

Infrastructure

Israel today enjoys a national highway system that crisscrosses the length and width of the country. Israel is in the final stages of building a complete north-to-south, four-lane toll road (Highway 6). Public transportation in Israel is second to none, with bus lines linking the entire country. Its rail system connects most cities north to south along the Mediterranean coastline, including lines that run from Tel Aviv to Jerusalem and south to the Negev Desert city of Beersheba. Israel's rail system is expanding to eventually link the entire country from its northern Lebanese border to the southern Red Sea port and resort city of Eilat on the Gulf of Aqaba. With a growing population in a relatively small geographic area, vehicular congestion during rush hours in and around its larger cities rivals that of any international large metropolitan area. Consequently, Israel and Israelis are depending more on public transportation. Israel is building a metro underground subway system in and around Tel Aviv, which will be linked to Israel's national rail system.

Israelis are renowned for being naturalist outdoor enthusiasts and enjoy picnicking, grilling, camping, hiking, and vacationing in or near the numerous state parks, natural springs, pools, rivers, and lakes and on the Mediterranean, Dead Sea, and Red Sea beaches. Many of Israel's state parks are treasured archaeological sites that date to the second millennium BCE (more than four thousand years ago). Israelis celebrate every archaeological excavation that uncovers early Hebrew-Israelite-Judahite history as confirmation of their ancestral roots to the land. There is a common saying in Israel that all Israelis are amateur archaeologists.

Housing

Because of limited real estate and the high cost of construction, most Israelis live in four- or five-room apartments in multistory buildings. Most homes and buildings, including their interior walls, are built from steel-reinforced poured concrete and concrete cinder blocks. Many homes, apartments, and government and commercial buildings are also given an outer layer of decoratively chiseled native stones, especially in Jerusalem, Haifa, and Nazareth and in most Arab towns, villages, and Druze communities in Israel's northern Galilee region. Jerusalem has a law requiring all buildings to be built of stone. This law was partially passed to make buildings in Jerusalem more resilient and able to withstand bombs and bullets because of its history of being much fought over. Structures of any kind, housing or commercial, are almost never built from lumber, as is the norm in the US. Lumber is scarce in Israel and not considered a sturdy or durable enough material to house and protect habitation.[74]

More than half of Israel's population lives in the central region of the country, known as ha-Mirkaz (the Center). This area is ever expanding north, south, and east of Tel Aviv and into the many adjacent municipalities that have grown and merged into what is now the overlapping urban sprawl of greater metropolitan Tel Aviv. Most Israelis choose to live in this area because it affords them greater employment opportunities. The downside is its high cost of living. Tel Aviv is not only Israel's largest metropolitan area; it is also Israel's commercial center, home to the IDF headquarters and Israel's cultural center, which houses its Philharmonic Symphony Orchestra, opera

---

[74] Israelis often ponder why Americans frame their homes with lumber, especially in tornado- and hurricane-prone regions. They often refer to American homes and buildings constructed from wood as temporary structures.

house, and numerous museums and galleries. Tel Aviv has a reputation like that of Paris and New York City for being "the city that never sleeps," because of its twenty-four seven entertainment and restaurant scene.

Military

Even before Israel attained statehood, Jews in pre-Israel Palestine had already formed defensive militias to protect their homes, settlements, and families. Some of these early established defensive militias (such as Hagana, Irgun, Palmach, Stern Gang, Lehi) became offensive and attacked both Arab militants and British military forces who were blockading the coast and preventing Jews from entering Palestine. After Israel attained statehood, the various Jewish militias came together under the leadership of the Haganah (which means "defense" in Hebrew) and became the Israel Defense Forces (Tsavah Haganah LeYisra'el צבא הגנה לישראל).

Military service is compulsory in Israel for all Jewish citizens upon graduation from high school following their eighteenth birthday. Non-Jewish citizens and permanent residents may serve in the military if they choose to with the approval of the Israel Defense Forces (IDF).[75] There are numerous Arab-Christian, Arab-Muslim, and Druze citizens of Israel serving in the IDF today.[76] In addition to post-service monetary benefits for having served in the Israeli military, as discussed above, there are employment benefits for having served and consequences for not having served. Veterans are given priority in employment over nonveterans. A complaint often heard by Arab Israelis is that they do

---

[75] Because our family's visa status in Israel was "permanent residents," when I turned eighteen, the IDF attempted to draft me into Israeli military. I was able to get a release from serving in the Israeli military because I am not Jewish.

[76] A Greek Orthodox priest in Nazareth, Father Gabriel Nadaf, is an advocate for Israeli Arabs to enlist in the IDF. In addition to having supporters, he has detractors. His life has been threatened, and his son was criminally attacked.

not stand a chance when competing for employment against Jewish Israelis, who as veterans are given employment preference.

Men generally serve in the IDF for three years of active duty and remain in the reserves until age fifty-five. Women generally serve for two years of active duty and are required to serve in the reserves until age thirty-eight, with exceptions made for family considerations. Although only Jewish Israelis and permanent residents are required to register for conscription and serve in the IDF, there are exceptions and exemptions, the biggest one being for non-Jews. Other exemptions are for pregnant women, Orthodox Jews attending seminaries (*yeshivot*), citizens with disabilities that prohibit them from serving, and conscientious objectors. Alternatives to military service are also an option in some cases. Normally, Israeli young people overwhelmingly support military service and eagerly anticipate their enlistment.

Israel's standing active military force is an estimated 175,000 troops and can surge to a wartime strength of 1.56 million within forty-eight hours. As in most countries, not all combat roles are open to women, but more roles are constantly being added. Today, Israeli women fly every aircraft in the IAF inventory, including fighter aircraft.

The order of battle figures given below should be understood in the context that Israel does not reveal exact numbers when it comes to its weaponry and strengths, so as not to give its adversaries an accurate understanding of its capabilities.

Army

Because of the Israeli Army's historical primacy as a service, Israelis often say "army" when they mean "military." The senior-ranking Israeli military officer, the chief of the general staff, is always an army major-general, a three-star general. There is only one major-general in the IDF.

The Israeli Army's personnel strength is reported as 134,000, making it the largest of the three services. The army is believed to have 1,730 tanks with several hundred more on order. Most of Israel's tanks today are extremely capable, state-of-the-art, indigenously built Merkava (Chariot) main battle tanks. To safeguard the tank's technology and capability, Israel does not export the Merkava. The Israeli Army is reported to have 2,783 self-propelled and towed artillery.

Air Force

After the IDF tests its new recruits for aptitude, intelligence, and physical ability, the Air Force gets first pick. The Israeli pilot-training attrition rate is 90 percent; by comparison, the US pilot-training attrition rate is 50 percent. Israeli pilots are Israel's first line of defense, so the IAF only accepts the best of the best. The IAF's personnel strength is 32,000, and its total number of aircraft is reported to be around 1,200. Of these, more than 500 are fighter aircraft, all US manufactured. Israel began receiving the most advanced US F-35 fighter aircraft in December 2017. Except for Japan and South Korea, Israel is the only non-NATO country to receive this fifth-generation, technologically superior, supersonic stealth fighter aircraft. In addition, the IAF has more than 350 cargo and transport aircraft and more than 350 attack and transport helicopters.

Navy

Although the Israeli Navy is the smallest of the three services, with nine thousand total active-duty sailors, in recent years, it has taken on a more important role in Israel's expanding regional offensive capability. Historically, the Israeli Navy has only had a coastal patrol mission, protecting Israel's long Mediterranean coastline and its Red Sea southern outlet and port, Eilat. For many years, Israel had only two older World War II–vintage submarines, but in recent years, the Israeli Navy has acquired three Dolphin-class submarines and new high-speed, state-of-the-art warships from Germany. Israel's new, more capable submarines give it a deep-water naval capability and complete its triad of nuclear-delivery methods. Other vessels in the Israeli Navy include eighteen missile-armed coastal patrol craft.

Nuclear Opacity

Israel does not discuss its nuclear program, either officially or speculatively. Israel maintains its silence, or "nuclear ambiguity," regarding any discussion of its real or hypothetical nuclear weapons program—a strategy also known as "nuclear opacity." Stated another way, Israel does not acknowledge or deny having a nuclear weapons program; it simply refuses to engage in any forum that has Israel's nuclear weapons program as an agenda item.

Israel was born surrounded by enemies vowing to destroy it and needed an aggressive defensive/offensive qualitative advantage. In 1949, almost immediately after the country attained statehood, Israel's first prime minister, David Ben-Gurion, directed Israeli scientists to begin a nuclear research center in the southern Negev desert, near the city of Dimona. Ben-Gurion stated, "What Einstein, Oppenheimer, and Teller, (all Jewish nuclear scientists) made for the United States, could also be done by [Jewish] scientists in Israel, for their own people." Israeli scientists developed a nuclear reactor and processing plant and shortly thereafter began exploring nuclear weapons development. Israel received a boost in its research and development under US President Dwight Eisenhower's "Atoms for Peace" program. In the 1950s, when France was also developing a nuclear weapons program, French and Israeli nuclear scientists began cooperating on research. It is now known that French scientists and the French nuclear program benefitted more from Israeli scientists and the Israeli nuclear program than did the Israelis from the French. Israeli scientists were more advanced in their understanding of nuclear weapons than were the French. Israeli scientists did the early nuclear heavy lifting in this cooperative program.

Israel is believed to have tested and detonated a nuclear device in the Negev Desert in 1963 and is thought to have produced its first nuclear weapon as early as December 1966. In 1979, Israel was suspected to have been involved in a joint nuclear test with South Africa on an island in the Indian Ocean. Israel is one of only eight countries to have developed nuclear weapons, becoming an unofficial member of the nuclear club that includes the US, Russia, France, Great Britain, China, India, Pakistan, and North Korea. Pakistan, North Korea, and Israel are the only three countries believed to have nuclear weapons that have not signed the Nuclear Non-Proliferation Treaty.[77] Although it denies it, Iran is believed to be developing nuclear weapons.

At the beginning of the twenty-first century, General Colin Powell, the former US chairman of the Joint Chiefs of Staff, estimated that Israel had two hundred nuclear weapons, while former US President Jimmy Carter estimated Israel to have three hundred nuclear weapons. Other estimates put Israel's nuclear arsenal as high as four hundred. Israel can deliver a nuclear warhead either via surface-to-surface missiles, via its indigenously produced Jericho missile, by aircraft, with the F-15 and F-35, or via its Dolphin-class submarines. Israel today possesses a true triad of nuclear weapons delivery methods.

Over the past two decades, Israel has seen a growing threat from Iran, whose leadership has repeatedly called for Israel's annihilation. Iran has in recent years replaced the traditional confrontational Arab states of Egypt, Syria, Jordan, Iraq, and Lebanon as the new face of opposition and existential threat.[78] Beginning in 2018, Iranian forces and proxies in Syria began cross-border rocket and missile attacks against Israel. It

---

[77] The Non-Proliferation Treaty (NPT) was developed by the United Nations in 1968 to limit the spread/proliferation of nuclear weapons and nuclear-weapons technology. The three original nuclear states, the United States, Russia, and Great Britain, first ratified the treaty in 1970 followed by France and China after they had developed nuclear weapons. Another 191 countries have since also signed the treaty. In 2003, North Korea announced that it was withdrawing from the treaty. Israel is not a signatory to the treaty, not because it plans to spread nuclear-weapons technology but because if it signed the treaty, it would appear to be admitting that it possesses nuclear weapons. This is a hollow argument, since 191 other countries who do not possess nuclear weapons have signed the treaty.

[78] Iran's supreme leader, Ayatollah Khamenei, said that "[the] barbaric Jewish state has no cure but to be annihilated." He also said, "The occupying regime in Jerusalem [should] be wiped off the face of the earth. ... This cancerous tumor of a state should be removed."

is estimated that Iran's Islamic Revolutionary Guard Corps (Farsi: سپاه
پاسداران انقلابی اسلامی) and other Iranian military forces number twenty
thousand in Syria. In addition to Iran's rhetorical threat, Tehran has
long been using proxies, specifically Hizb Allah[79] (حزب الله) in Lebanon,
and more recently has been funding and equipping Hamas[80] (حماس)
and Palestinian Islamic Jihad (Arabic: al-Jihad al-Islami fi Falastin
الجهاد الاسلامي في فلسطين) in the Gaza Stip.

Israel and Iran may be moving toward a nuclear showdown if Iran
produces nuclear weapons. Israel has twice destroyed Arab nuclear
facilities in the early stage of construction. First, the IAF bombed
and destroyed Iraq's Osirak nuclear facility in 1981, ending any hopes
the country had of developing nuclear capabilities, and then in 2007,
Israel destroyed Syria's Al-Kubar nuclear reactor, which was being
constructed with North Korean help in eastern Syria near Deir al-
Zor. Not wanting to admit that it was in fact constructing a nuclear
reactor, Syria initially only protested to the United Nations that Israeli
aircraft had overflown its airspace. Syria later, in a feeble attempt to
mask the facility's true purpose, publicly pondered why Israel would
want to attack "an abandoned World War II British air base." The
Syrians quickly bulldozed the bombed facility to remove evidence and
downplay its significance.

Israel is under no illusion that the only reason an adversary such as Iran
would develop a nuclear weapons program would be to annihilate the
Jewish state, as Iran has vowed to do on numerous occasions. There is
no doubt that if the world does not work in concert to stop Iran's not
only undeclared but denied nuclear weapons program, Israel will, at
the appropriate time, take out this developing threat, as it has stated
it would.

---

[79] *Hizb Allah* (حزب الله) is the correct Arabic-origin name for what is usually written in English
as *Hezbollah*, a transcription of the Iranian pronunciation. *Hizb* is Arabic for political party,
and *Allah* is Arabic for God, hence Hizb Allah.

[80] *Hamas* is a transliteration of the Arabic acronym for *Harakat al-Muqawamah al-Islamiyyah*
(Islamic Resistance Movement). As an acronym, it should probably be written in all capital
letters in English—*HAMAS*. Likewise, *Palestinian Islamic Jihad* is the English translation of
al-Jihad al-Islami fi Falastin.

In a memorandum of understanding signed by Israel and the US in 1965, Israel agreed that it "would not be the first country to introduce nuclear weapons to the Middle East." This position has evolved over the years in statements by several Israeli prime ministers and government spokespeople, first to "Israel will not be the first country to introduce nuclear weapons to the battlefield" and finally to "Israel will not be the first country to introduce weapons of mass destruction to the battlefield." Technically and factually, weapons of mass destruction have already been introduced to three Near East battlefields in the past fifty years; First, Egypt's President Nasser used them in the 1960s during the Yemen Civil War. Second, Iraqi President Saddam Hussein used chemical weapons in the 1980s against Iranian forces during the Iran-Iraq War and again against Iraqi Kurds after the 1991 First Gulf War. Third, chemical weapons were used by Syria's President Bashar al-Assad against opposition forces and civilians in the Syrian Civil War that began in 2011.

As a footnote to Israel's nuclear opacity policy, in 1986, the British Sunday *Times* newspaper printed a detailed account of Israel's nuclear weapons program at Dimona in the Negev Desert. Its source was a man by the name of Mordechai Vanunu, who claimed to work in the facility as a technician. The *Times* report included schematic drawings of a multistory underground facility, detailing rooms and chambers dedicated to known processes for the development of nuclear weapons. Israel initially dismissed the story and Vanunu's claim, but he was later captured in a Mossad kidnapping operation that brought him to Israel to stand trial for "treason, aggravated espionage, and collection of secret information with intent to impair state security." Given that he was captured, kidnaped, tried, and found guilty, there must have been some validity to Mr. Vanunu's claim, contrary to Israel's denials.

Notes

"Israel," *The Central Intelligence Factbook* (2019).

Robert O. Freedman, *Contemporary Israel* (Westview Press, 2009).

"Government: Political Parties in Israel", *Israel Science and Technology Directory* (2018).

"Israel Elections: Overview & Explanation," *Jewish Virtual Library* (2018).

Ashly Turner, "After US Embassy Makes Controversial Move to Jerusalem, More Countries Follow its Lead," *CNBC* (May 17, 2018).

Bill O'Reilly, "More Countries Following Trump in Moving Israel Embassy to Jerusalem," *Fox News* (July 9, 2018).

Raphael Ahern, "Paraguay Reverses Jerusalem Embassy Move; Fuming Israel Shuts Asuncion Mission," *Times of Israel* (September 5, 2018).

Mohamed Mamama, "Sisi Says Military Economy is 1.5% of Egypt's GDP, But How Accurate Is It?" *Mada (*November 2, 2016).

"Prices of Regulated Consumer Goods," *Ministry of Economy and Industry* (October 2, 2016).

"Israel Honors Priest Who Promotes Arab Enlistment in the Army," *Crux Catholic Media Inc.* (2018).

Stephen Farrell, "Israel Admits Bombing Suspected Syria Nuclear Reactor in 2007, Warn Iran," *Reuters World News* (March 20, 2018).

"Treaty on the Non-Proliferation of Nuclear Weapons (NPT)," *United Nations Office for Disarmament Affairs* (July 7, 2017).

"Headline: Revealed-The Secrets of Israel's Nuclear Arsenal/Atomic Technician Mordechai Vanunu Reveals Secret Weapons Production," *The Sunday Times* (October 5, 1986).

Ian Black. "Mordechai Vanunu Gets 18 Years for Treason-Archive, 1988," *The Guardian* (March 28, 1988).

Chapter 8

Nonstate, Low-Level Conflicts

Low-Level Conflicts

The signing of the Egyptian-Israeli Camp David Accords formalizing the first Arab-Israeli peace treaty ended major, multi-country warfare between Israel and its Arab neighbors. However, smaller-scale wars and lethal cross-border engagements took place before and continued after Camp David. In the 1970s, the PLO established armed camps in Lebanon and Jordan from which to attack Israel, with most of its fighters and their families living in Jordan. Jordan and Israel share a 192-mile-long border, the longest border between Israel and any of its neighbors. Jordan was an ideal base of operation for the PLO because it had a large, receptive Palestinian population with a pool of potentially like-minded individuals from which to recruit fighters. Although official Jordanian figures downplay the percentage of Palestinians in its population, independent sources place Jordan's Palestinian population as high as 70 percent. Having a base of operations in Jordan from which to attack Israel and quickly retreat made this an ideal location. Such an attack occurred in 1974 when a splinter group of the PLO, the Popular Front for the Liberation of Palestine (الجبهه الشعبيه لتحرير فلسطين), massacred twenty-five Israeli civilians in the northern city of Ma'alot (pronounced *ma-a-lot*).

Black September

In 1970, the PLO set up encampments with armed roadblocks and checkpoints in northern Jordan, challenging anyone wanting to pass through areas it controlled—including Jordanian civilians traveling to and from their homes and places of work—and, especially, denying free passage and control of the area to the Jordanian army. The PLO had in effect carved out an enclave and challenged Jordan's King Hussein over the right to control portions of his own country. In an ultimatum, King Hussein demanded the PLO take down its roadblocks and checkpoints and threatened military action to force the issue if the PLO refused to comply. The PLO did not want to give up its cherished foothold in Jordan from which to launch attacks against Israel and either did not take the king seriously or doubted that he had the political will to go against the PLO in the eyes of the Arab world, which was solidly behind it and its confrontation with Israel. The PLO refused to comply and dared the king to disarm it. The king, not known for being weak on defense and security, especially when his sovereignty and authority within his own country was challenged, waged war on the PLO in September 1970. The Jordanian Army defeated the PLO, forcibly evicting its fighters from Jordan and sending them and their families across the northern Jordanian border into Lebanon. Out of this bloody humiliation was born the PLO's Black September Brigade, (Arabic: Munathimat Aylool al-Aswad منظمه ايلول الاسود)—not from an armed engagement with Israeli forces but from a defeat at the hands of a fellow Arab army.[81]

---

[81] The arrival in Lebanon of armed PLO fighters, who were overwhelmingly Muslim, is credited with being the trigger that began the Lebanese Civil War, in which the country's Muslim majority demanded equal economic opportunities, power sharing, and representation in the Christian-majority government.

Operation Litani

After setting up residency and bases of operation in Lebanon, the PLO conducted numerous cross-border attacks on Israeli targets of opportunity, many of which were civilians. The PLO expanded its target list to include international airplane hijackings, attacks and massacres inside Israel on buses and hotels, and the murder of the Israeli military attaché to the US. On March 16, 1978, in response to continued cross-border attacks by the PLO from Lebanon, Israeli military forces launched a major operation called Operation Litani (Hebrew: Mevtsa Litani מבצע ליטני) to rid southern Lebanon of the PLO and give northern Israeli citizens security and quiet. Israeli armor and infantry units invaded southern Lebanon and held territory seven miles into Lebanon up to the Litani River. After a monthlong operation, the Israeli military was satisfied that it had cleared all PLO bases and fighters from southern Lebanon and began its withdrawal. Operation Litani did not, however, end PLO cross-border infiltrations or rocket and artillery attacks into Israel, which increased in frequency and lethality throughout the late 1970s and into the early 1980s. Cross-border attacks intensified in the early 1980s and escalated to the point where Israeli fighter aircraft were attacking PLO sites in Lebanon on a regular basis. This, in turn, drew into the fight the Syrian Air Force, which attempted to intervene on the side of the PLO. The IAF shot down numerous Syrian MiG aircraft and suffered no losses. In early 1982, the PLO shot and killed an Israeli diplomat in France, and the cross-border conflict became global. Finally, in early June 1982 when the PLO critically shot and wounded the Israeli ambassador to Great Britain, the Israeli government realized that the situation demanded a more forceful and escalated response.

Operation Peace for Galilee

In response to the attack on its ambassador to the UK, the Israeli Security Cabinet quickly gave the IDF the green light to launch a forty-eight-hour operation to once again go after the PLO, which had returned to south Lebanon. On June 6, 1982, the Israeli Armed Forces mounted a combined operation called Peace for Galilee (Hebrew: Mevtsa Shalom Hagalil מבצע שלום הגליל) to once again root out PLO bases of operation and fighters from south Lebanon up to the Litani River. The operation achieved its goal before the forty-eight-hour deadline, so the Security Cabinet gave the IDF authorization to continue chasing the PLO as far into Lebanon as possible within the forty-eight-hour period. The IDF was so successful in routing the PLO from south Lebanon that it was given the green light to continue chasing it past the forty-eight hours with the aim of destroying it as a fighting force. The IDF quickly found itself on the outskirts of Lebanon's capital, Beirut, where the fight turned into urban warfare, for which the IDF was not trained and in which it did not care to engage.

Israeli forces became bogged down in an unprecedented, three-year urban war from 1982 to 1985 and took unacceptably high casualties by Israeli standards. Israeli official casualty figures show 1,200 Israelis killed, while other sources reported this figure to be as high as 1,400. Operation Peace for Galilee took place in the middle of the Lebanese Civil War, which lasted fifteen-years from 1975 to 1990. During this war, Beirut was a free-for-all, with various factions, including the Lebanese Army, the Israeli Armed Forces, Christians, Muslims, Druze, the PLO, Hizb Allah, and both pro- and antigovernment militias, all fighting one another for control and power. Israel's war in Lebanon was referred to by Israelis as "Israel's Vietnam," since it had evolving goals, no end in sight, and no exit strategy. The high casualties coupled with public resentment produced a groundswell of Israeli popular opposition to the war. This became the beginning of Israel's Peace Now movement.

Within days of the beginning of the war, Israel was besieging Beirut and bombing the PLO mercilessly. The PLO appealed to the United Nations, and an agreement was reached to have the several thousand surviving PLO fighters evacuated by ship to Tunisia. This was accomplished by September 1, 1982, after which Israel withdrew from its siege and took up defensive positions around the city of Beirut. Christian Phalange Militia (Arabic: al-Kataa'ib al-Lubnaniyyah الكتائب اللبنانيه) fighters approached Israeli commanders to tell them that PLO fighters were still inside two Palestinian refugee camps, Sabra and Shatila (Arabic: Sabra wa-Shatila صبرا وشاتيلا). The Phalange requested that Israeli forces step aside and allow them to avenge an earlier feud. Israeli forces allowed the Phalange Militia to enter the refugee camps. After two days of free access to the camps, the Phalange Militia withdrew, and the world became aware of a horrific massacre. It quickly became clear that there were no PLO fighters in the camps and that the Phalange Militia had murdered as many as two thousand noncombatant men, women, and children. Israelis and the world were incensed by the massacre. The Israeli government commissioned an investigation, which concluded that although the IDF did not participate in the atrocity, it could have prevented it by denying the Phalange Militia access to the camps. The commission recommended that Israel's defense minister, Ariel Sharon (pronounced "sha-rone"), be fired and barred from ever holding a ministerial-level position again. The events of Sabra and Shatila only made the cries for Israel to withdraw from Lebanon even louder.

Before PLO fighters could evacuate to Tunisia, Western powers, including the United States and France, sent troops to safeguard the boarding of PLO fighters onto ships bound for Tunisia. Following their evacuation, the US and France withdrew their forces, only to return them shortly following the Sabra and Shatila massacre. PLO chairman Yasser Arafat, always looking to blame the West for Palestinian misfortunes, claimed that the massacres would not have taken place if the foreign peacekeeping forces had not departed.

For Israel's military to penetrate so far into an Arab country and assault its capital was without precedence. In past wars, Israeli ground forces had deliberately halted offensive operations short of Arab capitals, as in the 1967 and 1973 wars, when Israeli forces were within artillery striking distance of Damascus. Israelis took to the streets by the hundreds of thousands in opposition to continued Israeli action in Lebanon. Israeli forces remained outside the Lebanese capital until 1985, when they withdrew to the Litani River and established a twelve-mile security zone in southern Lebanon. Israel patrolled this security zone with the help of the Army of South Lebanon (ASL), a militia of south-Lebanese Christians that Israel trained, equipped, and funded. Israeli forces eventually withdrew completely from Lebanon in 2000, an unprecedented eighteen years after its forces first entered the country.[82]

A new, shadowy Islamic militant organization appeared on the Near East scene called Islamic Jihad (Arabic: Harakat al-Jihad al-Islami حركه الجهاد الاسلامي), with connections to Hizb Allah and Iran (see chapter 7). On April 18, 1983, the group took responsibility for driving a suicide truck bomb into the American embassy in Beirut, killing 63, 17 of them Americans. On October 23, 1983, the US Marine Corps barracks, located at the Beirut International Airport, was attacked by a suicide truck bomber, killing 241 US Marines, sailors, and soldiers. Within minutes of this attack, the French military barracks were also attacked by a truck bomber, killing 58 French soldiers. And again, on September 20, 1984, the American diplomatic mission in Lebanon, which had moved into the embassy annex, was attacked by a suicide car bomber, killing 24 people, 2 of them American. Hizb Allah announced that the attacks against the US and France were in response to Western powers' intervention in the Near East.[83]

Operation Desert Storm

In the summer of 1990, two years after the end of the Iran-Iraq War, Iraq's president, Saddam Hussein, had the world's fourth-largest standing army, well equipped and trained but idle; his treasury was

[82] Upon its withdrawal, Israel repatriated SLA soldiers and their families into Israel. They are today settled and integrating into Israeli society. A few who could not integrate well returned to Lebanon. They understood that upon their return, they would be arrested, tried, and given prison sentences; some were executed.
[83] Although Iran denied involvement in the bombings, it erected a monument in Tehran dedicated to the "1983 martyrs."

depleted, and his country was in debt from the expense of war. He looked for a remedy from his neighbor to the south, Kuwait. He claimed Kuwait owed Iraq several billion dollars in agreed-upon payments it had withheld during the Iran-Iraq War. Kuwait rejected Saddam Hussein's claim. Two months after reassuring Arab leaders at the Arab League Summit Conference on May 30, 1990, that he would not attack Kuwait, Iraqi forces invaded Kuwait on August 2, 1990, and in two days had completely occupied the country to the Saudi Arabian border. Heeding concerns raised by Saudi Arabia that Saddam Hussein might continue his land grab southward into Saudi Arabia's oil-rich fields down the western shores of the Persian/Arabian Gulf, US President George H. W. Bush (Bush forty-one) immediately sent US Air Force squadrons from both US and European bases to show his resolve and demanded Saddam Hussein immediately withdraw his forces from Kuwait. Saddam Hussein continued to show defiance, and within weeks, President Bush had assembled an international coalition of thirty-five countries to oppose Saddam Hussein and threatened the use of military force to evict Iraq from Kuwait if it did not withdraw voluntarily. It was imperative that this coalition include Arab and Muslim countries, such as Egypt, Syria, Saudi Arabia, and Turkey, who were indignant at Saddam Hussein for reneging on his word not to invade Kuwait. Equally significant was the fact that Saddam Hussein had invaded a fellow Arab-Islamic country and his forces were now literally raping, pillaging, and plundering noncombatant Kuwaitis.

Seeing that the world, including the Arab world, was overwhelmingly against him, Saddam Hussein attempted to deflect attention away from his invasion of Kuwait by making numerous erroneous, side-stepping claims. He wrongfully claimed that Kuwait was the nineteenth province of Iraq, that the border between Iraq and Kuwait was drawn incorrectly, and that Kuwait possessed Iraqi territory. He attempted to bargain by saying that he would withdraw from Kuwait when all other foreign forces withdrew from all Arab lands. This was a reference to Israel holding territory in Palestine that it had taken in the 1948 and 1967 wars, as well as the US and foreign coalition forces now assembling in

Saudi Arabia, Bahrain, and Qatar and the Syrian forces still in Lebanon from the Lebanese Civil War. Not an overly religious person, Saddam Hussein also attempted to play the devout-Muslim card by having himself photographed and video recorded praying in the desert near his invasion forces.

Playing the Palestinian card and continuing to deflect attention from his having invaded Kuwait by attempting to rally the Arab world around an issue of mutual importance, Saddam Hussein declared himself in a broadcast speech to be the defender of the Palestinian people and used a veiled threat to "scorch half of Israel" if the coalition forces attacked him. Knowing that he possessed chemical weapons and had in fact used them against Iran during the Iran-Iraq War and against the Kurdish people of Iraq, Israel understood Saddam Hussein's veiled threat to mean that he was threatening to affix chemical or biological agents to his North Korean-provided SCUD surface-to-surface missiles, which had adequate range to reach Israeli cities. The next day, Israeli defense minister Moshe Arens counter-threatened Saddam Hussein with not so veiled language, saying that if he (Saddam), Iraq, or any other country were to attack Israel's population with weapons of mass destruction, Israel's response would be "immediate, not in-kind, and overwhelming." Arabs suddenly saw a scenario wherein coalition forces would attack the Iraqi Army in Kuwait, Saddam Hussein would respond by firing SCUD missiles at Israel, and Israel would retaliate with its air force against Iraq. In such a scenario, Arab coalition partners would be in an untenable position where they would be fighting a war on the same side as the Israelis against a fellow Arab country. This presented an unacceptable situation for the Arabs, some of whom stated that they would not take part in a war against Iraq with Israel as a de facto partner. Saddam Hussein was deliberately trying to put a wedge between the Arab world and the West, specifically the US, to get Arab coalition partners to break ranks.[84]

---

[84] Arab countries were just beginning to heal from Egypt's peace with Israel and had earlier in the year returned the Arab League headquarters from Tunis to Cairo.

The international coalition force swelled to 670,000 personnel and 2,250 aircraft; of these, 425,000 soldiers, airmen, and sailors and 1,800 aircraft were from the US. On January 15, 1991, President Bush gave Saddam Hussein one final ultimatum: withdraw from Kuwait or face a new kind of warfare that would destroy his army. There was a last-minute attempt at diplomacy between US Secretary of State James Baker and Iraqi Deputy Prime minister Tariq Aziz to reach a resolution to the looming showdown, but it was to no avail. In the early morning hours of January 17, 1991, the forty-three-day coalition air campaign began. The next night, January 18, Saddam Hussein began launching SCUD missiles against Israel and coalition Gulf countries.[85] Israel and the Gulf countries, mindful that Saddam Hussein might affix chemical or biological warheads to the SCUDs, sounded air raid sirens as soon as the missiles began raining down.

The Israeli public demanded that its military (Air Force) attack Iraq's SCUD launchers. There was a loud outcry in Israel reminding its leaders and the world of the possibility that Jews might once again be gassed as their families had been one generation earlier in Europe by the maniacal Hitler, only this time it would be in their own country by an Arab tyrant. The US implored Israel not to retaliate so as not to jeopardize the integrity of the coalition. The US and Western powers were sensitive to the need to keep the Arab coalition partners in the fight against Saddam Hussein because they did not want it to appear that Western countries alone were waging war against Arabs, or against the Arab world, as Saddam Hussein had tried to frame it. The US assured Israel that coalition forces would exert the maximum effort to locate and destroy Iraqi SCUD launchers and missiles, warning that Israel entering the war would only jeopardize the delicate Arab coalition and be counterproductive to Israel's long-term interests. Although Israel reluctantly heeded the US request not to enter the war, voices within Israel complained that this was the first war in which Israel

---

[85] In the months leading up to the war, Israel distributed gas masks to every Israeli and to all tourists. Israelis practiced gas-attack drills, and its Civil Defense department instructed citizens on how to construct above-ground chemical-biological safe rooms. Chemical and biological agents are heavier than air; thus an elevated room would increase survivability.

was involved that it willingly sat on its hands and did not engage the attacker to protect Jewish life, the basic reason for which the Jewish state was created.

To shoot down incoming SCUDs, the US sent Patriot missile batteries to Israel and coalition Gulf countries that were coming under Iraqi SCUD missile attacks. Not designed to shoot down ballistic missiles, Patriot missiles were initially incapable of hitting incoming SCUDs and were not effective in preventing them from hitting their intended targets. The presence of the Patriot missiles was primarily effective in psychologically lifting the spirits of the traumatized people under attack.[86]

Coalition forces initially launched a campaign to rid Kuwait of the occupying Iraqi forces by waging a massive and relentless air bombardment on Iraq's military infrastructure, specifically targeting command and control centers in both Iraq and Kuwait, the Ministry of Defense and Intelligence headquarters, radar sites, and numerous other strategic military sites and installations. When Saddam Hussein still refused to pull his forces out of Kuwait, coalition forces began a ground attack on February 24 that mercilessly destroyed Iraq's military. Four days later, Iraqi forces were routed from Kuwait, and Saddam Hussein agreed to a cease-fire, which went into effect on February 28, 1991. As Iraqi forces withdrew from Kuwait, they ignited six hundred Kuwaiti oil wells, emitting tons of choking carbon monoxide and other toxins into the air. Iraqi forces ruptured another sixty oil wells, spewing millions of gallons into the desert, and ruptured oil storage tanks on

---

[86] The Patriot Missile System was designed to shoot down air-breathing targets (aircraft), not ballistic missiles such as the SCUD. Early in the war, there was little warning of an impending attack before a SCUD missile landed. However, as the war progressed, Raytheon Corporation, the Patriot's developer, reprogramed its software to better detect incoming SCUDs traveling beyond Mach speed, and the warning time increased to ten minutes, allowing enough time to alert and secure targeted populations. The Iraqi military only fired SCUDs at night to conceal its launch positions from patrolling coalition's search-and-destroy aircraft. Israel's major cities—metropolitan Tel Aviv, Jerusalem, and Haifa—were the primary targets. Every evening before dark, tens of thousands of Israelis would evacuate their homes in these cities and scatter to farther locations that were not being targeted.

the coast, releasing six million barrels of crude oil into the Gulf, which killed animals, birds, and sea life for miles. For his madness and crimes against nature, Saddam Hussein was dubbed the world's number-one environmental terrorist, and a new term was created and conferred upon him: "ecoterrorist."[87]

Saddam Hussein wisely heeded Israel's warning not to attack Israel with chemical or biological agents and only affixed conventional high-explosive warheads to his SCUDs, which destroyed numerous Israeli homes and buildings and terrorized the population. A total of forty-one SCUDs were launched at Israel within a forty-one-day period, resulting in one thousand Israeli injuries but only one death directly caused by a SCUD explosion. Many people at the time claimed that it was nothing short of miraculous that only one person was killed by the forty-one SCUDs that rained down on Israeli cities. There were, however, other reported Israeli deaths due to heart attacks and other traumas triggered by the incoming SCUDs.[88]

Although coalition countries deliberately did not report the number of Iraqis killed or wounded, it is estimated by independent sources that at least twenty-thousand Iraqi soldiers lost their lives in the forty-three-day war, and probably another twenty thousand were wounded. The war is estimated to have cost $61 billion. Gulf countries that stood to benefit the most from ousting Saddam from Kuwait paid $36 billion, and Japan, whose Self-Defense Forces did not participate, paid $16 billion. The $9 billion balance was absorbed by the various other coalition countries. The money was given to coalition partners to offset expenses such as airlifts and fuel and to replace expended and destroyed equipment. An estimated 81 Iraqi military aircraft and 3,700 tanks were destroyed, and 7,000 Iraqi prisoners of war (POWs) were taken.

---

[87] It was first estimated that it would take two years to put out all the oil well fires, but with huge monetary incentives and multinational cooperation, the fires were extinguished and oil wells were capped in nine months.

[88] Following the war, the US gave Israel $650 million to offset infrastructure damage caused by SCUD missiles and approximately a dozen F-15 fighter aircraft. This was viewed as a thank you to Israel for staying out of the war and not breaking up the Arab coalition partners.

A total of 147 coalition troops were killed, 75 aircraft were destroyed, and there were 26 POWs. In a bizarre move to save themselves and their aircraft, Iraqi pilots flew 137 aircraft to their longtime archenemy neighbor, Iran, with whom Iraq had fought a bloody eight-year war from 1980 to 1988. As the saying goes, war makes strange bedfellows.

Notes

"1974: Teenager Die in Israeli School Attack," *BBC* (May 15, 1974).

Andrew Killgore, "For Israel, Southern Lebanon Means the Litani River," *Washington Report on Middle East Affairs* (September/October 2006).

Yaqub, Salim. "The Daring Move that Crippled the Middle East Peace Process." *The Washington Post.* (November 20, 2017.

"The Lebanon War: Operation Peace for Galilee (1982)," *Israel Ministry of Foreign Affairs* (2013).

They Came in Peace. DIA Public Affairs (October 22, 2013).

Tyler Rogoway, "Operation Desert Storm by the Numbers on Its 25th Anniversary," *Foxtrot Alpha* (January 16, 2016).

Jerry M. Long, *Saddam's War of Words* (University of Texas Press, 2004).

Thomas L. Friedman, "After the War: Israel; US to Give Israel $650 Million to Offset Costs of the Gulf War," *The New York Times* (March 6, 1991).

Chapter 9

Palestine and Palestinians

Palestinian Ethnogenesis

By the seventh century CE, the Byzantine Empire had become weakened and too vast to control to the point that it was close to fragmenting and vulnerable to external assault (see chapter 3, "Byzantine Empire"). That external assault came from Arabian armies, who were fighting out of zeal under the banner of their new religion, Islam, with the battle cry "the religion of Muhammad is by the sword" (Arabic: "Deena MuHammad bi-as-Saif" دين محمد بالسيف). After first conquering the Arabian Peninsula, Muslim armies poured out of Arabia and quickly subjugated Southwest Asia, the Near East, and Northeast Africa. In 637, Jerusalem fell to the invading Arab-Muslim armies, and for the next eight hundred years, the region came on-and-off under Arab-Muslim rule.[89] This eight-hundred-year rule was interrupted for

---

[89] The first Islamic dynasty, the Rashidun Caliphate, ruled and consolidated power in Arabia from 632 to 661 CE, after the death of Islam's founder. The second was the Umayyad Caliphate, which ruled from Damascus from 661 to 750 CE and conquered all the Near East, including Palestine and lands extending east to Persia and west to Libya in north Africa. The third was

about two hundred years from 1099 to 1291 by European Crusaders, who ruled the Holy Land, which encompassed today's Israel-Palestine, Lebanon, Syria, and western Jordan. Prior to the middle of the seventh century, around 640, there was no Arab political rule, no Arabic culture, no Arabic language, no Arabic religion (Islam), or anything else Arabic in the Near East outside of the Arabian Peninsula and certain points north in the greater Arabian Desert. The region we today call the Arab world simply did not exist before the Arab-Muslim conquest in the middle of the seventh century. Prior to this time, the Near East was overwhelmingly Christian and Jewish and culturally and literarily Hellenized Greco-Byzantine.

Under the Roman Emperor Constantine, the Roman Empire split, with the eastern half later becoming the Byzantine Empire, with its capital established in Constantinople (Istanbul) in 330. The Byzantine Empire became a theocracy and ruled much of Central and Eastern Europe, Asia Minor, the entire Near East/Holy Land, and North Africa for 1,123 years, making it the longest-lasting empire to rule in the Near East. During the period of intermittent Arab rule, Palestine was ruled as part of three successive Arab-Muslim dynasties, which eventually stretched from Spain in the west to the banks of the Indus River in the east.

At the beginning of the seventh century, Palestine and its inhabitants, who came under Islamic dynasties, were ruled by foreign Arab-Muslim administrators appointed by the caliphs. Palestine's indigenous majority was largely composed of Aramaic-speaking Hellenized Christians and Jews, as was most of the Levant. Over time, this population become Arabized culturally, linguistically, and religiously, losing more of its original identity with every successive generation. At no time during the centuries of Islamic Arab rule did these people think of themselves as a distinct, politically unified people, as "Palestinian

---

the Abbasid dynasty, which ruled from Baghdad from 750 to 1517 CE and expanded from the Indus River in the east to the Iberian Peninsula in the west and encompassed all of North Africa. These Islamic empires/dynasties were ruled by caliphs (Arabic: *Khulafaa'* خلفاء), who were the political and spiritual successors to Islam's prophet Muhammad.

Arabs," or as Palestinian anything; the term and concept simply did not exist during the Arab-Muslim empires' rule in the Near East. The population of Palestine during the Muslim dynasties was first a mix of ancient inhabitants, including Phoenicians, Canaanites, Edomites, Ammonites, Moabites, and Aegean Philistines, and later a mix of Egyptians, Assyrians, Babylonians, Persians, Greeks, Romans, western Europeans (Crusaders), and finally Arab invaders who all added their DNA to the local gene pool.

In 1516, the Ottoman Turks defeated the reigning empire and ended Arab (but not Muslim) rule in Palestine as well as in much of the Near East. Unlike Arab-Muslim empires of the Near East, the Ottoman Turkish rulers were not considered by Muslim Arabs to be a legitimate religious Islamic dynasty because Arab Muslims did not regard Ottoman sultans (rulers) as the rightful spiritual successors, or caliphs, of Muhammad, even though from the fourteenth century onward, Ottoman sultans used the title *caliph*. Interestingly, Turkey was one Near Eastern country where the Arabic language did not take hold, even though the religion of Islam did. Therefore, Turkey did not become completely Arabized and is thus not today part of the Arab Near East, but it is absolutely part of the Muslim Near East and Muslim world. During their four-hundred-year rule of the Near East, the Ottoman Turks did not impose the Turkish language on the peoples and lands they ruled.[90] Thus, the inhabitants of Palestine and all the other lands that the Arab Muslims had previously conquered continued to speak Arabic and identify with the Arab culture. After centuries of Arab cultural dominance, the indigenous inhabitants of Palestine and their descendants lost their pre-Arab-Muslim roots and cultural identity, became completely Arabized, and began thinking of themselves exclusively as Arabs. They became nominally Arabs simply because they could now only identify culturally, linguistically, and over

---

[90] The Turks are a Central Asian people from north of modern Iran who migrated into Asia Minor after converting to Islam. Turkish is a non-Semitic Turkik language. The Turks wrested control of eastern, southern, and central Asia Minor from the Byzantine Empire during the eleventh century. In the centuries that followed, they increased their control of Asia Minor, capturing Constantinople in 1453 and thereby putting an end to the Byzantine Empire.

time religiously with their new rulers, the Muslim Arabs, not because they themselves were Arabs racially or ethnically.

With the defeat and eviction of the Ottoman Turks from the Near East and Palestine at the end of World War I, Arabs naturally thought of Palestine as part of the greater Arab world and expected it would come under Arab rule as promised by Great Britain in the McMahon-Hussein Correspondence (see chapter 4).

The Palestinian Narrative

With the United Nations–mandated partition of Palestine in 1948—and the creation of the Jewish State of Israel but not a Palestinian Arab state—came the beginning of the Palestinian Catastrophe (Arabic: Nakbah النكبه). The Nakbah brought an end to the Palestinian dream of an independent state encompassing all of Palestine and created 650,00 Palestinian refugees.

The Palestinian and Arab argument against the creation of a Jewish Israel in what they considered exclusive Arab lands stated that the territory was inhabited by a majority Arab population whose ancestry and roots went back generations. Some argued that regardless of what had happened to Jews in Europe under the Nazi regime, not one Arab was responsible for putting one Jew in a concentration camp, gas chamber, or crematorium or for killing European Jews. So why was the world taking out the Jewish tragedy on the Arabs of Palestine and giving half of their lands to yet another outside power to rule? They continued by asking not so rhetorically, "When do Palestinians get to rule themselves in Palestine?" As discussed in chapter 4, the argument ended, "if new international canon allows for the descendants of a people who lived in a land two thousand years earlier to uproot its current inhabitants, then people the world over would be required to uproot themselves and return to the lands of their ancestors." Throughout the history of the world, since the original Homo sapiens first came out of Africa, people have migrated, inhabited new lands, empires have come and gone, and the past simply becomes history.

The Palestinian personal narrative since 1948 is that the Jews stole Palestine, the Jews evicted Palestinians from their homes, the Jews made Palestinians a stateless people and a people with no identity. They conclude that ancient ancestral residency is not a license to uproot and evict.

Palestinian Demographics

Today, there are approximately 10 million Palestinians worldwide; 2.1 million live in Israel and hold Israeli citizenship.[91] As in Israel overall, the Palestinian literacy rate is among the highest in the world—96 percent in the West Bank and between 93 and 95 percent in the Gaza Strip. There are an estimated 5 million Palestinian refugees who live in refugee camps in Lebanon, Syria, Jordan, the West Bank, and the Gaza Strip. They are housed, educated, medicated, and fed by the United Nations Relief and Works Agency for Palestine (UNRWA).

The West Bank

The West Bank is an area of only thirty by sixty miles. Its narrowest point is between Jerusalem and the Jordan River, and at its closest, it is fifteen miles from Tel Aviv. Among the West Bank's nearly 3 million inhabitants, there are 585,000 Israelis who live in what the United Nations and much of the international community consider to be illegal settlements. These settlements range from small start-up communities of a few dozen people to the medium-size city of Ariel, which has a population of 18,000. Ariel's population swells to 26,500

---

[91] There are 3.5 million Palestinians living in Jordan, about one-third of the total Palestinian population: 2.8 million in the West Bank and 1.9 million in the Gaza Strip. The Palestinian population is relatively young, with the average age in the West Bank being 22.5 years and that in the Gaza Strip being 15 years.

when 8,500 students commute daily to attend the University of Judea and Samaria, located within its city limits. The West Bank is politically governed by the Palestinian Authority (Arabic: as-Saltah al-Falastiniyya السلطة الفلسطينية), which was established as a result of peace talks between Israel and the Palestinians, known as the Oslo Peace Accords, that were held in Oslo, Norway, in 1993 and 1995. The Palestinian Authority (PA) is the Palestinian virtual government in exile, which has its de facto capital in Ramallah (رام الله) about six miles north of Jerusalem in the West Bank. The PA is governed by a cabinet and President, Mahmoud Abbas (a.k.a. Abu Mazin), who replaced Yasser Arafat. The PA has its own armed police force, which works with the Israeli security forces and military to police and secure the area. The Israeli military has de facto free rein to enter the West Bank and conduct search operations for suspected Palestinian attackers. In 2003, in response to near-weekly attacks from the West Bank into Israel that resulted in the deaths of civilians and soldiers alike, Israel began building a twenty-six-foot-high concrete security barrier between Israel and the West Bank. The barrier spans 225 miles, almost the entire length of the Israeli–West Bank contiguous border. Israel stated that building the barrier was necessary to control West Bank Palestinian access to Israel, to keep Palestinian terrorists out of Israel, and to save Israeli lives. Israel claims that since the barrier's construction, incidents of terror attacks inside Israel have been reduced by over 95 percent. Israel considers the wall effective, necessary, and justified. Palestinians, on the other hand, consider the wall a land grab that has cut off some Palestinians' homes from their agricultural fields and places of work. The wall is a stark, unilateral statement of separation between Israel and the Palestinian Authority's jurisdiction in the West Bank.[92]

---

[92] Construction of the barrier began after a suicide-homicide attack at the Park Hotel in the city of Netanya; thirty Israelis were killed, and 160 injured. Hamas, the Gaza-based terrorist organization, claimed responsibility for the attack.

The Gaza Strip

When the United Nations partitioned Palestine in 1948, the Gaza Strip, plus an additional strip of land that straddled the Egyptian-Israeli border and extended south into the Negev Desert, was designated to be part of the Palestinian-Arab state. If Palestinian statehood had materialized, the Gaza Strip would have been cut off from the rest of the Palestinian state located in the West Bank and the Galilee. The Gaza Strip was annexed by Egypt after the first Arab-Israeli War in 1949, taken by Israel in the 1956 Sinai War, and retuned to Egypt when President Eisenhower intervened and promised Israel security from its adversaries. Israel again took the Gaza Strip in the 1967 Six-Day War and held it until it completely dismantled its settlements in the region and withdrew its forces in 2005.

Gaza Strip is the name given to a strip of land on the southeastern corner of the Mediterranean coast, two miles wide by nine miles long, extending from just north of the city of Gaza to the city of Rafah on the Egyptian border. It has a population of approximately two million. Hamas split from and violently overthrew the PA in Gaza in 2007 and today governs its population with a conservative, hardline, Islamic, militant iron fist. When it overthrew the PA, it murdered PA administrators and security forces and dragged their bodies through the streets of Gaza City and other towns and cities in the Strip to demonstrate and announce the beginning of its reign of terror. The Hamas charter states that its aim is the annihilation of Israel and its replacement with an Islamic state. In 2018, Hamas considered rewriting and softening its charter for more favorable international sympathy and to reconcile with the PA. The rewrite did not materialize and talks with the PA collapsed. Mediterranean waters off the Gaza coast are blockaded by the Egyptian and Israeli navies, and the movement of Gaza's population is controlled by a militarized border by both countries.

Unemployment in the Gaza Strip is estimated to be as high as 70 percent. There are very few industries in Gaza other than education, medicine, retail, service, agriculture, food service, and concrete, as well as some small family businesses and humanitarian distribution centers from the UNRWA and other international charitable organizations. Gazans receive millions of dollars annually from various European and Arab countries—primarily Qatar, Saudi Arabia, and other rich, oil-producing Gulf countries—as well as from the PA. Payments from the PA were temporarily but unsuccessfully halted in 2018 to pressure Hamas to return Gaza to PA rule. Gaza residents cannot freely travel outside of the strip because Egypt and Israel militarily control its borders. It is exceedingly difficult for Gaza's residents to obtain travel visas to leave the Strip. One of the few reasons one may travel outside the Gaza Strip is medical emergencies, for which Gazans may travel to Arab (usually Jordanian) hospitals, European hospitals, and surprisingly Israeli hospitals, which often open their services to Gazans as well as Arabs from other surrounding countries, such as Syria and Jordan. Gazan young people have very few opportunities for employment or to improve their conditions and do not see much hope for their future. For this reason, it is fertile ground from which terrorist organizations like Hamas and Palestine Islamic Jihad (PIJ) may recruit fighters for their respective cause.[93] These militant Jihadist organizations promise young men and women monetary compensation and better living conditions for their families, as well as personal heavenly rewards in the afterlife, if they agree to martyr themselves for the Palestinian cause. It's an attractive win-win proposition for some young people, who believe they have no other options for escaping their miserable conditions while at the same time leaving the world enshrined as martyrs and heroes and also helping their families.[94]

---

[93] There are two primary militant/terrorist organizations operating in the Gaza Strip: Hamas and PIJ. Both have been declared terrorist organizations by the United Nations and much of the world. The self-proclaimed Islamic State (IS, or ISIS, which stands for the Islamic State in Iraq and Syria) attempted to set up an Islamic caliphate in portions of Syria and Iraq from 2015 to 2018 and is known to recruit and have cells in the Gaza Strip. Egypt has been waging a continuous low-level war with IS and Islamic Jihad in the Sinai Peninsula for a decade.
[94] When the retired IDF chief of the general staff Ehud Barak ran for office in 1999, he stated that if he were a young man in Gaza with no future and no hope, he most likely would become

Israel has many reasons to be concerned about Hamas and PIJ, because Tel Aviv and central Israel, where approximately half of its population lives, is only thirty-seven miles from the northern border of Gaza. Over the years, Hamas has randomly and indiscriminately fired rockets and mortars into Israel, with no possibility of hitting any military targets because of the rockets' woeful inaccuracy. They can only terrorize Israeli citizens living near the border. In recent years, Hamas's rockets have improved in range and have been able to hit areas as far away as Israel's Ben-Gurion International Airport, thirty miles away; the outskirts of Jerusalem, fifty miles away; and the Negev Desert city of Beersheba, fifty-six miles away. As Israel celebrated its seventieth anniversary in 2018, the weekly Hamas and PIJ-sponsored demonstrations and border attacks from the Gaza Strip intensified to a near daily cross-border barrage. These attacks have included incendiary balloons and kites that not only have terrorized Israeli residents living near the Gaza border but have burned ten thousand acres of Israeli farmland at a cost of millions of dollars and have thus threatened farmers, their livelihoods, their lives, and the lives of their families. For months, Hamas and PIJ attempted to breach Israel's barbed- and razor-wire border defenses, which drew tear gas and live fire from Israeli soldiers, an outcome the terrorist organizations often welcomed in order to win the international public relations war. Israel has also discovered and demolished numerous infiltration tunnels (Israel refers to them as "terrorist tunnels") extending under the border and reaching as far as nearby Israeli residential communities. Although the tunnel diggers would never admit to it, the understanding is that they were built so that Hamas and PIJ could infiltrate the country and attack and kill Israeli soldiers and civilians or kidnap them and then hold them for ransom, use them as bargaining chips in prisoner exchanges, or use them to extract demands from Israel, as they have done in the past. There is no other possible explanation for the tunnels. They are certainly not designed to reach out across no-man's-land to promote peaceful cross-cultural understanding and coexistence. Israel, which

---

a terrorist and attack Israel. Although many Israelis were incensed by Barak's words, his party won the elections, and he was chosen as Israel's prime minister.

controls all commercial material coming in and out of Gaza by land, including concrete, rebar, and other building materials, constantly complains to the international community that Hamas and PIJ are using these materials not to build schools, hospitals, and infrastructure, as they claim, but to construct infiltration/attack tunnels.

After more than seven decades of Israeli statehood, no country or organization has yet come up with a workable solution for the Gaza Strip, the West Bank, or the greater Palestinian-Israeli conflict. In January 2020, the Trump administration unveiled its peace plan for the region. It was presented as a platform for the beginning of direct talks between Israel and the Palestinians. Israel accepted the plan in principle as a starting point, but it was rejected outright by the Palestinian leadership as not even a starting point (see "Attempts at Peace" below). For there to be a workable solution, both sides will have to become realistic and willing to compromise, qualities not yet sufficiently exhibited by either side.

Intifada/Uprising

After four decades of waiting on Arab leaders' to defeat and destroy Israel on the battlefield and create a Palestinian-Arab state as promised and two decades of Israeli military occupation and rule following Israel's takeover of the Gaza Strip and West Bank in the 1967 Six-Day War, tensions within Palestinian society reached a boiling point in 1987. Palestinian society had exceeded its limits of its patience and tolerance of subjugation and would no longer accept the reality of the "facts on the ground," as Israelis referred to the new normal. Palestinians' response to these frustrations would be loud and would take the form of a multiyear and violent intifada (انتفاضه), or uprising.

First Intifada: 1987–1993

The First Intifada began with an incident in the Gaza Strip in December 1987, when an Israeli military vehicle ran over and killed four Palestinian men. The incident brought thousands of Palestinian civilian demonstrators into direct confrontation with Israeli security forces. The confrontations quickly spread in the form of grassroots strikes throughout the Palestinian-Arab communities of Jerusalem and Bethlehem. The unrest then spread to other cities in the West Bank, as well as cities inside Israel proper, such as Jaffa, Nazareth, and Umm al-Fahm.[95] The uprising was a culmination and expression of the frustrations felt by Palestinians who had lived under Israeli occupation in the West Bank and Gaza for twenty-years, and it later grew to include Israeli Arabs, who had lived in Israel for thirty-nine years since it had attained statehood in 1948.

The confrontations began as running street battles against Israeli police and security forces at military checkpoints, where Palestinian young men burned tires and threw stones. There were also general strikes and business closings to express indignation and outrage at having to live under Israeli military occupation and rule. A new phase of attacks against Israeli security checkpoints and civilians took on an especially deadly and indefensible dimension: homicide-suicide bombings. As was the case with the street battles, these attacks were usually carried out by young Palestinian men and, later, women. They would strap on explosive vests, go to public places— restaurants, discotheques, open markets, malls, fast-food kiosks, buses, or anywhere they could be assured of high casualties—and detonate the vests, killing themselves and all who were within lethal range of the explosion. Israeli military and security forces fought back with what many called a heavy-handed response, which escalated from tear gas and rubber bullets to small arms

---

[95] The strikes and business closings were intended to hit Israel's tourism industry, which is a major source of revenue. These strikes and confrontations in high-tourism locations, like Jerusalem and Bethlehem, succeeded in curbing tourism, which was felt not only by Israeli merchants and service industries but also by Arab merchants whose businesses were primarily located in Jerusalem's Old City and Bethlehem, where Pilgrims frequented.

fire. Death and injury rates were high on both sides, especially among Palestinian militants, who became increasingly bold in their direct confrontations with Israeli security forces. Because of the perception of heavy-handedness, Israel lost the public relations battle in the minds of the world public. Israeli security forces were compelled to employ nonlethal force to confront young Palestinians who had no regard for their own lives and were ready to die in full view of rolling cameras.[96] This was a no-win public relations disaster for Israel, as images of the daily confrontations were broadcast nightly into homes across the world by the international media. The First Intifada ended following the signing of the first Oslo Peace Accords in September 1993. It is estimated that 1,500 Palestinians and 185 Israelis lost their lives during the First Intifada.

Second Intifada: 2000–2005

The Second Intifada is said to have been triggered by Israeli Prime Minister Ariel Sharon's visit to the Temple Mount/Haram al-Sharif in Jerusalem. In reality, the cause was a combination of Islamic outrage that Sharon had visited the Temple Mount/Haram al-Sharif, also the site of the al-Aqsa and Dome of the Rock mosques, and the frustrations of some within the Palestinian Authority leadership who were not satisfied with the slow-to-no progress of the Oslo Accord, which had called for negotiations with Israel that would, it was hoped, lead to Palestinian statehood by 2000. It was reported that Palestinians were looking for an excuse to initiate violence against Israel in hopes of forcing Israel to negotiate seriously. Prime Minister Sharon's visit to the Temple Mount gave them that excuse.

---

[96] Israel labels all homicide-suicide bombers as terrorists and subscribes to a simple definition for terrorism: the deliberate attack on unarmed, noncombatant civilians with lethal force for political, racial, or religious motives. This definition later also included attacks by Palestinian militants on armed Israeli security forces. Put another way, if someone terrorizes another with deadly force, the attack is terrorism, and the attacker is a terrorist.

The modus operandi of the Second Intifada was like that of the First Intifada: homicide-suicides and bombings of Israeli security forces and civilians, who were easy targets of opportunity. The Second Intifada's indiscriminate murder of unarmed, noncombatant civilians came to a head in 2002 during a Passover dinner celebration at the Park Hotel in Israel's coastal city of Netanya. As mentioned earlier in this chapter in a footnote under "The Gaza Strip," a young Palestinian homicide-suicide bomber walked into the Park Hotel's dining room and detonated his explosive vest where families were celebrating the end of the Passover with a traditional evening meal after a day of fasting. The terrorist killed 30 Israeli civilians and injured 160 others. This bombing triggered a massive search operation by the IDF called Operation Grapes of Wrath (Hebrew: Mevtsa Za'am Anavim מבצע זעם ענבים) in the West Bank, which lasted three weeks and involved hundreds of Israeli forces descending on cities, towns, and villages to search for the Palestinian perpetrators and to root out terrorist cells. The operation focused on the larger cities of Nablis and Jenin. The Park Hotel bombing was also the trigger that persuaded Prime Minister Sharon and the Israeli government that a concrete security barrier was needed between the West Bank and Israel, and so construction began. The Second Intifada claimed the lives of an estimated 3,000 Palestinians and 1,000 Israelis. Before detonating their explosives, homicide-suicide bombers yell "Allahu Akbar اللّٰه أكبر," as Muslims often do when killing in the name of jihad (holy war).[97]

---

[97] *Allahu Akbar* is usually translated into English as "God is Great." This translation is not completely accurate linguistically nor specifically in its Islamic context. *Allah* means "God," and *Akbar* is the comparative form of the word *big*; thus a literal translation would simply be "God is bigger." The Arabic word for great is *atheem*. So, if we translate the phrase *God is Great* backward from English to Arabic, it would be "Allahu Atheem" (the *u* at the end of the word *Allah* is a case ending). Thus, a more accurate translation that captures the term's Jihadi-Islamic essence is "God is Omnipotent," "God is Supreme," or "God is without equal." The phrase is also often used by Muslims as a rallying battle cry in the context of "God be Praised/Praise God." Therefore, the simple English translation of *God is Great* leaves its meaning totally undertranslated and undervalued.

Third/Continuing Intifada: 2015–Present

In 2015, Palestinian militants began a campaign of terror against the Israeli military and Israeli civilians, both in the West Bank and within Israel. Although the attackers' goal was the same as in the first two intifadas (i.e., to randomly kill any Israeli targets of opportunity, whether they be security forces or noncombatant, unarmed civilians), their modus operandi had changed. The methods of choice since 2015 have been vehicular rammings, stabbings, and shootings. Unarmed Israeli civilians have become the primary targets during this unofficial intifada. They are attacked and killed at bus stops, in restaurants, or simply walking or standing on sidewalks. This new wave of terror does not appear to be linked to any organization or to be directed by any central leadership, nor does it require any extensive training, since the weapons are readily available and the targets are random targets of opportunity.

Vehicular assaults (rammings) and stabbings are exceedingly difficult to anticipate and defend against and are therefore usually successful. Vehicular attackers are often unable to escape the scene after an attack because the ramming usually renders their vehicles undrivable. As they attempt to flee by foot, these perpetrators are often quickly shot by an armed Israeli soldier, security guards, or other individuals licensed to carry concealed weapons. Armed Israelis and security cameras are ubiquitous throughout the country, making the chances of an attacker getting away extremely low. The attackers can be characterized as copycat, lone murderers.[98]*

Twenty-First-Century Nonstate Subwars

There have been five minor wars, or subwars, so far this century between Israel and its confrontational nonstate neighbors. These

---

[98] It is estimated that since this new wave of violence started in October 2015, approximately 80 Israelis have been killed, 1,167 wounded; more than 380 Palestinians have been killed in 201 stabbings, 217 shootings, 71 vehicular rammings, and one car bombing (the number of Palestinian wounded is unavailable).

wars have been primarily with Hizb Allah in Lebanon and Hamas in Gaza. During these wars, the IDF has thrown nearly everything in its arsenal at its adversaries, from attacks by infantry, tanks, and artillery to naval bombardment and ground attacks by aircraft. Its enemies have primarily used short- and long-range rockets, mortars, and missiles, which they randomly fire at Israel, usually not hitting anything of any military or strategic significance but only terrorizing the Israeli population. Chronologically, these subwars were the war across the Lebanese border with Hizb Allah in July 2006, the first Hamas war in Gaza from December 2008 to January 2009, the second Hamas war in Gaza in November 2012, the third Hamas war in Gaza from July to August 2014, and the fourth Hamas war in Gaza in May 2021.[99] Many in Israel have criticized the way the IDF executed the 2014 and 2021 Hamas wars. Critics of these wars said that Israeli forces should have entered the Gaza Strip with a larger force and dealt a heavier blow to the organization's command, control, and infrastructure. There continues to be voices in Israel that say the situation on the border with Gaza will not improve until Israel attacks Hamas and PIJ with full force in a major fifth engagement to completely destroy the infrastructure of these militant organizations. There are some Israeli strategic thinkers who say that once Hamas and PIJ are dismantled and dislodged, Israeli forces should remain and permanently occupy the Gaza Strip. The near-weekly cross-border rocket, mortar, and missile attacks from Gaza into Israel have dramatically increased since mid-2018 to the point where many Near East watchers predicted that a fifth Israeli-Hamas war was inevitable. Since withdrawing from the Gaza Strip in 2005, Israel has averaged one Gaza war every every 4 years. The next war may come sooner than 4 years.

---

[99] In the second Hamas war in 2012, Hamas fired more than 1,000 rockets, mortars, and missiles into Israel, hitting Jerusalem and Tel Aviv. Israel responded with more than 600 air strikes against Hamas targets in Gaza. Israel deployed its Iron Dome defensive system for the first time and destroyed more than 450 targets. In the third Hamas war in 2014, Hamas and PIJ fired 3,360 rockets and missiles at Israel, and Israel destroyed 4,762 Hamas and PIJ targets. Israel also destroyed numerous infiltration/concealment tunnels leading into Israel. Casualties were 70 Israelis killed and 2,000 Gazans killed. In the fourth Hamas war in 2021, Hamas launched 4,360 rockets and missiles into Israel and Israel destroyed over 1,000 Hamas and PIJ targets. 230 Palestinians and 7 Israelis were killed.

Attempts at Peace

Following numerous wars and numerous attempts at peace, Israel and its Arab neighbors, primarily the Palestinians, have yet to find a formula to peacefully coexist. The 1979 Camp David Accords between Egypt and Israel and the 1994 Israeli-Jordanian Peace Treaties have so far been successful. The 2020 Abraham Accord and diplomatic normalizations between Israel and non-neighboring Arab states were discussed in chapter 7. Unfortunately, a resolution to the Israeli-Palestinian conflict continues to be elusive and remote. Israel and the Palestinians have made no fewer than seven attempts to resolve their disputes and move in the direction of anything resembling reconciliation and coexistence.[100]

On January 28, 2020, the Trump administration revealed the latest and much-awaited Israeli-Palestinian peace initiative, billed as the "deal of the century." The plan offered a version of a two-state solution of sorts, with Israel maintaining West Jerusalem as its undivided capital and Palestinians being given the opportunity to establish their capital in East Jerusalem. Among other specifics, it allowed Israel to maintain and annex all its settlements on the West Bank (Samaria and Judea) and called for $50 billion in investments to boost the Palestinian economy. One of the more unusual aspects of the plan was the digging of a highway tunnel from the Gaza Strip on the Mediterranean to Palestine's land-locked West Bank territory. It did not allow for the repatriation of Palestinian refugees living outside Israel and did not grant control of the Old City of Jerusalem to the Palestinians—two nonnegotiable terms for Palestinians. Consequently, the "deal of the century" was billed as the "failure of the century" by the Palestinian Authority leadership. In fact, the PA, headed by President Mahmoud

---

[100] The seven Palestinian-Israeli attempts at peace and coexistence are: the 1991 Madrid Conference; the 1993 Oslo I Accord; the 1993 Oslo II Accord; the 1995 Wye River Summit; the 2000 Camp David Summit; the 2007 Annapolis Conference; and the 2020 Trump Administration "deal of the century" (see below). In 2002 and 2007, the Arab League offered full recognition by its twenty-two member nations to Israel if it would withdraw from and return all Arab territories taken since the 1967 Six-Day War, including East Jerusalem, thus making it once again a divided city. Israel has rejected this offer as unrealistic because it would leave Israel with no strategic geographic depth, returning it to indefensible borders.

Abbas, rejected the deal before it was revealed, claiming it would only favor Israel because it was written by the US, Israel's longtime ally. Mahmoud Abbas later rejected it a second time, saying, "No, no, one thousand times no." The Arab League initially embraced the deal as a good starting point, but after three days of Palestinian pressure, the League fell in lockstep with the PA and rejected it entirely. Before it was released, it was billed as only a good starting point and a basis for beginning a dialogue and negotiations between Israel and the Palestinians, not a final, all-or-nothing, take-it-or-leave-it proposal. It called for a final agreement to be negotiated in direct, face-to-face talks between the Israelis and the Palestinians. Time will tell if this plan will be the spark that launches a new and serious dialogue or whether it will join the other failed attempts on the trash heap of history. The question remains: will these decades-old rivals continue the status quo of violent confrontation, or can they find a solution to coexist in the same neighborhood? If they fail, both sides will continue to condemn their unborn generations to a future of endless warfare and anguish. The big unknowns are whether there is enough goodwill on both sides to achieve coexistence and peace and how far each side is willing to go for the sake of current and future generations. Unfortunately, at this point in history, the odds do not look favorable for anything resembling accommodation and a workable solution.

Ongoing Security Concerns

Although Israel has had a respite from major pan-Arab wars for more than four decades, there are some concerns that point to a possible near-future full-scale war. Israel today enjoys relatively uneasy cohabitation with its neighbors. First and foremost is its concern over Iran's nuclear program. These concerns are real, because Iran has repeatedly made specific threats against Israel and other countries of the Near East. Iran has in no uncertain terms said that its aim is to wipe Israel off the map (see more detail below). Although Israel is geographically located in the Near East and has peace treaties with two former enemy countries, Egypt and Jordan, it remains economically, commercially, and socially isolated from all its neighbors. The future of Egypt is always uncertain, especially since the Muslim Brotherhood and its hatred for Israel is a powerful force just below the surface, as evidenced by it having won national elections in Egypt in 2012. What will happen in post-civil war Syria is a big unknown, especially with Syria's close political and military ties with Iran. Lebanon, which is heavily influenced by Shiite Hizb Allah and, some would say, consequently virtually controlled by Iran, is a much-divided country with its large Christian population of over 40 percent. These factors plus its failed economy put Lebanon today one car bomb away from returning to civil war and disintegration. Iraq is still very fractured with much below-the-surface Sunni discontent toward the Shiite-majority government. With a high Palestinian population, Jordan's King Abdullah II is always walking a tightrope. And finally, Israel is always concerned over its growing indigenous Arab population, which gave rise to the three intifadas (see chapter 10, "Demographics").

Iran, Israel's Existential Threat

The most serious existential threat to Israel today comes from Iran. Before the overthrow of Shah Mohammad Reza Pahlavi and the establishment of the Iranian Islamic Republic (IIR) in 1979, Israeli-Iranian relations were excellent, with Israel buying oil from Iran and Iran trading with Israel. After the accession to power of the Mullahs and Ayatollahs in Iran, Israel and Iran have become archenemies; Iran has labelled Israel the "Little Satan" and has reserved the "honor" of the title "Big Satan" for the US. Iran has replaced Arab countries as the leader of confrontation states with Israel. Iranian leadership has made no attempt to conceal its hatred and contempt toward the Jewish state.[101]

---

[101] Iranian and other threats toward Israel include the following: "Israel is a cancer that must be cut out" (Mahmoud Ahmadinejad, Iran's past president). "The occupying regime in Jerusalem [should] be wiped off the face of the earth. ... This cancerous tumor of a state should be removed" (Ayatollah Khamenei, supreme leader, Islamic Republic of Iran). "Israel will cease to exist in 25 years" (also Ayatollah Khamenei). "The fake regime will disappear from the international scene in the near future" (Brigadier General Hossein Salami, IRGC lieutenant

Following the 2003 US-led overthrow of Saddam Hussein's Sunni-minority regime in Iraq, a leadership vacuum arose in the Persian/Arabian Gulf and throughout the Near East that has since been filled by Iran. As brutal as his regime was, Saddam Hussein was able to contain Iran's spreading of the Shiite apocalyptic worldview and its desire for regional control. Without Iraq's check on Iranian hegemonic aspirations, Iran has been able to spread its influence and control throughout the region and beyond. Iran has created a violent Shiite crescent of terror, both directly with its Islamic Revolutionary Guard Corps (IRGC) and indirectly through proxies. Iran has extended this arc of instability across the Near East from the Gaza Strip on the Mediterranean, north to Lebanon, east to Syria, southeast to Iraq, and south to Yemen at the southern tip of the Arabian Peninsula on the Red Sea. Iran has fostered chaos throughout the Near East and is thereby changing the face of traditional alliances in the region. In the Gaza Strip, Iran supplies arms and money to its proxies, Hamas and PIJ, for their near-weekly rocket and missile attacks on the Israeli civilian populations living near the border and their violent confrontations with the Israeli military when they attempt to breach the border barrier. Iran has had a relationship with the enormously influential Shiite Hizb Allah organization in Lebanon for more than four decades, providing it everything from small arms and missiles to training and financial assistance for its confrontation with Israel. In Syria, Iran has provided troops and equipment to support the Syrian Alawite (a minority branch of Shiite Islam) government of the al-Assad regime against various Sunni-led opposition groups in its ongoing civil war, which began in 2011. Additionally, the Assad regime allows IRGC forces, estimated to number more than twenty thousand fighters, to launch drone and missile attacks into Israel from Syria. In Iraq, Iran supports the Shiite-led government with arms, military training, and advisors, which results in Iran having significant influence over Iraq's national

---

commander). "Our holy goal is to liberate all of Palestine, and if the Jews do not go, they will die" (Sheikh Ahmed Yassin, cofounder of Hamas). "We are not fighting so that you will offer us something, we are fighting to eliminate you" (Husay Abbas al-Musawi, former head of Hizb Allah).

and security affairs, especially regarding its regional foreign policy. In the Persian Gulf, Iran has supported Shiite minorities gaining greater political influence in Saudi Arabia, Bahrain, and Qatar. And in Yemen, Iran is backing the Houthi rebels in a proxy civil war against the Sunni-led, Saudi-backed government, supplying the rebels with arms and financial assistance. Iran's support for revolution and instability extends beyond the Near East to the Americas, where it is silently supporting the regimes in Cuba, Nicaragua, and Venezuela.

Today, this Iranian-Shiite arc of encirclement is confrontational, provocative, violent, expansionist, and supportive of destabilizing Islamic-militant proxies and terrorist organizations that did not exist ten years ago. Israel is greatly concerned, vigilant, and realistic about Iranian intentions. Despite Iran's numerous denials, the world community, led by Israel, believes Iran is in fact working to develop nuclear weapons. Without offering specifics but still implying that it would use force if needed, Israel has repeatedly and strongly articulated that it will, without hesitation and unilaterally if necessary, prevent Iran from acquiring nuclear weapons.

In anticipation of Iran's development of nuclear weapons, which could be mounted on long-range missiles capable of reaching Israel and much of the Near East, Israel's defense industry has produced the world's first operational antiballistic missile defense system, the Arrow. Israel today possesses a multitiered, overlapping, comprehensive air-defense umbrella consisting of the Arrow, David's Sling, and the Iron Dome. The Arrow III is designed to intercept long-range ballistic missiles outside the earth's atmosphere. The Arrow II is designed to intercept long-range ballistic missiles within the earth's atmosphere. David's Sling is designed to intercept medium-range targets and drones, and the Iron Dome is designed to intercept short-range rockets and mortars. David's Sling and the Iron Dome have both been repeatedly operationally tested in real-world intercepts and have proven to be over 90 percent successful. The Arrow II and III systems have successfully intercepted targets in trial tests but have yet to be war tested, because no country has yet fired a ballistic missile at Israel since these intercept systems became operational. Before launching an unconventional lethal attack on Israel, a potential adversary might well consider that Israel has offensive nuclear weapons and a triad delivery system—air, ground, and sea. It would not be wise for any adversary of Israel to threaten it with annihilation, because Israel's response, as has been stated by a former Israeli defense minister, would certainly be "immediate, not in-kind, and overwhelming."

Israel lives in a rough neighborhood and fights for its existence every day. Former Israeli Prime Minister Benyamin Netanyahu has stated, "We are soon headed for a full-out war between Israel, Iran, Syria, and Hizb Allah." The world can be assured that Israel is preparing to protect and preserve itself and its citizens against all enemies, conventional or otherwise.

Notes

"The Demographics of the Arab World and the Middle East from the 1950 to the 2000s," *I.N.E.D.* (2005).

"Population of Cities in Palestine (2021)," *World Population Review* (2021).

"United Nations Relief and Works Agency for Palestinian Refugees in the Near East, 2018 Annual Report," *unrwa.org* (2018).

Walter Laqueur and Barry Rubin, *The Israel-Arab Reader* (Penguin Books, 2016).

"Jordan," *The Central Intelligence Factbook* (2019).

"The Lebanon War: Operation Peace for Galilee (1982)," *Israel Ministry of Foreign Affairs* (2013).

Sana Hussein, "Remembering the First Intifada," *Middle East Monitor* (December 9, 2017).

"Fatalities in the First Intifada," *The Israeli Information Center for Human Rights in the Occupied Territories* (September 28, 2000).

Jeremy Pressman, "The Second Intifada: Background and Causes of the Israeli-Palestinian Conflict," *The Journal of Conflict Studies* (Fall 2003).

"Passover Massacre at Israeli Hotel Kills 19," *CNN World* (March 27, 2002).

Daniel L. Byman. "The Oslo Accords at 25, the Second Intifada at 18. Will There Be A Third?" *Brookings* (September 12, 2018).

"War of Terror 2015–2018," *Israeli Ministry of Foreign Affairs* (December 13, 2018).

"Future Government of Palestine," *United Nations General Assembly 181* (November 29, 1947).

Yosi Klein Halevi, *The Israeli Paradox*, (Harper Collins Publisher, 2018).

"The Human Cost of the Conflict," *Israel-Palestine Times* (December 14, 2018).

Salim Yaqub, "Imperfect Strangers: Americans, Arabs, and US-Middle East Relations in the 1970s," *The Washington Post* (November 20, 2017).

Raphael Ahern, "Ministers say Israel Close to Retaking Gaza, Hamas Leaders' Days are Numbered," *Times of Israel* (November 21, 2018).

Martin Gilbert, *The Rutledge Atlas of the Arab Israeli Conflict* (Taylor & Francis Publisher, 2012).

Wafa Sultan, *A God Who Hates: A Courageous Woman Who Inflamed The Muslim World Speaks Out Against the Evils of Islam* (St. Martin's Press, 2009).

Udi Shaham, "2017 in Numbers: Terrorists Kill 20 Israelis, 3,617 Palestinians Arrested," *The Jerusalem Post* (December 20, 2018).

Stuart Winer and Marissa Newman, "Iran's Supreme Leader Touts 9-Point Plan to Destroy Israel," *The Times of Israel* (November 10, 2014).

"IRGC Commander: Israel Will Disappear," *The Iran Observer* (October 2015).

Chapter 10

Enough, Maspeek, Kifayah

Demographics and the Eight-Hundred-Pound Gorilla

Yasser Arafat, the founder of the PLO and the Palestinian Authority's first president, stated that the Arab womb is Palestinians' secret weapon against Israel. He stated that it was the duty of every Palestinian woman to have ten children. By so doing, Israel's Palestinian-Arab population would eventually outnumber the Jewish-Israeli population. Once achieved, assuming Israel remains a democracy, the Palestinians would not have to wage war against Israel but would simply go to the polls and vote themselves into office. In this scenario, Jewish-ruled Israel would instantly cease to exist and would be replaced by a Palestinian-Arab-majority country. This is the nearly unspoken but whispered eight-hundred-pound gorilla in Israel's room. The demographic time bomb looming over the horizon (plus the Iranian factor discussed in chapter 9), is what keeps Israeli leaders awake at night. For this reason, Israeli lawmakers are attempting to pass laws, such as the 2018 Nation-State Law, with the stated aim of "maintaining the Jewish character of Israel."

Not all Israeli leaders and social demographers agree that the indigenous Arab population will for certain eventually outnumber Jewish-Israelis or the non-Arab population. They point to the Ultra-Orthodox Jewish community, which has an even higher birth rate than does Israel's Arab population. They also expect Jewish immigration to Israel to increase for various reasons, including the rise of worldwide anti-Semitism, specifically in Europe. There are reports that because of increased anti-Jewish sentiments and hate crimes, the Jewish community in France, which numbers between five-to-seven-hundred- thousand, is on the verge of sending large waves of immigrants to Israel. Recently, with the worldwide COVID-19 pandemic, Jews who have contemplated immigrating to Israel have begun to see Israel as a safer country in which to live, since Israel enjoyed early and continued successes in aggressively containing the spread of the virus. Another factor that would help maintain Israel's Jewish majority and reduce its Arab population's percentage is Palestinian migration away from Israel as Israel's Arab population becomes more discouraged about living as second-class citizens in a Jewish-majority country. Considering Israel's attractive reputation as a Near East superpower military and the perception that Israel is a safer location for themselves and their families, Israel is looking more attractive to Jewish communities around the world. Israel's hope is that many of these Diaspora Jews will immigrate to Israel in the next few decades and boost Israel's Jewish population, which would in turn further delay the date Jews in Israel might lose their majority.

Ishmaelites and Isaacites

The Arab-Israeli conflict can be seen as a sad story of two related tribes, the Ishmaelites and the Isaacites—two tribes connected to Near Eastern Semitic clans of Mesopotamia. The Ishmaelites claim to have a relationship to the patriarch Abraham through Ishmael, Abraham's firstborn. Abraham is recognized as a major prophet in the religion of Islam and is claimed by Arabs to be their ancestral father. The claim of direct blood kindship to Abraham is not supported by accurate historical scholarship (see "Refutation of Arab Kinship Claims to Abraham" below).

The Isaacites are the descendants of Isaac, the second-born son of Abraham, the patriarch of the Hebrew people. They have over time been identified as Hebrews, Children of Israel, Israelites, Judahites, Judeans, Jews, and most recently Israelis. Abraham is undisputedly the patriarch and father of the Jewish people. Regardless of the historical facts (or mythological non-facts) of the narratives, the descendants of both Ishmael and Isaac claim to be tied to one another and to the same land, Canaan, through a common ancestor, Abraham, and through a promise made by God for Abraham's sons to inherit this land. Each side asserts that its claim is more legitimate and maintains that its people are the rightful inheritors of the land, either because of divine decree, covenant, residency, historical and political connection with and control of the land, or a combination of all of the above.

Refutation of Arab Kinship Claims to Abraham[102]

It is common to hear that the Jews are Abraham's descendants through Isaac and Jacob and that the Arabs are his descendants through Ishmael. Although it is a nice, compact explanation of Near Eastern demographics, is it correct? In a word, no, and the following is why.

Scholars know more about the (recorded) history of the Near East than any other region of the world. *History* here means only written sources information, not legends or archaeological remains from which specialists draw inferences. The earliest written records from this region date back to about 3000 BC. The history of Britain, by comparison, begins with Julius Caesar's campaigns there in the first century BC,

---

[102] This section (up to "Enough! Maspeek! Kifayah!") is a historically accurate, edited summary of the ethnogenesis of the Arab peoples and a refutation of a legend of kinship to the Jewish patriarch Abraham that is popular among Jews, Christians, and Muslims. It was contributed by Daniel Reilly, who is an ancient Near East Scholar, an expert in biblical and Semitic languages, and a former lecturer in modern Arabic at Baylor University. He prefers the historical dating designation BC and AD rather than BCE and CE.

and the history of the Americas begins in 1492; there are no readable, datable written sources from the pre-Columbian period.

The earliest known Near Eastern civilization is that of the Sumerians, a people who, among other major technological advancements, invented writing and who occupied what is now known as southern Iraq sometime around the end of the fourth millennium BC. It was from one of their famous cities, Ur, that Abraham would begin his migration over a thousand years later in the early second millennium BC. While the Sumerians ruled ancient Iraq for most of the fourth and third millennia BC, another large demographic group, the Semitic-speaking Akkadian peoples (who would later be identified as Babylonians and Assyrians), lived under Sumerian hegemony in northern Iraq. By this time, there were already Arabs living in the Arabian Peninsula. And of course, Egypt was already a flourishing Eastern Hamitic civilization, with Pharaohs reigning over upper and lower Egypt. The pyramids were built not long after 3000 BC, about a thousand years before Abraham was born.

Moving through time another thousand years or so to about 2000 BC, a little before Abraham's birth, another Semitic-speaking people group known as Amorites ("westerners" to the Sumerians) occupied and ruled Ur and other southern Mesopotamian cities. It is most likely that Abraham himself was an Amorite. Also, during this time, there were major cities and states in the lands of the eastern Mediterranean, such as Syria and the area we now know as Israel. There were Indo-European peoples in what is now Iran (the Persians), northern Syria (the Hurrians), and Asia Minor (the Hittites and others), as well as the lands surrounding the Aegean (Greeks).

We know of many wars, invasions, and migrations throughout this area that took place over the next 2,500 years, from about 2000 B.C. to AD 500. For instance, as seen in chapter 1, the Philistines were an Aegean people related to the Greeks who migrated to the coastal plain of Canaan (Palestine) about the same time as the Exodus. And as we have seen, it is their name that the Romans gave to the land of Israel. Persians and Greeks came, conquered, and colonized the Near East during the latter half of the first millennium BC, and then at the end of that millennium, Roman rule began to spread throughout the Mediterranean basin. It was the Romans' practice to reward retiring soldiers with farms and estates in subjugated lands, thus bringing Italians and others in the Roman armies to the Eastern Mediterranean as permanent residents. Thus, by the end of the New Testament period, all the lands of southwest Asia, which we now call the Near East, were populated by a great mix of peoples known and unknown, related and unrelated.

By the birth of Muhammad, about five hundred years after the deaths of Peter and Paul, there were many ethnic groups living in the lands we now know as Israel, Jordan, Syria, Iraq, Lebanon, and Egypt. Within one hundred years of Muhammad's death, the Muslim armies would conquer all these countries, the rest of North Africa, and half of Spain. Along with the new religion of Islam, they imposed the Arabic language on the peoples of these regions, who natively spoke languages such as Aramaic, Greek, Latin, Coptic (Egyptian), and Berber. The people of these regions became Arabs through the adoption of the Arabic language. Thus, an Arab from Tunisia and an Arab from Iraq have no blood relation to one another and are not Arabs racially as are the Arabs of the Near East. They are only Arabs because they speak Arabic and because they eventually adopted Arabic culture as their own. An Arab from Syria, in addition to having Arab DNA, may have ancestors who were Assyrians, Phoenicians, Hurrians, Jews, Hittites, Persians, Greeks, Romans, Armenians, or any combination of the above. This also applies today to the people who call themselves Palestinians.

So how does Abraham or Ishmael fit into this picture? At the time of Muhammad, Jews and Christians lived in the Arabian Peninsula from what is now southern Jordan to Yemen at the southwestern tip of the peninsula. Many of the Arabs (people living in this area) had converted to either Judaism or Christianity. Muhammad learned biblical stories and legends from these Jews and Christians and would later incorporate those stories into his Qur'an. It had been the Jews' practice for a long time to refer to the inhabitants of the regions southeast of Palestine (Israel) as "Ishmaelites," by which they may have meant nothing more than camel caravanners. The Jews probably believed that their southeastern neighbors were in fact descendants of Ishmael, and indeed, Ishmael's descendants—as well as Abraham's descendants via Keturah (Genesis 25:1–4)—may well have contributed to the gene pool of the Hijaz (northwestern Arabia). But is there any reason to say that the Arabs of Mecca, whether in Muhammad's day or one to two thousand years earlier or later, were or are the descendants of Abraham through Ishmael? No. There had been Arabic-speaking peoples in that area in Abraham's day and for perhaps more than a thousand years before. Muhammad accepted at face value what he learned from Jews and Christians and incorporated it into Islam. Therefore, an oversimplified Jewish way of identifying their neighbors became codified into three religions. But that oversimplification does not explain the complexities that we know of the demographics of the Near East.

Enough! Maspeek! Kifayah!

The disputed land of the "sons of Abraham" is of course that part of the former Ottoman province of Syria, known prior to the establishment of the State of Israel as Palestine, which includes all present-day Israel. Palestinian Arabs refer to this entire region, including the West Bank (Samaria and Judea) and the Gaza Strip, as "Occupied Palestine." The two tribes, the Ishmaelites and Isaacites, are obviously today's Arabs and Jews, respectively. As seen above, both Arabs and Jews claim Abraham to be their forefather and patriarch, the Arabs through Ishmael, Abraham's first son by his second wife, Hagar, and the Jews through Isaac, Abraham's second son by his first wife, Sarah.[103] Modern-day claims and counterclaims to the land of Israel-Palestine and the

---

[103] Interestingly, Arabs and Israelis today in an almost ironic, mythical joking manner refer to one another as patrilineal cousins (Arabic: Awlaad 'Amm [اولاد عم] | Hebrew: bnei dod [בְּנֵי דוד]).

conflict that has ensued over this tiny land is known to the world as the Palestinian-Israeli conflict, or more broadly the Arab-Israeli conflict. Although this relatively young conflict that has troubled the Near East and the world is in fact only about one hundred years old, it has roots in events that go back almost four thousand years. Both sides have paid dearly for their tenacious claims to this ancient land, in blood sacrifices of tens of thousands of human lives and in the waste of the human condition and enterprise.

The reason this issue is of importance to the world is that it has over time grown to draw allies to each of its respective camps and has polarized governments and people throughout the world. Consequently, the world has been mired in the Arab-Israeli problem for the past one hundred years, since the end of the Ottoman Empire's rule in the Near East in 1918. The monetary cost to the world has been in the hundreds of billions of dollars, and on two occasions during the Cold War, this regional conflict became a potential trigger of nuclear war between the United States and the Soviet Union, as the superpowers took sides and threatened each other with a nuclear response if either one entered the fight in support of its allies.

As a result of the stakes involved over the rights of land ownership and possession, both sides have developed passionate positions on the issue, which have flared into regional Near Eastern warfare and violence and spilled over to other countries outside of the Near East, committed both by and against the parties concerned. This violence has been exported and directed against those who are perceived to be supporters of Jewish/Israeli claims to the land. The conflict continues to escalate, with attacks and counterattacks both by Arab militants against Israeli civilian and military targets and by the Israeli military against Arab militants.

Israel's prime minister from 1969 to 1974, Golda Meir, is credited with the following two quotes: "If the Arabs lay down their weapons tomorrow, there will be peace. If Israel lays down its weapons tomorrow,

Israel will be annihilated." And "We [Israelis] can forgive the Arabs for killing our children. We cannot forgive them [the Arabs] for forcing us to kill their children. We will only have peace with the Arabs when they love their children more than they hate us." These two quotes are known and can be quoted almost verbatim by many Israelis who have lived with the near constant state of warfare for the past seven decades.

It is time to get realistic about the problem and solve it for the sake of all its victims and in the name of all that is sane. Otherwise, where and when will the conflict end and at what unimaginable continued, future cost in human suffering and blood? What is the alternative? What will the future look like if no workable solution is found? When does the madness stop? What price must be paid by the societies involved and, most sadly, the thousands of innocent victims, both living today and yet unborn? To all the hatred and bloodshed, I say, "Enough! *Maspeek* מספיק! *Kifayah* كفايه!"[104]

---

[104] *Maspeek* and *kifayah* are the Hebrew and Arabic words respectively for *enough.*

Notes

Raoul Wootliff, "Final Text of Jewish Nation State Law Approved by the Knesset on July 19," *Times of Israel* (August 2, 2018).

Kyle Mackie "Why Israel's Model Minority is Leading the Protest Against the Nation-State Law," *Ha'aretz* (July 26, 2018).

Maajid Nawaz, "Israel must be a secular state for all citizens," *The Guardian* (June 16, 2009).

Chapter 11

Mistakes and Missed Opportunities

This chapter will review the numerous historical mistakes made and opportunities missed by all concerned that have produced the dilemma known as the Arab-Israeli conflict. Had some of these egregious errors not been made and opportunities not been missed, the region might have been more peaceful today and may have looked quite different than it does.

Great Britain: Creating the Nightmare[105]

The first mistake was made when Great Britain very generally stated in the 1917 Balfour Declaration that "His majesties government views with favor the establishment of a Jewish homeland in Palestine." Perhaps at this early date, Great Britain did not want to be more specific so as not to inflame Arab concerns. However, because it was

---

[105] It is easy with one hundred years of hindsight to look back at these historical events and pass judgment with today's clearer vision and perspective.

such a broad statement, it required Great Britain six years later to issue the 1922 White Paper on Palestine to specify that it did not intend to make all of Palestine available to the Zionists but that Jews would be allowed to establish a nation-state somewhere within Palestine. The White Paper also placed an annual quota on how many Jews could immigrate to Palestine and effected a naval blockade preventing Jews from entering Palestine. This blockade often intercepted Jews escaping the Nazi Holocaust, who were often returned to Europe only to again fall victim to the Nazis' Final Solution, extermination. The British act of blockading and limiting Jewish immigration to Palestine was at the core of the creation of Jewish underground militias, which fought the British to circumvent the blockade. The White Paper in effect walked back and contradicted the earlier sentiments and goodwill of the Balfour Declaration toward the Jews. In two official declarations, Great Britain raised the hopes of persecuted world Jews and then offended, insulted, and made itself the enemy of both Arabs and Jews— not a good start—which sowed seeds of discontent and inflamed the conflict that is still ravaging the region to this day. Arabs, specifically Palestinians, would argue that the first great mistake that created the nightmare was Great Britain's arrogance in thinking it could legally and morally give away another people's land and home to a third party, for whatever reason.

In this era after World War I and the dissolution of the Ottoman Empire, Great Britain was in the business of creating countries in the Near East as part of its promise to Sharif Hussein of Makkah and the Arabs in the McMahon-Hussein Correspondence of 1915. Great Britain created a country it initially called the Amirate of East Jordan, a name later changed to the Emirate of Transjordan, then the Hashemite-ruled Arab Kingdom of Syria, and finally, as it is known today, the Hashemite Kingdom of Jordan. Arab inhabitants of Palestine at this time did not think of themselves as a distinct Palestinian nation but rather as Arabs or sometimes as Syrian Arabs. A more balanced approach Great Britain could have taken, which might have shown that it was taking into consideration all the nationalistic aspirations of the region's inhabitants, would have been for it to have simultaneously created two separate Arab and Jewish countries in the territory in the Levant over which it had been given a mandate by the League of Nations: one a Jewish nation in all of Palestine, to which Arabs would have certainly objected, and the other an Arab nation in the twice-as-large region of Trans-Jordan (known in antiquity as Ammon and the Ammonite Kingdom). This newly created Arab nation would have stretched from the Jordan River east to the western Iraqi Desert and from the Syrian border in the north to the Red Sea port city of Aqaba in the south. Iraq was another country Great Britain arbitrarily created by drawing lines in the sand, uniting three former provinces of the defeated Ottoman Empire: the northern Kurdish region with its capital in Mosul, the central Arab-Sunni region with its capital in Baghdad, and the southern Arab-Shiite region with its capital in Basra.

Great Britain missed another opportunity to make its country creation more inclusive of the region's inhabitants after Jewish leaders convinced it to allow them to establish a Jewish state in Palestine in 1918. Although there was some attempt to bring Arab leaders into the discussion, Great Britain should have made more effort to do so and should have reached an amicable agreement with the major Arab players as to what a Jewish state in the middle of the Arab Near East would look like. Bringing Arab leaders on board with the possibility of a Jewish state in Palestine is not as far-fetched as might first appear. At this time, Arabs did not have any animosity toward Jews, who had become culturally Arabized, had lived peacefully in Arab lands for centuries, and were not considered a threat. The sharif of Makkah, Sharif Hussein bin Ali of Saudi Arabia, is reported to have stated in the Makkah daily newspaper *Al Qibla* that Palestine was a "sacred and beloved homeland of its original sons [the Jews] … the return of these exiles to their homeland will prove materially and spiritually an experimental school of their [Arab] brethren." In effect, the attitude of the leader and representative of the Arab world in the post–World War I Near East was one of welcome to their long-displaced Jewish kin. There are other conflicting historical accounts stating that Hussein considered Palestine (at some point in the post-Ottoman Near East) to be Arab land. But assuming the former scenario was the reality, this would have been yet another missed opportunity in the early years.

At the end of World War I, it was in fact France, as a partner to the secret Anglo-French Sykes-Picot Agreement, that could have been the deal maker but that was in fact the deal breaker in the Near East. Arab leaders at the time stated that if France would drop its post–World War I plans to control Syria and Lebanon as a colonial power per the Sykes-Picot Agreement, Arabs would allow the Jews to establish a state in Palestine, most likely encompassing all of Palestine. France was still in the pre–World War I Napoleonic mindset of colonial rule and coveted control over this portion of the world that had newfound petroleum wealth—a region in which it had colonial interests and over which it had control going back more than eight hundred years to the Crusades. What a missed opportunity not to have formalized an understanding between Jewish and Arab leaders, which could have included Arabs as partners in the establishment of a Jewish state in the Near East.

Jewish and Israeli Mistakes

In their post–World War I zeal to begin the process of nation building and promote Jewish immigration to Palestine following the promises made by Great Britain to Jewish leaders through the Balfour Declaration, Jews misrepresented Palestine as "a land without a people for a people without a land." This was, of course, inaccurate, since Palestine was inhabited by a mostly Arabized population of several hundred thousand. During this period, the indigenous Palestinian population did not think of itself as a separate people from the rest of the Arab world but thought of itself as either Arab or Syrian. *Syrian* comes from the Arabic word for the Levant, *ash-Shaam* (الشام), which is also another Arabic name for Syria, greater Syria, and even specifically Damascus. They often referred to themselves as "Shamiyeen" (شاميين, translated as "Shamites"). Jewish immigrants to the land expecting it to be "without a people" were often surprised to find that the land was in fact inhabited.

Palestine had for centuries been essentially forgotten, neglected, underdeveloped, and poor and had vast malaria-carrying, mosquito-infested swamps; Mark Twain's 1867 book *Innocents Abroad* recounts the abysmal condition of the region. The land may have been sparsely populated, neglected, and poor, but it was not "without a people."

Immediately prior to attaining nationhood in 1948, Jewish militias committed murderous atrocities against Arab towns and villages in areas designated for the Jewish state by the United Nations' Partition Plan. They committed these murderous attacks to frighten and terrorize the Arab population in hopes that they would leave and escape to surrounding Arab countries, as many indeed did. One of the most notorious and infamous such massacres occurred in the Arab village of Deir Yassin near Jerusalem in April 1948, committed by the Jewish militias of Irgun and Lehi. The massacre, which killed between one hundred and two hundred Arab villagers (some accounts are even higher) and involved men, women, and children, torture, rape, and dismemberment, was condemned by both Jewish leaders and the international community. This incident triggered a counterattack by Arab militants on a hospital convoy four days later, which resulted in the death of seventy-eight Jewish medical personnel. Incidents such as this were widespread between Arabs and Jews during Palestine mandate years and only deepened the hatred, animosity, and mistrust between the two groups. Stories of massacres such as Deir Yassin are told and retold in the Arab community as though they occurred last week and have caused deep, irreparable distrust and hatred seven decades later.

A big strategic error that Israel committed occurred during Operation Peace in the Galilee when Israeli military forces went after the PLO and other militants in Lebanon in 1982. The Israeli military was given a forty-eight-hour window to pursue PLO fighters into southern Lebanon who had been attacking and terrorizing Israeli residents in northern Israel. The forty-eight-hour window became stretched out to eighteen years and was extremely costly to Israel monetarily, in terms of lives lost and soldiers maimed and injured, and especially in terms of its reputation and standing in the international community. Israel had never before attacked, surrounded, and besieged a neighboring Arab country's capital as it did in the Lebanon war. Israel should have stayed the course and, after having defeated the PLO and other militants, withdrawn to Israel. At a minimum, Israel should have withdrawn from Beirut to its self-declared South Lebanon Security Zone, as it eventually did from 1985 to 2000. It was during this period that the world began to be less sympathetic toward Israel because of its perceived heavy-handedness and use of the entire weight of its armed forces to invade and occupy a neighboring Arab country for so long. Prior to this period, when the PLO hijacked aircraft internationally and held countries hostage to its demands, murdering Israeli civilians, athletes, and diplomats, and massacring Israeli civilians in schools and communities in northern Israel, the world was for the most part sympathetic to Israel in its justified retaliations against terrorism. Israelis have a saying that may be paraphrased as "only when Jews are suffering and dying does the world feel sympathy toward us."

Another example of a time when Israel lost international goodwill was during the First Intifada/Uprising from 1987 to 1993, when Israeli military and security forces used harsh, on-the-spot punitive measures against Palestinian militants that were recorded and documented by the international press. These measures included breaking the arms and bones of young Palestinian militants who threw rocks and Molotov cocktails at Israeli security forces. Consequently, Israel was portrayed in the international press as responding with a disproportionate, harsh, heavy-handed, and torturously cruel overuse of force against rock- and Molotov cocktail–throwing Palestinian youth. During the first and second intifadas, Israel continued to lose more of the moral high ground it may have had in the minds of the international community and drew many people, especially Europeans, into the Palestinian camp.

Israel's continued construction of Jewish settlements in the West Bank (Samaria and Judea), which it captured from Jordan in the 1967

Six-Day War, is considered by much of the international community to be illegal, an obstacle to peace, and not conducive to resolving Israel's dispute with the Palestinians. It is considered illegal because under international law, these settlements are constructed on lands taken in warfare. Israelis view it very differently, claiming these lands were liberated from Jordan in the defensive war of 1967 and that they are in fact the heart of ancient biblical Israel, as Israel's ethnogenesis began in the Judean hills. This historical claim of that land being at the heart of ancient Israel is accurate and is supported by both written records and archaeology. It is estimated that today nearly six hundred thousand Israelis live in the West Bank. This figure continues to grow, as recent Israeli governments have granted more permits for the construction of new settlements in this region.

Israelis, beginning with Prime Minister Ariel Sharon in the 1980s, have labeled these permanent Jewish communities in the West Bank "facts on the ground" (i.e., six hundred thousand Israelis living in the West Bank is an undisputed factual reality). Before embarking on such an extensive settlement construction project and settling so many Israelis in the West Bank, it would have been preferable for the Israelis to have first come to an agreement with the Palestinians about the area's ultimate disposition. Such an agreement would most likely have also had the international community's endorsement. The reality is that Israel knows the Palestinians would never agree to concede West Bank land for Israel to establish permanent settlements and very probably eventually annex.

The most recent Israeli mistake was the July 2020 proposed annexation of approximately 30 percent of the West Bank. Why? Annexation of this area is simply not necessary for Israel's security, economy, international standing, or any other rational reason. The vast majority of Israel's almost six hundred thousand Jewish inhabitants in the West Bank overwhelmingly rejected this annexation. They contend that this plan opens the way for an eventual Palestinian state in the West Bank, which would physically cut them off and isolate them from Israel proper.

They fear that there would be no guarantees that such a Palestinian-Arab state would not eventually surround them and morph into the Gaza Strip model, with a Hamas or Hamas-like militant Islamist state that would be bent on their destruction. Jordan's King Abdullah II has come out strongly against the annexation and has even hinted that it could jeopardize the Israeli-Jordanian peace agreement. Israel can ill afford to have its peace treaty with Jordan nullified; it has given Israel quiet and security on its eastern border for almost three decades. Although Egypt has not come out as strongly as has Jordan against annexation, Israel would assuredly antagonize the Egyptian and entire Arab world population if it went through with annexation. Israel can continue to control these areas as it has done for the past fifty-three years, since June 1967, without risking losing the scarce goodwill it has in the international community or the rapprochement it has recently developed with Arab countries, particularly with the Arabian Gulf countries. More ill than good can come from annexation, and therefore there simply is no need or urgency for annexation. It is not wise, not necessary, and not advisable.[106]

Possibly the biggest existential problem and misstep by Israel and Israeli policy has been its forcible rule and control of a people who do not wish to be ruled. Palestinian Arabs living under Israeli rule today, both in Israel proper and within control of Israeli security forces in the West Bank, number approximately 5 million—2.1 million in Israel and 2.8 million in the West Bank. With a total Jewish Israeli population of 6.5 million, Arab Israeli citizens make up 20 percent of Israel's population, and the combined 5 million Palestinians make up almost 45 percent of the total Arab and Jewish population either directly or indirectly under Israeli control. For its own short-and long-term best interests, Israel needs to get out of the business of occupying lands and controlling people who not only do not want to be controlled but who in many cases harbor ill will toward the Jewish state and

---

[106] Israel suspended this proposed annexation in August 2020 after its earth-shattering announcement that it would be normalizing diplomatic relations with the United Arab Emirate (UAE). Apparently, suspending annexation was the cost of a peace treaty.

would in a heartbeat side with forces bent on Israel's destruction. At a minimum, Israel's Arab population is a very real potential fifth column that could eventually bring Israel down as a Jewish state from within. The original socialist Zionist dream, espoused by Israel's first prime minister, David Ben-Gurion, that Arabs and Jews could build a common, peaceful community under Jewish rule was naïve at best and has so far proven to be unworkable and unrealistic. The sooner Israelis and Palestinian Arabs are separated from one another, the better. Just as India relinquished control over its huge Muslim populations in its eastern and western provinces and created East and West Pakistan and eventually Bangladesh, so too should Israel relinquish the segment of territory under its control with large Palestinian-Arab populations and allow for the creation of a Palestinian-Arab state. The only limiting factor to such a creative option is a lack of imagination and a fear of risk taking. Undoubtedly, Israelis who might oppose such an arrangement would point to Hamas's violent, hardline, Islamist, militant takeover of the Gaza Strip in 2007 and argue that following such a withdrawal by Israel, the West Bank could also become a similar hotbed of extremists bent on Israel's destruction. Such a withdrawal would be understandably risky to Israel's security and would need to come with a heavy proviso.

A withdrawal of Israel from Palestinian-majority lands would come with the following important stipulations, which would put the international community, as well as the newly created Palestinian state, militants, activists, Jihadists, terrorist, militaries, and any other group who would choose not to live in peace side by side with the Jewish State of Israel, on notice: First, should Israel be attacked from this newly created state, the Israeli military would be fully justified in counterattacking the areas from which the attack originated to eliminate the threat. Second, each kilometer that Israeli forces retake in their pursuit of attacking militants would immediately become annexed into Israel without further discussion. Palestinians who have learned the lessons of history and wish to live in peace in an independent Palestine should have no problems with these conditions. Militants and extremists who oppose this arrangement would not only be repeating history's mistakes but would once again squander an opportunity for statehood and continue to have nothing.

There are other, smaller mistakes and errors of judgment made by Israel over the years and obstacles it has put up to peaceful coexistence, such as Israeli forces permitting the Phalange Christian Militia to enter and massacre Palestinian noncombatant civilians in the Sabra and Shatila Refugee Camps in Lebanon in 1982, and Prime Minister Ariel Sharon's visit to the Temple Mount in 2000, which triggered the Second Intifada.

United States Mistakes

Arabs have long claimed that the US has always been biased in favor of Israel, ever since the Truman administration recognized Israel diplomatically in 1948 when it attained statehood, following the United Nations vote to partition Palestine. The reality is that the US would also almost certainly have recognized a Palestinian-Arab state diplomatically at the same time had the Arabs not rejected the UN partition plan and waged a war of extermination on Israel. Therefore, this claim that is at the heart of Arab complaints about US bias in favor of Israel is baseless in its premise. Arabs will also point to the evident US bias toward Israel when President Eisenhower guaranteed Israel's security against its adversaries in exchange for Israel withdrawing from the Sinai Peninsula, which it had captured from Egypt in the 1956 Sinai War. The US gave these assurances because it needed Israel to return the Sinai Peninsula to Egypt so that Egypt could retain honor and needed to end a state of war in which the Soviet Union threatened the use of nuclear weapons. As a result of Eisenhower's assurances of security to Israel, the US has continued to sell qualitative-edge weaponry to Israel even as it has sold the same weapons systems to Arab countries. It was obvious by 1956 that the entire Arab world, backed by the Soviet Union, would be relentless in pursuing its goal of annihilating the Jewish state, which was completely isolated in the Near

East. The Arab-Israeli conflict had now become another front line in the Cold War as the Soviets looked for willing client states.

All during the Cold War, the US had been Israel's primary weapons benefactor, as the Soviet Union was the primary weapons benefactor of most of the Arab states in confrontation with Israel. The Soviet Union was not the exclusive supplier of Arab countries. Great Britain was the primary weapons supplier of Jordan, and the US became Egypt's primary weapons supplier after 1979 following the Egyptian-Israeli peace treaty. Arab Gulf countries that had long come under the protection of the British Empire purchased most of their weapons from Great Britain and later also France. Saud Arabia, which was not in direct confrontation with Israel, also purchased most of its weaponry from the US. Although they were not direct combatants, Saudi Arabia and other oil-rich Arab Gulf countries were financial backers of Arab states in confrontation with Israel, such as Egypt, Syria, and Jordan.

US policy and actions have not always been helpful or necessary in advancing Near East peace. An argument can be made that it was not necessary for the US Congress in 1995 to recognize Jerusalem as Israel's capital and authorize the US to move its embassy there from Tel Aviv. Then in 2018, when the Trump administration moved the US embassy to Jerusalem, it was viewed by much of the world as not only unhelpful but proof to Arabs of US bias and even obstructionism and provocation. The US could have maintained the international community's position of waiting for the Palestinians and Israelis to ultimately decide the status of Jerusalem in a final negotiated agreement. Also, it did not resolve any urgent issue when in 2019 the US Trump administration recognized Israel's 1981 annexation of the Golan Heights, which it (Israel) had captured from Syria in the 1967 Six-Day War. Neither one of these US actions changed any facts on the ground or contributed to Arab-Israeli peace.

Arab and Palestinian Mistakes and Missed Opportunities

Without question, the first, biggest, and most tragic opportunity missed by both the Arabs and Palestinians was not accepting the 1947 United Nations Partition Plan of Palestine. Simply put, had the Arabs accepted the United Nations Partition Plan, as did the Jews, Palestinians would today have a country. Granted, it would not have been everything they wanted—all of Palestine—but as the Jews, who also would have preferred all of Palestine, something from nothing would have given them *something*. Not only would Palestinians have a country today, but it would be 50 percent larger than the area they and the Arab world are now demanding that Israel withdraw from to create a Palestinian state. This area is 50 percent smaller than that given to the Palestinians by the United Nations in the partition plan because Arabs lost 50 percent more territory to the Israelis after they declared war on the newly created Jewish state in 1948—their first attempted war of annihilation. The Arab League has repeatedly called on Israel to withdraw from the West Bank and allow the Palestinians to establish a Palestinian state. Arabs today, with twenty-twenty hindsight, are willing to settle for this diminished Palestinian state and have twice, in 2002 and 2007, stated that if Israel were to withdraw to the pre–Six-Day War boundaries, all twenty-two nations of the Arab League would recognize Israel's right to exist in peace and would normalize diplomatic relations with the Jewish state. Repeated wars with Israel have only proven to be more devastating in loss of territory, honor, and dignity. By not accepting the original United Nations Partition Plan and continuing down the road of military confrontation with Israel, the Palestinians and Arabs have not only created but have intensified the shame and misery of their own Nakbah, catastrophe.

The next big, missed opportunity for the Arabs came immediately following the June 1967 Six-Day War. Shortly after the war, Israel offered to withdraw from the captured territories of the Sinai Peninsula, the West Bank, the Gaza Strip, and the Golan Heights if the Arab world would recognize Israeli's right to exist and abandon their state of war with the Jewish state. In response to this initial offer, the Arab League met in Khartoum, Sudan, in August 1967 and issued their infamous three nos: "No to Israel, no to negotiation, no to peace." This short-lived window of opportunity quickly closed, and all concerned began rearming and preparing for the next inevitable war.

In the 1970s, when the PLO began its guerilla attacks on unarmed Israeli civilians, schools, children, and athletes and began hijacking international aircraft and assassinating Israeli diplomats, there was not much international sympathy for their cause. Again, during the intifadas of the late 1980s through the early 2000s, when Palestinian militants attacked Israeli civilians in restaurants, clubs, hotels, and bus stops, including through random stabbings and vehicular assaults (ramming), Palestinians lost some of the international goodwill they might have had. Their cause might have been more effective all these years with the international community had they resorted to nonviolent civil disobedience along the lines of Gandhi's opposition to the British colonial rule and the successful nonviolent civil disobedience of the black-majority population to oppose South African apartheid rule.

During the 1990s, the United States attempted to broker diplomatic negotiations between Israel and the Palestinians. The US used its good offices to shuttle ideas between the Palestinians and the Israelis through US Secretary of State James Baker. In his frustration at being unable to get concessions from Yasser Arafat, chairman of the Palestinian Authority, James Baker accurately characterized Arafat as someone who "never missed an opportunity to miss an opportunity." This can also be said about Palestinian leadership over the years, which has been accused by other Palestinians as not always acting in the Palestinian people's best interest. These critics point out that no Palestinian leader has yet to deliver on promised statehood for the Palestinian people. Criticism of Arafat can be extended to apply to subsequent Palestinian leaders, who have also "never missed an opportunity to miss an opportunity."

Other US presidents and administrations have since attempted to broker peace between the Palestinians and Israelis—first in 1995 at the Wye River Summit in Maryland and again in 2000 at Camp David, Maryland. The 2000 Summit was attended by US President Bill Clinton, Israeli Prime Minister Ehud Barak, and Palestinian Authority President Yasser Arafat. Ehud Barak, in a generous gesture, offered the Palestinians statehood in large portions of the West Bank and the entire Gaza Strip, even offering East Jerusalem as the Palestinian capital. Arafat and the Palestinians were once again consistent in their rejection of this deal as well. And finally, as discussed earlier, true to form, the Palestinian leadership under Palestinian Authority President Mahmoud Abbas rejected outright the Trump administration's proposal for peace in 2020, even before it was made public. This was followed in late 2020 by the Palestinian Authority objecting to and rejecting normalizing relationships between Israel, the United Arab Emirates, Bahrain, and Morocco. The Palestinians had been given an opportunity in early 2020 to become a part of the greater Trump administration's "deal of the century" initiative with a $500 million economic investment and development package. The Palestinian leadership once again chose to continue to reject to all proposals and as a result is being left behind as Arab-Israeli relations normalize and move forward.[107]

Many Palestinians have claimed that Arab leaders in general have also not always had Palestinian best interests at heart. They complain that

---

[107] In 1988, when I was an assistant air attaché in the US Defense Attaché Office at the US embassy in Tel Aviv, Israel, I had an encounter with a young Palestinian day laborer with a work permit to enter Israel. Since I speak his Palestinian Arabic dialect natively, I befriended him and let him know that I worked in the American embassy. I proposed to come to his home in Gaza, sit down with his family, and have them share with me anything they wanted about their condition and their perspective of the Palestinian-Israeli conflict. The young man said yes, that would be a possibility and that he would be happy to welcome me to his home, where he would drive a knife into my back and kill me. Thinking maybe I had miscommunicated my proposal, I again repeated my offer, telling him that through me he and his family could have a direct voice to the US government to express whatever perspective they wished. He again said he would welcome me to his house and then drive the blade of a long knife into my back and kill me. Knowing clearly that he had understood me well, I shook my finger in his face and told him that if he and his people approached such offers of assistance with his attitude, neither he nor the Palestinians would ever have a country of their own. I turned my back and left, never seeing him again.

Arab leaders have often selectively played the Palestinian card when it suited them and their agendas du jour. Two examples were when Nasser of Egypt used the Palestinian cause to bolster his leadership role in the Arab world in the 1950s and 1960s and when Saddam Hussein in the 1990s wanted to garner Arab support to deflect attention from the fact that he had invaded and occupied Kuwait.

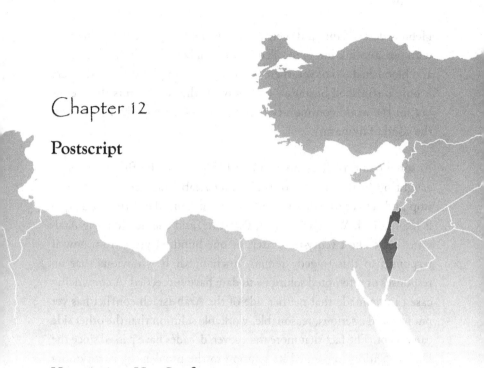

Chapter 12

Postscript

Negotiation, Not Confrontation

This story began by identifying the Hebrew people's ethnogenesis and discussing the attempts made by the descendants of these early Hebrews to hold on to a land they believed was divinely given to them. We followed their descendants as they were evicted and exiled from their land and dispersed, hated, and persecuted to the point of near extermination because they were different. Yet all the while, they tenaciously clung to the dream that they would someday return to their ancestral home—"Next year in Jerusalem." We saw their descendants miraculously surviving, beating the odds, and reconstituting themselves in their ancestral homeland after almost two thousand years, like the mythical phoenix rising from the ashes. Israel is today the only country in the world whose people live in the same land and speak the same (updated) language as their ancestors more than three thousand years before. It is in many ways a romantic, unique human survival story unmatched in the world. Unfortunately, we ended the journey with the

Hebrew descendants and their neighbors not being able to live in peace
with one another but embroiled in seemingly endless hatred, warfare,
and bloodshed. As of yet, there is no happy ending to this story. There
is only unfinished business—not only for the combatants themselves
but for the world community of nations—which must be resolved for
the good of humanity.

At some point, belligerents and non-belligerents who find themselves
caught up in the tragedy of the greater Arab-Israeli conflict need to
stop and reflect on what the future might look like if the status quo
is maintained. What will Israel, Palestine, and the neighboring Arab
states look like twenty-five, fifty, or one hundred years from now if
responses to this tragedy remain unchanged? It is obvious that no
responses or attempted solutions to date have succeeded. A convincing
case can be made that neither side of the Arab-Israeli conflict has yet
put forward a serious, reasonable, workable solution that the other side
can accept. The fact that more than seven decades have passed since the
United Nations presented its solution to the problem by partitioning
the land demonstrates that a workable formula has not yet been found
that satisfies even the minimum requirements of the majority of both
sides of the conflict.

For the sake of not repeating history's mistakes, many Palestinians
today, including many in the Arab world, would accept the creation
of a Palestinian state that the United Nations proposed in 1947, even
though they refused it at the time (i.e., a two-state solution, one
Palestinian-Arab and the other Jewish-Israeli). Four major wars, three
uprisings, numerous smaller-scale subwars, and the tragic deaths of tens
of thousands of people have made Palestinians realize what the Jews
realized in 1947: that something from nothing is not only something
but is better than nothing. An alternative to the current dead-end
stalemate of attack, revenge, avenging the revenge, and unending
killing and hatred must be found. A workable solution that would give
both parties some of what they want should be the goal. If "everything"
is all the territory of Israel-Palestine, then both sides simply cannot

have everything. The impossibility of both sides having everything is a confirmation of the law of physics that governs time and space: two objects cannot occupy the same space at the same time. Meeting the demands of the extremists on both sides, who want the entire land of Israel-Palestine, is a nonstarter and an impossibility. Compromise by both sides is the only option. By definition, compromising means that neither side will get all that it wants and will have to give to receive. What is certain is that the status quo lacks imagination, is not sustainable, and has repeatedly proven unworkable.

A solution must be found that incorporates the spirit of what an Israeli, quoting an old saying, once said to me: "If you want an omelet, you must break some eggs," which is to say that you must give up some of what you want—"eggs"—in order to get the more important portion of what you want—"an omelet." A receptive population and a willing leadership on both sides must first decide if they want an "omelet." Assuming each side is willing to do what is necessary, which is not yet a given, a negotiated solution must be the means to a resolution.

For more than seventy years, both sides have tried war, killing, homicide-suicide, murder, targeted assassinations, and terror to no avail. None of the killings have persuaded either side to give up its dream of possessing all the land. The armed approach has not worked, necessitating a different approach. A first step in a negotiated solution is for each side to put forward representatives with the authority to speak for their respective constituents. Negotiated settlements always results in neither side getting everything it wants. Both sides must focus on the big picture and be willing to give up something for the sake of the bigger goal. Anyone hoping to mediate a compromise between the Israelis and Palestinians must be well versed in the conflict's history, think outside the box, and above all not take sides in this conflict between these quarreling "half-brother" tribes. It is enough that more than 300 million Arabs and the 1.3 billion Muslims around the world overwhelmingly take the Arab or Palestinian position, and that the approximately 6.7 million Israeli Jews and an estimated 12 to 15 million Jews around the world, plus millions of non-Jews around the world, take the Israeli position in this conflict.

Ironically, the United Nations, which in 1947 voted to create Israel and a Palestinian-Arab state and which was formed by the international community to resolve and prevent conflict, has not been an honest broker in the Palestinian-Israeli conflict. On the contrary, the United Nations has over the past four decades one-sidedly taken the Palestinian position and repeatedly voted in resolution after resolution to oppose and condemn Israel. This antagonism toward the Jewish state began with the 1973 Yom Kippur/Ramadan War. Following Israel's fourth defeat of combined Arab forces, OPEC (the Organization of Petroleum Exporting Countries) began using oil sales as a political weapon, primarily against Western industrial powers who supported Israel and who were heavily dependent on Arab oil exports to fuel their economies. Led by Saudi Arabia, OPEC began by raising prices and cutting deliveries of petroleum, which created an immediate international gasoline and fuel oil shortage. This de facto blackmail of the industrialized world to change world opinion against Israel and toward the Arab world was dubbed the 1973 Gasoline Crisis/Oil Embargo. Long lines of motorists waited at gas stations in industrial centers around the world. Specifically hard hit was the US, which had become accustomed to having cheap gasoline to fuel the world's largest and most fuel-inefficient automobiles. Gradually, the oil embargo worked, and industrialized countries, primarily in Europe, began to reduce their traditional political and economic support for Israel and started outwardly supporting the Arab/Palestinian perspective, which was reflected in numerous votes both in the General Assembly and the Security Council of the United Nations. As an outgrowth of this world shift away from supporting Israel, many European countries also signed on to the Arab-led political and economic embargo against Israel and Israeli products.

A prime example of the extreme United Nations bias in favor of the Palestinians and against Israel is a recent decision made by the

United Nations Education, Scientific, and Cultural Organization (UNESCO). Among other responsibilities, UNESCO is charged with identifying, recognizing, and preserving World Heritage sites. In a 2016 Palestinian-sponsored resolution, UNESCO recognized the Temple Mount in Jerusalem by its Arab/Muslim name, *Haram al-Sharif* (Noble Sanctuary). This UN resolution made no reference to this site as being originally Mount Moriah, or the Temple Mount, Judaism's holiest spot on earth and the location of King Solomon's and King Herod's respective First and Second Temples. Judaism's claim to this site predates any Arab or Muslim claim by 1,700 to 2,500 years. This resolution was deliberately worded to maximize Arab claims to the site and minimize or even eliminate its original Jewish identity. In the Palestinian-Israeli conflict, the United Nations has unfortunately become an agent of polarization and conflict perpetuation, not one of conflict prevention and resolution.

The effort to solve the problem is not best served by having the world line up behind one side against the other. To do so is counterproductive and irresponsible and only perpetuates the problem. By taking one side against the other, one becomes part of the problem and not its solution. Well-meaning mediators to this tragic quagmire must be true, honest brokers, not flame stokers. In order to pursue the happiness of both sides in this conflict, anyone genuinely interested in solving the Palestinian-Israeli conflict must not be pro-Palestinian (and anti-Israeli) or pro-Israeli (and anti-Palestinian) but must be both pro-Palestinian and pro-Israeli. An honest broker should want the best for both people.

Painting in broad strokes and acknowledging that these options for a resolution are at best general ideas that require more specifics, the four proposals that follow are intended only as starting points to begin a dialogue, with the aim of ultimately reaching a compromise and bringing peace to this unholy, blood-soaked Holy Land.

Option One: Status Quo, Continued Military Confrontation (One-State [Israel] Solution)

A continuation of the status quo will only perpetuate the current state of confrontation into the foreseeable future. The status quo option of no resolution and no peace would have Israel keep all the land it currently controls, possibly obtaining and controlling more Arab land in future armed conflicts and wars, not only from the Palestinians but also from some of its other neighbors, such as Syria and Lebanon. This option is probably the worst-case scenario for all concerned and would not resolve the situation. It would not get the Palestinians any land, which is at the core of their dissatisfactions, and would almost assuredly guarantee future wars, bloodshed, and suffering, as well as a deepening of the animosity and hatred on both sides. Israel must ask itself, as both assassinated Egyptian President Sadat and Israeli Prime Minister Rabin undoubtedly did: What might the future look like if Israel continues to militarily control another people and rule over lands whose majority population is Palestinian Arab? Israel must also ask what the future response of the greater Arab and Muslim worlds might be to the continuity of the status quo? The combined Arab population is many times more numerous than the Jewish population of Israel. There are more than 300 million Arabs living in the Near East and only 6.8 million Jewish Israelis—a ratio of approximately sixty to one (60:1). Israelis often point out that if it were not for Hitler and the Holocaust, there would potentially have been 12.8 million Jewish Israelis today. Worldwide, there are today approximately 1.3 billion Muslims, who most likely sympathize with the Palestinian-Arab cause, and only an estimated 11 to 15 million Jews in the world who could support the Israeli agenda.

One Muslim country, Pakistan, currently possesses nuclear weapons, and Iran is likely to obtain nuclear weapons soon unless international or Israeli action is taken to prevent it. As we have seen, Israel has repeatedly warned that it will not tolerate a nuclear Iran and will destroy Iran's nuclear weapon research facilities if it feels imminently threatened. Israel's willingness to use force against Iranian nuclear facilities is continuously reiterated by the Israeli leadership. What will become of the future nuclear aspirations of regional Arab and Muslim countries if Iran goes nuclear? Saudi Arabia has already stated that it would seek nuclear weapons capabilities if Iran developed nuclear weapons. How long will Pakistan be ruled by level-headed moderates, and what might happen if Pakistan becomes ruled by not so sober leaders who might choose to rattle the saber of the "Islamic Bomb" toward Israel? Such a threat by Pakistan or any other adversary would be dangerous, considering the open secret that Israel has had nuclear weapons capabilities for at least fifty years, an ample stockpile of warheads, and a triad delivery system. With its nuclear opacity policy, Israel remains a sleeping nuclear giant that should not be provoked.

Weapons of mass destruction (WMDs) notwithstanding, the sheer size of the combined Arab and Islamic militaries would overwhelm Israel in a future pan-Arab-Israeli conventional conflict. As one Saudi senior military officer said to me, "The Arabs are relatively weak militarily today, but they will not always remain so into the future." If a future pan-Arab-Israeli conventional war— or an expanded holy war that included other non-Arab but Islamic countries—did take place, Israel could not possibly survive against such overwhelming odds by taking a defensive posture. Given this scenario, Israel, which is the size of New Jersey, would have no choice but to quickly escalate to a nuclear option and lay waste to the armies and possibly capital cities of attacking countries. With its current arsenal of several hundred nuclear warheads and a state-of-the-art delivery system of supersonic fighter aircraft, surface-to-surface missiles, and undetectable stealth submarines, this is not that far-fetched a scenario. Faced with annihilation, Israel would have no other choice than to employ what has been called the "Samson option." If that were the case, Muslim-majority countries with nuclear capabilities and other Arab and Muslim countries that may have nuclear weapons or other WMDs in the future, would most likely attack Israel in kind with their combined nuclear, chemical, and biological weapon arsenals—not an optimistic scenario for maintaining the status quo in the ongoing Arab-Israeli conflict.

Option Two: Partition Plan 2.0 (Two-State Solution)

As discussed in chapter 11 under "Jewish/Israeli Mistakes," the two-state-solution option is based on the premise that neither the Palestinians nor the Israelis want to live in a country controlled by the other. Such a model has been tried for more than seven decades and has proven largely unworkable. For the sake of the happiness of both peoples, neither side needs to rule over the other. Israel's experience in so doing since 1948 has proven to be at best unbecoming of a people who are to be "a light unto the world" and at worst ugly and a national stain. At a minimum, the goal of this plan is for both parties to own part of the land and live in peace and security as neighbors. For this plan to work, both sides must agree to a compromised solution, with the understanding that neither side will be able to have it all.

Partition Plan 2.0 would partition Israel-Palestine based on current demographic concentrations, with some adjustments, into separate Palestinian-Arab and Jewish-Israeli countries. Israel, for the most part, would control much of its pre–Six-Day War territory, and the Palestinian Arabs would control much of the West Bank and the Gaza Strip. This plan is, in effect, a geopolitical update of the 1947 United Nations Partition Plan and would be an opportunity for the Palestinians to press reset to the partition plan they originally rejected, with some land exchanges and border adjustments to give Israel its much-needed defensible borders and a modicum of strategic depth. To give Israel its demanded security requirement, there would be a caveat in this plan that a joint Palestinian-Israeli security force would be responsible for securing the two countries' contiguous international borders, and Palestine would gradually—over so many decades—build a self-defense force/military in cooperation with Israel. The basis of such a security arrangement already exists between Israel and the Palestinian Authority

Security Forces in the West Bank, per the Oslo accords of 1993 and 1995.

This new Partition Plan 2.0 would symbiotically link Israel's and Palestine's economies, which would be a winning formula for both sides. The linked economies would become the glue that would bind the two peoples and make any future thought of armed confrontation out of the question. If the region does establish a workable, peaceful, and secure environment, international tourism would be another element that would feed this two-state solution's success. Many in the international community have been hesitant to visit the region because of its historical turmoil and conflict. If this plan proved successful, Israel and Palestine would not be able to build resorts, hotels, or other elements of tourism and pilgrimage infrastructure fast enough to accommodate the pent-up worldwide demand. A third positive element of economic cooperation and ties would be the long-discussed proposed Red Sea–Dead Sea Canal Project with its proposed resorts (see footnote in chapter 6 under "Water Concerns"). In addition to Israel and Jordan, the Palestinians would benefit immensely from this water conservation and tourism bonanza.

With this plan, Israel could maintain its capital in West Jerusalem, where most of its government offices are located, and the Palestinian state could designate East Jerusalem as its capital. Israel has held both East and West Jerusalem for over the past half century, since taking East Jerusalem from Jordan in the 1967 Six-Day War. Even though Israel has always stated that the status of Jerusalem is not negotiable and not on the table for discussion, Prime Minister Ehud Barak offered East Jerusalem to the Palestinians as their capital in a peace proposal in 2000. Again in 2020 the Trump Administration's Palestinian-Israeli "deal of the century" offered East Jerusalem as a Palestinian capital. Although the Palestinian government in exile has its de facto working capital in the city of Ramallah north of Jerusalem, the Palestinians have always stated that one of their uncompromising positions would be to have the Old City of Jerusalem as their capital. If Partition Plan

2.0 is to have any chance of success, there would have to be agreed-upon assurances that Jerusalem's holy sites would be accessible to all, regardless of religion, ethnicity, or nationality. The status of Jerusalem will have to be negotiated and a workable compromise agreed upon that would not completely satisfy all factions but would respect those who wish to access and worship in this most contested city.

Some critics of Partition Plan 2.0 say there already exists a two-state solution: Israel and Jordan. The reality of the demographics seem to support this contention, since by most credible estimates, the Palestinians make up well over 50 percent of the population of Jordan today. Why, these critics add, is there a need for a second Palestinian state?

For the naysayers, hardliners, Palestinian nationalists, and extremists—and the Iranian regime—who would never consider a plan that recognized a sovereign Jewish Israel in the Near East, a historical review is needed to clarify factual connections and claims to this land.

Jewish historical identification with this disputed land of ancient Canaan predates any Arab presence or claim by at least 1,400 years. Uncompromising naysayers need to reflect on their version of history and be reminded that by all accounts, including theirs, Abraham had two sons, Ishmael and Isaac. By regional, historical, cultural, societal, and religious custom and tradition, *all* sons are entitled to inherit a share of a father's wealth. The claim that only Abraham's firstborn is entitled to a portion of the land inheritance is simply not legal and has no regional precedent or validity. Since Muslims, who make up the majority of the Near East population, accept the Hebrew scriptures as valid, with some exceptions, they acknowledge God's promise to Abraham that he and his descendants would inherit the land "from the [Nile] river of Egypt to the great [Euphrates] river." This sounds like the entire region of the Near East was promised by God to the descendants of Abraham—*all* the claimed descendants of Abraham, the Ishmaelites and Isaacites, Arabs and Jews. The biblical account did not stipulate where each descendant tribe of Abraham should live in this vast land that God would give Abraham's sons. He simply said that the sons of Abraham would inherit this land. Approximately four thousand years later, the descendants of Abraham are today arguing and fighting over which lands, if any, each could claim as their inheritance.

Assuming one accepts the Arab argument that Arabs today are the sons of Ishmael, it seems obvious that they have fared well in the Near East with their share of the inheritance. As one looks at today's Arab world through the Arab narrative, there is no doubt that Ishmael's sons have truly been well blessed. Arabs have inherited the lion's share of the Near East, with Arabs today occupying well over 90 percent of the entire Near East (minus Turkey and Iran, which are not Arab and are not contested in the Arab-Israeli dispute). Additionally, Arabs today possess the portion of the Near East containing more than two-thirds of the world's known oil reserves. Going by the Arab narrative, it is evident that at least the descendants of the firstborn son of Abraham have prospered well in both wealth and vast land holdings in the Near East. The question today is whether the second son of Abraham, Isaac, and his descendants, the Jews, are also entitled to any of God's promise and inheritance. The answer is an unequivocal yes. The real question, then, is whether the naysayers will find it in their hearts to accommodate their "kid brother" (Isaac) and allow him and his descendants to live in peace in their share of the inheritance, a small sliver of land between the ocean and the desert.

Unfortunately for this plan, Israel's 2020 Benjamin Netanyahu–led center-right–center-left (Lekud–Blue and White) coalition government was not interested in a two-state solution. Following Israel's 2021 forth election in two years, for the first time in twelve years Israel has a government without Benjamin Netanyahu as its prime minister. With left-wing parties and an Arab-Muslim party in its coalition, how accommodating this new government will be to a two-state solution is yet to be seen.

197

Option Three: Status Quo Minus Armed Conflict (Demographically Driven One-State [Eventual Palestinian] Solution)

Option three, also discussed in chapter 10, is probably the most threatening to Israel's long-term existence, as all Israelis and Israeli leaders are keenly aware. Its premise is that Arab Israelis will eventually outnumber Jewish Israelis if the Arab Israelis maintain a higher birthrate.[108] Assuming Israel maintains its character as a liberal democracy where all citizens have the right to vote, it would only be a matter of time before the Arab residents and citizens of Israel outnumbered the Jewish residents and citizens of Israel. When, not if, this day arrives, Arab-Israeli citizens will simply vote themselves in as the majority in parliamentary (Knesset) elections, and the country will instantly cease being a Jewish-ruled nation. Israel will become a Palestinian-Arab-majority-ruled country without Palestinians having to resort to armed struggle or warfare.

This eventuality is one that future Israeli governments will do everything within their powers to delay and prevent. One way Israel might delay the inevitable would be through statistical manipulation. Israel might minimize its officially reported Arab population by manipulating census statistics or by simply not taking population counts in certain Arab-majority regions. Israel might also manipulate statistics by changing who it identifies as citizens with full voting rights. This is already on the horizon, as seen in Israel's 2020 proposal to annex 30 percent of the West Bank, wherein Israel stated that Arabs living in these newly annexed areas would not be counted as citizens and therefore would not have voting rights. Understandably, most Arab states, the Palestinian Authority, and Hamas have all come out against the annexation plan. There are some reports, however, that many Palestinians in the West Bank are privately, and some not so privately, saying that they would

---

[108] To counter this scenario, there have been some recent statistics that show that the Jewish-Israeli birthrate has reached parity with and even slightly surpassed that of the Arab-Israeli birthrate.

favor not just a 30 percent partial annexation by Israel but a total annexation of all of the Palestinian territory in the West Bank, because life under the established, robust Israeli economy with its generous social welfare system would be preferable to life under an unknown Palestinian government. Realistically, Israel already controls most of the West Bank militarily.

While expressions by Palestinians of a desire to be annexed by Israel may initially sound pleasing to Israeli ears, there is a built-in risk should Israel eventually annex the entire West Bank or even large portions with majority Palestinian populations. By so doing, Israel would instantly absorb nearly three million Palestinians and be required to categorize them as citizens or residents or otherwise deal with their legal status under Israeli control, doing so in full view of the international community that is already critical of Israeli geopolitical hegemonic aspirations. With full annexation, the combined Arab population of Israel and the West Bank would be close to five million, or 45 percent of Israel's population. As suggested, Israel would undoubtedly do all within its legal power to minimize the citizenship and voting rights of Palestinians it absorbs. Israel could do this with stipulations, such as that Palestinians would not be eligible for Israeli citizenship or have the right to vote if their ancestors were not citizens of Israel by a specified date—perhaps the date of Israel's independence in May 1948 or the beginning or end of the Six-Day War when Israel took control of the West Bank—or if they do not meet some other similar residency grandfather-clause requirement. All these citizenship voting restrictions would be obvious schemes to deny Arab residents of Israel voting rights, thereby limiting their ability to gain representation and thus a voice in Israel's Parliament.

Another option to reduce the population of Arab-Israeli citizens might be to provide incentives for Arabs to leave the country voluntarily. In 2005, the mayor of Bat Yam, a southern satellite city of Tel Aviv, stated that he would pay for transportation and provide a $20,000 monetary incentive for any Arab family wishing to leave the country voluntarily and permanently. Some Arab Israelis may well take this option to seek a better life for themselves and their families, away from both second-class citizenship and daily occupation, and to remove themselves from the ever-present threat of war. Many Christian Arabs—who often live in the traditional Israeli-Christian-Arab centers in Galilee, as well as other territories administered by Israel, mainly in and around the Jerusalem-Bethlehem corridor and the West Bank—feel themselves an unwelcome minority within a minority (i.e., a minority within the majority-Muslim Arab community, which itself is a minority within the greater Israeli Jewish majority) and have been steadily leaving Israel. As a result of this exodus of Arab Christians from the birthplace of Christianity, Christian Arabs have quickly lost their majority status within the Israeli Arab population to Muslim Arabs. Christian Arabs made up the majority in these areas as recently as the 1980s. Assuming this trend continues, it is expected that someday in the not too distant future, the only Christians remaining in Christianity's birthplace will be caretakers, the foreign priests and nuns overseeing shrines like the Church of the Nativity in Bethlehem, the Church of the Holy Sepulcher in Jerusalem, the Church of the Annunciation in Nazareth, and the few sites of Jesus's ministry on the western shores of the Sea of Galilee.

Forcible deportation of a portion of its Palestinian population to the surrounding Arab countries would be one of the least civilized and less desirable option for Israel to reduce its Palestinian-Arab population and retain a demographic Jewish majority. During an election campaign in the 1980s, while running for leadership of the conservative party (and ultimate the position of prime minister), Ariel Sharon appealed to the right-wing electorate by saying that Israel should load all Arabs in Israel onto busses and trucks and deport them to the nearest Arab border. Ariel Sharon was, in effect, proposing ethnic cleansing of Israel's Arab population.

The demographic clock of non-Jewish Israelis slowed down for Israel in the 1980s and 1990s when Israel received an influx of more than nine hundred thousand ostensibly Jewish immigrants from the collapsing

Soviet Union. In addition, Israel has absorbed more than ninety thousand Ethiopian Jewish immigrants since the end of the twentieth century. Even though about half of the Russian immigrants were not actually Jewish, the nine hundred thousand Russians and the ninety thousand Ethiopians have bought Israel some time before the inevitable demographic time bomb goes off and Arab citizens of Israel become the majority. However, unless Israel can stop the growth of its Arab population relative to its non-Arab population, in fifty to one hundred years, the demographic inevitability will occur and Jewish Israelis will become a minority in their own country.

What might this country look like with a minority-Jewish population governing a majority-Arab population? In a word, apartheid, such as the world experienced in South Africa in the twentieth century. Most countries boycotted and sanctioned South Africa, eventually bringing down the apartheid regime. The fate of South Africa might await a future Israel if it chooses this option.

As a final note concerning this option, on a recent trip to Israel, I asked some Jewish Israeli friends how they would respond if the demographic time bomb went off resulting in an Arab-majority country. I was not completely surprised when many of them said they would simply leave Israel if this were to happen. They stated unequivocally that they would not live in a country dominated by Arabs and Muslims. What a sad historical footnote, I thought to myself, if—after decades of hatred, terrorism, war, and family separations; hundreds of thousands of dead and injured; rivers of blood and tears; years of international attention and efforts by foreign ministries, heads of state, defense departments, and the United Nations; and hundreds of billions of dollars of infrastructure and weapons purchases and deployment—it all ended as a hundred-year failed experiment in nationhood. There must be a better solution for the sons of Abraham.

Option Four: "A Return to Canaan" (Single-State Solution, No Israel, No Palestine)

The final option would in many ways be a variation of option three. It would recognize the inevitable demographic parity of the Arab population of Israel and would create an inclusive state for all, minus ethnic or religious partisanship. In reality, there is less enthusiasm in the Arab world today for a two-state solution as presented in option two, outside of some in the Palestinian camp who strongly advocate for it. On July 21, 2020, Jordan's foreign minister, Omar al-Razzaz, stated in an interview with *The Guardian*, "You close the door on a two-state solution, I could very well look at this positively, if we're clearly opening the door on a one-state democratic solution." Since the Netanyahu government announced its plan in July 2020 to annex more than 30 percent of the West Bank, many Arab and Palestinian realists, especially in the West Bank, have also begun to raise their voices to advocate for a one-state, secular, democratic solution.

As stated earlier, not only is having everything one wants impossible but demanding it is the biggest, most unrealistic nonstarter. Compromise is the only remaining civilized option. Under this single-state solution, a single, democratic, secular Palestinian-Israeli state would be created based on the equality of all its citizens under the law. This option would mean the creation of a non-ethnic-based, religiously unaffiliated, all-inclusive government under which all were equal under the law— objectively the best solution. Unfortunately, this option will be rejected by hardliners on both sides as dead before arrival, because it forces hardliners to give up their unrealistic dreams of possessing everything.

The United States could provide a blueprint for this form of government, which would have a constitution and an essential bill of rights that would protect all its citizens and establish a legal, level playing field for all ethnic and religious groups. Under this option, Jewish Halakha and Islamic Shari'a religious laws would not only have to take a back seat to national secular law but would have very narrow jurisdiction. Religious law could only be administered with regard to marriage and family matters, as the Islamic Shari'a and Jewish Halakha courts in Israel currently do. This option would institute a national unity government that would not favor any one group but be ruled by democratic principles and majority rule of one person, one vote. A system could be established where heads of state rotated between Arabs and Jews, as in the Lebanon model instituted following the Tai'f Accord of 1990, which mediated an end to the Lebanese Civil War. Under this option, there would be no state religion, no Jewish-Israeli state, and no Islamic-Arab state. It would be a secular state that is free from, free of, and free for religion. It would not be an atheist state by design but one where people would be free to worship or not as they choose. Under this single-secular-state solution, there would be no state sponsorship of religion.

This new country could not have the word *Israel* or the word *Palestine* in its name, nor any reference to either group, and its flag could not have the current Israeli or Palestinian colors or symbols, such as the Star of David, or any reference to a religion. To have a new beginning, the origin of this country's name must predate Jewish and Arab histories and claims to the land. This back-to-the-future/forward-to-the-past country would be called simply New Canaan.

كنعان الجديده כנען החדשה

Notes

Michael Safi and Jassar al-Tahat, "Jordan could 'look positively' one-state solution if Palestinian-Israeli rights equal," *The Guardian* (July 21, 2020).

Glossary

Abdullah I, King. The first king of the Hashemite Kingdom of Jordan. Abdullah I was assassinated while praying in the al-Aqsa Mosque in Jerusalem because he was holding secret talks with Israeli government leaders.

Abiru/Apiru/Hapiru/Habiru (Aviru). Written in a variety of ways, a proto-Israelite people who many scholars believe were the ancestors of the Hebrews/Israelites.

Aelia Capitolina. The name the Romans gave to the city of Jerusalem after its destruction and reconstruction following the Second Jewish Revolt against Rome from 132 to 135 CE.

Al-Aqsa Mosque. A silver-domed mosque built on the Temple Mount in Jerusalem, on the site of the first and second Jewish temples. Muslims call the site "al-Haram al-Sharif" (the Noble Sanctuary) and believe that their prophet Muhammad ascended to heaven in a dream from this location. It is considered Islam's third holiest site after the cities of Mecca and Medina in Saudi Arabia.

Al Qibla. Mecca's daily newspaper.

Al-Azm, Khalid. Syrian Prime Minister from 1948 to 1949. He admitted in his memoirs that Arab leaders were partially to blame for the creation of the Palestinian refugees because Arab leaders encouraged Palestinian Arabs to leave their lands in Palestine that were designated to become Israel.

Arab Boycott. Following the 1967 Arab-Israeli Six-Day War, Arab countries threatened to boycott French goods if France continued to sell Mirage fighter aircraft to Israel. Arab states have since extended this boycott to include all Israeli-produced goods and threaten to boycott any country or company doing business with Israel.

Arafat, Yasser. Founder and chairman of the Palestine Liberation Organization (PLO).

Army of South Lebanon (ASL). A Christian militia organization funded, trained, and equipped by Israel to help Israel keep the PLO and other militant organization out of southern Lebanon.

Arrow missile. An Israeli antimissile defense system funded by and coproduced with the US. The Arrow is designed to intercept intercontinental ballistic missiles.

Ashkenazi Jews. Jews from Eastern Europe.

Asia Minor Agreement. *See* Sykes-Picot Agreement.

Baal/Ba'al. The primary Canaanite god whose Hebrew translation means "Lord" or "Master."

Balfour Declaration. A formal British declaration made in 1917 by the British foreign secretary, Sir Arthur James Balfour, that said that Great Britain would be favorable to Jews establishing independent self-rule and a homeland in Palestine following the defeat of the Ottoman Empire in World War I.

Bar Kokhba, Simon (Hebrew: Shim'on). Leader of the Second Jewish Revolt against Rome from 132 to 135 CE, now often referred to as "The Bar Kokhba Revolt."

Bar-Lev Line. Israel's massive defensive system along the ninety-three-mile length of the East Bank of the Suez Canal. The defenses included sixty- to eighty-foot-high sand berms with fortified observation and firing positions every one thousand yards. The fortifications were built after Israel captured the Sinai Peninsula from Egypt during the 1967 Six-Day War.

Bedouins/Bedu (al-Badu [البدو]). Nomadic Arab tribespeople who have lived in the Near East for millennia. Bedouins, who once numbered in the hundreds of thousands, are today fast disappearing as they become settled in towns and villages.

Berlin University Granite. An extrabiblical inscription on a granite slab attesting to the existence of the nation-state of "Israel" in Canaan dating to 1,400 BCE.

biblical maximalists. Biblical scholars who accept the existence of an ancient Israel as early as the late second millennium BCE.

biblical minimalists. Ancient Near East scholars who reject the existence of an ancient Israel, including the existence of the Davidic-Solomonic dynasties. They claim there is insufficient extrabiblical evidence to confirm the existence of an ancient Israel. With the discovery of several extrabiblical archaeological sources, biblical minimalists have been for the most part discredited. *See also* extrabiblical.

Black September Brigade. A militant branch of the Palestine Liberation Organization (PLO). Named for their defeat and eviction from Jordan by Jordan's King Hussein in 1970 and subsequent flight to Lebanon.

British-French mandate. Control of much of the Middle East given to Great Britain and France as a mandate by the League of Nations following World War I. The mandate gave Great Britain control of the area from the eastern Mediterranean to the Persian Gulf—an area covering today's Israel-Palestine, Jordan, and Iraq—and France the area of Syria-Lebanon. Great Britain and France were to control these lands until such time as their inhabitants could develop the instruments of government for self-rule and independence.

British White Paper on Palestine. A 1922 British government statement/document further defining the Balfour Declaration of 1917.

caliph. A political and spiritual successor to Islam's Prophet Muhammad.

Camp David Accords (a.k.a. the Egyptian-Israeli Peace Treaty). The first Arab-Israeli peace treaty signed between Egypt and Israel at Camp David, Maryland.

Canaan/Canaanites. The land and its inhabitants on the eastern Mediterranean shores between roughly modern-day Lebanon to the north and the Sinai Peninsula to the south. In antiquity, Canaan was inhabited by non-confederated, western-Semitic-speaking, independent Canaanite tribes.

Church of the Holy Sepulcher. A shrine in Jerusalem built over the believed sites of the crucifixion (Golgotha) and burial of Jesus. The site was first identified and preserved in the fourth century CE by Queen Helena, Constantine's mother.

Church of the Nativity. A shrine in Bethlehem built over the believed site of the birthplace of Jesus. The site was first identified and preserved in the fourth century CE by Queen Helena, Constantine's mother.

Constantine. The first emperor of the Easter Roman Empire who built his capital in Constantinople (today's Istanbul in Turkey). Constantine lifted the ban on Christianity, essentially legalizing it. This led to Christianity's growth and, eventually, to it becoming the official religion of the Eastern Roman/Byzantine Empire and later that of the Western Roman Empire.

Crusader kingdoms. Territories in the Holy Land under Christian-European rule for approximately two hundred years, from 1099 to 1291 CE.

Davidic-Solomonic dynasties. The combined rule in Judea and Samaria of King David and his son Solomon from 1009 to 925 BCE.

David's Sling. An Israeli defensive missile system, codeveloped with the US, designed to intercept aircraft, drones, rockets, and medium-to-long-range rockets and cruise missiles.

Dead Sea Scrolls. More than eight hundred document fragments written primarily on parchment (specially treated animal skins) and papyrus. Many of the scrolls contain the earliest texts of the Hebrew Bible, which predate all other biblical manuscripts by a thousand years. The first scrolls were found accidentally in 1947 by a Bedouin shepherd boy looking for his lost goats.

death penalty. Israel does not have a death penalty. Following World War II, Jews who established the institutions of government in Israel decided that they had seen far too much state-sponsored killing during the Holocaust and were not interested in passing laws that would institutionalize taking lives. There have been two exceptions, with special laws passed to execute an Israeli Army officer for treason in the 1950s and for executing the Nazi war criminal Adolf Eichmann in the 1960s.

Diaspora. The exile and dispersion of the Jewish people from their ancestral homeland beginning with the Babylonian exile in 586 BCE. Some consider the Diaspora to have begun over seven centuries later in 135 CE, following the Roman defeat of the Second (Bar-Kokhbah) Jewish Revolt against Rome.

Dome of the Rock. A mosque built in 691 CE on the site of the first and second Jewish temples on Mount Moriah in Jerusalem. Referred to in Islam as the Haram al-Sharif (the Noble Sanctuary).

Druze. A secretive religion that began as a sect of Islam in the tenth century CE. Its approximately one million adherents live primarily in Israel, Syria, and Lebanon. Druze are not nationalistic and serve in the various militaries of the countries in which they live.

Dreyfus Affair. The sham court-martial of Captain Alfred Dreyfus, a French Jewish artillery officer, which stripped him of his military commission because he was Jewish. Captain Dreyfus was later retried, found innocent, and reinstated in the French military.

Eastern (Oriental) Jews. Jews living in Arab-Islamic and North African countries during the Diaspora. Usually refers de facto to culturally Arabized Jews who immigrated to Israel from these countries after Israel attained statehood in 1948.

El (אל). The name for the god commonly worshiped by people who lived in the ancient Near East from western Mesopotamia to the eastern Mediterranean. The name *El* is of Semitic origin.

Elohim. A name of Semitic origin and one of the names used for the God of the Hebrew Bible/Old Testament. It is plural in form, but when used in reference to the God of Israel, it is singular in meaning. It was common in the ancient Near East to interchange the singular and plural forms of the noun for God when referring to a singular concept of the deity. Some scholars agree that since Abraham believed in a single, all-powerful God that was creator of the universe, Abraham's God represented, and in fact was, all the other recognized gods in one, hence the plural.

extrabiblical sources. Sources of factual, historical information outside of the Hebrew Bible. Examples include confirmations of the existence of a tenth-century Israel found in the Egyptian Merneptah Stele, the Berlin Granite inscription, and the Tel Dan inscription.

Farouk/Farouq, King. The last king of Albanian dynasty that ruled Egypt for 150 years after 1800. In 1952, King Farouk was overthrown in a bloodless military coup that ended the Egyptian monarchy.

French mandate. *See* British-French mandate.

Gaza Strip. A two-by-nine-mile geographical land area located on the southeastern Mediterranean coast on Israel's southwest border. It has a Palestinian population of approximately two million. The Gaza Strip has been ruled by a strict Islamic militant organization, Hamas, since 2007, after the group violently overthrew the Palestinian Authority. Palestinians want to create an independent Palestinian state that would include the Gaza Strip and the West Bank.

Golan Heights. A high plateau/escarpment overlooking the Galilee region in northern Israel. The region was captured by Israel from Syria during the 1967 Six-Day War and annexed in 1981. In 2019, US President Trump recognized Israel's annexation of the Golan Heights.

Hamas (حماس, acronym of Harakat al-Mukawamah al-Islamia). The Sunni-Islamic militant organization that forcibly overthrew the Palestinian Authority and PLO rule in the Gaza Strip in 2007. It has been declared a terrorist organization by most of the international community. Hamas has fought three wars with Israel, in 2008, 2012, and 2014. Since March 2018, the organization has been flying incendiary kites and balloons into Israel, burning thousands of acres of Israeli farmland and attempting to breach the Israeli border on a weekly basis. Hamas has dug numerous infiltration tunnels from the Gaza Strip into Israel, which Israel continues to discover and demolish.

Haredi Jews (see also Orthodox/Ultra-Orthodox Jews). Jews who take a literal, strict interpretation of Jewish scripture and adhere strongly to Hebrew Bible (Old Testament) dietary laws as well as lifestyle restrictions and proscriptions. Haredi Jews are nonsecular and nonconformist.

Hasmonean dynasty. A period of Jewish self-rule in the Land of Israel from 166 to 37 BCE. The Hasmonean dynasty was ushered in by the Maccabean Revolt against the Seleucid (Greek) Empire in the second century BCE.

Helena, Queen. Mother of the Byzantine Empire's first emperor, Constantine. Queen Helena is credited with identifying, preserving, and building shrines over Christian holy sites, such as the Church of the Nativity in Bethlehem and the Church of the Holy Sepulcher in Jerusalem.

Hellenism. The advanced and enlightened Greek culture that began in the fourth century BCE. Hellenistic Greek culture led the world in almost every field, including math, science, astronomy, medicine, law, architecture, and government.

Herod the Great. A Roman-installed king of Judea who reigned from 37 to 4 BCE. Jewish leadership rejected Herod's legitimacy as their king because his mother was not Jewish but a Nabatean (Arab) princess.

Herzl, Theodore. A Hungarian Jewish journalist who, after attending the Dreyfus trial in France, wrote the book *The Jewish State* (*Der Judenstaat*), in which he concluded that Jews would only be safe from world persecutions when they ruled themselves in an independent Jewish state. His call was the beginning of political Zionism, which eventually led to the establishment of the independent Jewish State of Israel in Palestine.

Hizb Allah (Hezbollah). The Shiite-Islamic political and military organization that controls much of the behind-the-scenes politics of Lebanon. Established by Iran in the 1980s, it is Iran's proxy and has been declared a terrorist organization by much of the international community. Israel fought a war with Hizb Allah in 2006. In 2019, Israel discovered and destroyed five infiltration and attack tunnels dug by Hizb Allah from Lebanon into Israel. Many Middle East observers predict a more intense war between Israel and Hizb Allah in the near future. Hizb Allah claims to have 150,000 rockets and missiles poised to fire at Israel.

Hussein Ibin Ali. The leader of the Arab armies in the Arabian Peninsula during World War I.

Hussein bin Talal. King of the Hashemite Kingdom of Jordan from 1951 to 2000. King Hussein replaced his grandfather, King Abdullah I, who was assassinated because he was holding secret talks with Israeli leaders.

Irgun. A Jewish underground (illegal) militia in pre-Israel Palestine that used lethal guerilla terror tactics to attack Arabs and British forces in the region.

Iron Dome. An Israeli defensive missile system designed to intercept short-range rockets and mortars.

Israelites. The collective name given to the Hebrew tribes during the period of their conquest and settlement in Canaan in the late second millennium BCE. In the tenth century BCE, *Israel* was the name of the northern Hebrew kingdom, which had its capital in Samaria/Shechem, modern-day Nablis/Nablus.

Israel's War of Independence. The first Arab-Israeli war, which took place from May 1948 to March 1949 following the United Nations' partition of Palestine into separate Arab and Jewish countries. Arabs rejected the partition plan, and five Arab countries, Lebanon, Syria, Jordan, Egypt, and Iraq, declared war on Israel with the intent of destroying the Jewish state. The war ended with the signing of an armistice (cease-fire) after Israel took control of 50 percent more territory than it was given under the United Nations Partition Plan.

Islamic Jihad. A shadowy Islamist terrorist organization that first immerged during the Lebanese Civil War in the 1970s and 1980s.

Islamic Jihad, believed to be the forerunner of Hizb Allah, claimed responsibility for truck bombings of the US embassy and the US Marine Corps barracks in Beirut in 1983. Today, there are Islamic Jihad cells operating throughout the Middle East, especially in the Gaza Strip and the Sinai Peninsula.

Islamic Revolutionary Guard Corps (IRGC). Iran's military arm that provides funding, weapons, and military support to proxies throughout the Middle East, including such organizations as Hizb Allah in Lebanon, Palestine Islamic Jihad and Hamas in the Gaza Strip, and the Houthi Shiite rebels in Yemen. The IRGC maintains more than twenty thousand troops in Syria in support of the al-Assad regime and to launch attacks on Israel.

Islamic State (IS). Also known as the Islamic State in Iraq and Syria (ISIS/ISIL) and by its Arabic acronym DAISH. IS attempted to establish a strict, brutal, militant caliphate in portions of Syria and Iraq from 2015 to 2019. At its height in 2018, IS controlled as much as one-third of Syria. IS was an outgrowth of Osama Bin Laden's al-Qa'idah (Al-Qaeda).

Jebus/Jebusites. A Canaanite tribe who inhabited Jerusalem (Jebus) until the late second millennium BCE. King David conquered Jebus in 1000 BCE, renamed it Jerusalem, and made it the capital of his kingdom.

Jerusalem Embassy Act. A bill with unanimous, bipartisan support passed in 1995 by the US Congress authorizing the US to move its embassy from Tel Aviv to Jerusalem.

Josephus, Flavius. Born Yosef Ben Mattityahu, Josephus (37–100 CE) was a Jewish commander during the First Jewish Revolt against Rome, 66–70 CE. He later became a Roman citizen and is credited with being the preeminent first-century historian of the Roman Near East.

Judahite/s. The people and culture of the southern Hebrew kingdom that resided in Judea.

Kfir aircraft. A supersonic fighter aircraft developed by Israel, based on the French Mirage-3 aircraft.

Khutspah. A term sometimes used to characterize modern Israelis' brash, unapologetic, in-your-face boldness bordering on aggression.

Knesset. The Hebrew name for Israel's Parliament.

Khrushchev, Nikita. Soviet Union premier from 1958 to 1964.

Law of Return. The Law of Return was one of the fist laws passed by Israel in 1950. It granted immediate citizenship to anyone who could prove his or her Jewish identity. One's Jewishness has traditionally been determined matrilineally, the reason being that most people know who their biological mother is but cannot always be 100 percent certain of their biological father. With the advent of DNA testing, an Israeli rabbinical court decreed in 2017 that one's Jewishness can today be established patrilineally.

Lawrence of Arabia. The identity/persona given to the British military officer Thomas Edward Lawrence by a US journalist, Lowell Thomas. Thomas wrote romantically of Lawrence's exploits fighting with Arab armies during World War I to evict the Ottoman Turks from regional control.

League of Nations. An international organization established in 1920 following World War I to prevent future wars. The organization did not have the support of many nations, including the United States, and was dissolved in 1946 in favor of the United Nations.

Lehi. A Jewish underground (illegal) militia in pre-Israel Palestine that used lethal guerilla terror tactics to attack Arabs and British forces in the region.

Liberty, **USS.** A US signals intelligence collection ship that was attacked by Israeli air and naval forces on the fourth day of the 1967 Arab-Israeli Six-Day War. A subsequent investigation by Israel concluded that the attack was one of mistaken identity caused by the fog of war. US naval personnel on board the USS *Liberty* at the time refute this conclusion, claiming the ship was flying the US flag and was clearly marked.

Maccabean Revolt. *See* Hasmonean dynasty.

McMahon-Hussein Correspondence. A series of letters between Sir Henry McMahon, the British high commissioner in Cairo, and Sharif Hussein Ibin Ali, the Emir of Mecca. The letters maintained that if Arab armies joined forces with the British to evict the Ottoman Turks from the Near East, Arabs would be free to rule themselves in Arab lands following the war. Although it was not a formal agreement, it was a clear understanding between the two men.

Masada. A mountaintop desert fortress and palace built by King Herod the Great. The fortress was taken over by Jewish fighters and their families during the First Jewish Revolt against Rome in 70 CE. Jewish defenders held the Roman Tenth Legion at bay for three years, from 70 to 73 CE, until Roman soldiers and slaves built an earth ramp bridging the valley, allowing the Roman soldiers to breach Masada's defenses. The nine hundred Jews who had held out in the fortress killed themselves rather than be captured, enslaved, or killed by the approaching Roman Legion.

Merneptah Stele. An Egyptian inscription on a granite monument providing extrabiblical evidence of the existence of the nation-state of "Israel" dating to 1,200 BCE.

MFO (Multi-Force Observers). A multinational observer force established to monitor the Egyptian-Israeli border because of the 1979 Egyptian-Israeli Camp David Peace Treaty.

Mossad. Israel's state security organization.

Moslem Brotherhood. A transnational, conservative Sunni Islamist organization whose intent is to establish a pan-Islamic state. It supports Islamist political parties and provides funding and weapons to militant terrorist organizations.

Mubarak, Hosni. Egypt's president from 1981 to 2011 who succeeded Anwar Sadat after he was assassinated by the Moslem Brotherhood. Mubarak was forced to resign in 2011 following massive antigovernment demonstrations during the Arab Awakening (so-called Arab Spring).

Mutual Defense Pact of 1967. An agreement signed between Egypt, Syria, and Jordan prior to the 1967 Six-Day War. The agreement called for its signatories to come to the aid of one another should war break out between any one of them and Israel.

Nasser, Jamal Abdul al-. The charismatic president of Egypt from 1955 to 1980 who came to power in a bloodless military coup that overthrew the last monarch of Egypt, King Farouk. Nasser rallied the Arab world in opposing Western colonialism and led Arab confrontation against Israel.

nation-state law. A law passed by Israel's Knesset (Parliament) in 2018 restating Israel as a Jewish state. The law removed Arabic as one of Israel's official languages, leaving Hebrew as its single official language.

Nakbah. The term Arabs use for the creation of the Jewish state of Israel because of the United Nations' 1948 partition of Palestine. It has also come to represent the non-creation of a Palestinian-Arab state and the exiling of 650,000 Palestinian Arabs, as well as the refugee status of four-generations of their descendants.

Neapolis. The name given by the Romans to the formerly Israelite city of Sheckem/Shchem. The city was renamed to erase Israelite connection to the city after Rome defeated and evicted the Judeans from the Land of Israel in 135 CE. After Arab Muslims conquered the region in the seventh century CE, the pronunciation changed from Neapolis to Nablis/Nablus because of the absence of the letter *p* in Arabic.

Nesher aircraft. A supersonic fighter aircraft developed by Israel, based on the French Mirage fighter aircraft.

Netanyahu, Benjamin. Israel's longest-serving prime minister, who has served from the 1990s through 2021.

"Next year in Jerusalem." A Jewish prayer that began following the exile of the southern Kingdom of Judah to Babylon in 586 BCE.

nuclear opacity (nuclear ambiguity). Israel's official policy of no comment regarding its nuclear weapons program. It has long been believed by the international community that Israel has possessed nuclear weapons since as early as 1966. Israel is estimated to have more than three hundred nuclear devices that are deliverable via a triad delivery system that includes surface-to-surface missiles, aircraft, and submarines.

Nuseibeh. The surname of the Muslim family that was given the key to the Church of the Holy Sepulcher by Salah ad-Deen (Saladin) because various Christian denominations and orders constantly fought over its possession. The key has been passed down through the generations for almost nine hundred years and remains in the hands of the Nuseibeh family to this day.

Oriental Jews. *See* Eastern Jews.

Orthodox/Ultra-Orthodox Jews. *See* Haredi Jews.

Palestina (Palestine). The name the Romans gave to the Land of Israel in 135 CE following the defeat and eviction of the Jews in the Second Revolt against Rome.

Palestinian Authority (PA). A governing body established by the 1993 and 1995 Oslo Peace Agreements, which gave Palestinians partial self-rule in the West Bank and the Gaza Strip.

Palestine Islamic Jihad (PIJ). A subgroup of the greater Islamic Jihad militant organization.

Palestine Liberation Organization (PLO). A Palestinian militant organization created by Yasser Arafat in 1964 to use lethal force to attack Jewish and Israeli targets in and outside Israel.

Palestinian refugees. Arab refugees who were either evicted by Israeli forces or fled from their homes in Palestine in 1948 and 1949 after Palestine was partitioned by the United Nations and following the 1967 Arab-Israeli Six-Day War.

Peleset. *See* Sea People.

Phalange. A Lebanese Maronite Christian political party. During the Lebanon Civil War from 1975 to 1990, the Phalange Militia was responsible for massacring innocent Palestinian civilians in the Sabra and Shatila refugee camps. *See also* Sabra and Shatila Massacre.

Philistia. The land of the Philistines, and area that includes today's Gaza Strip, extending south into the Sinai Peninsula and north to the modern Israeli city of Ashkelon.

pogroms. Eastern European persecutions of Jews beginning in the late nineteenth century (1880s).

Qumran. The location in the Judean Desert where the Dead Sea Scrolls were found. The residents of Qumran are believed to have belonged to a strict monastic Jewish sect called the Essenes, which flourished from the first centuries BCE to the first century CE. Qumran was destroyed by the Romans in 70 CE during the First Jewish Revolt against Rome. *See also* Dead Sea Scrolls.

Qur'an (Koran). Muslim holy scripture. Claimed by Muslims to be the literal, verbatim word of God as dictated to Islam's Prophet Muhammad by the Angel Gabriel in Arabic. The Qur'an was later written in the Arabic script by Muhammad's followers after his death in 632 CE.

Rabin, Itzhak. Israel's prime minister for two terms in the 1970s and 1980s. Rabin was Israel's chief of the general staff of the Israeli Armed Forces during the 1967 Six-Day War. He was assassinated by a Jewish extremist who objected to his peace initiatives to the Palestinians.

Sabbath laws. Jewish religious laws that prohibit work on the Sabbath (Saturday). Orthodox and observant Jews do not travel by motorized vehicle on the Sabbath and are limited in the amount they can walk by the distance to the nearest synagogue. Orthodox Jewish parliamentarians in Israel's Knesset (Parliament) routinely attempt to pass laws that impose Sabbath limitations on the entire country, the majority of whose population is either secular or nonobservant.

Sabra and Shatila Massacre. A massacre of between six hundred and two thousand Palestinian civilians (the exact figure is much disputed) by the Phalange Christian Militia during the Lebanese Civil War in September 1982. The Israeli Army controlled access to these camps and allowed the Phalange Militia to enter on the pretext that armed PLO fighters were hiding in the camps. The attack was apparently made to avenge an earlier massacre of Phalange Christians by the PLO. When the international press corps entered the camps, they found no PLO fighters or weapons. The massacre cost Israel's defense minister, Ariel Sharon, his job because the Israeli commission of inquiry blamed him for not preventing the PLO fighters from entering the camps, which would have averted the massacre.

Sadat, Anwar. President of Egypt who led Egypt into the 1973 Yom Kippur/Ramadan War. He replaced Nasser in 1970 and was assassinated in 1981 by the Moslem Brotherhood as he sat in the reviewing stand celebrating Egypt's crossing of the Suez Canal and victory over the Israeli Bar-Lev Line defenses on the Suez in the 1973 Ramadan War.

Salah ad-Deen (Saladin). The Kurdish-Muslim commander who conquered Jerusalem and took it back from the Crusaders in 1187 CE.

Sea People. A group of people/tribes who migrated from the Aegean region to the eastern shores of the Mediterranean in the mid to late second millennium BCE (approximately 1700 to 1200 BCE). Among these people, according to Egyptian inscriptions, were a group called the Peleset, who are believed to be the Philistines known from the Hebrew Bible.

Sephardi/Sephardic Jews. Jews from the Iberian Peninsula (Spain and Portugal).

Six-Day War. The third Arab-Israeli war fought from June 5 to 10 in 1967 between Israel and a coalition of forces from Egypt, Syria, and Jordan. Threatened with annihilation, Israel launched a preemptive attack against the massive Arab armies poised on its borders. In six days, Israeli forces defeated the combined armies and air forces, capturing the Sinai Peninsula from Egypt; the West Bank, including East Jerusalem, from Jordan; and the Golan Heights from Syria.

Suez Crisis/Campaign of 1956 (a.k.a. the Sinai War of 1956). The second Arab-Israeli war precipitated in 1956 by Egypt's President Nasser, who nationalized the Suez Canal Company, evicted British military forces controlling the canal, and mobilized Egyptian armed forces on Israel's southern border, threating to destroy the Jewish state. Israel attacked the Egyptian forces, removing them from the Sinai Peninsula and pushing them across the Suez Canal. Within two days of the Israeli attack, a joint Anglo-French airborne force landed on the Suez Canal, wresting it from Egyptian forces.

Sykes-Picot Agreement (a.k.a. the Asia Minor Agreement). A secret formal agreement between Great Britain and France stating that they would divide the Near East into spheres of influence to exploit the region strategically, politically, and economically, following the defeat of the Ottoman Empire in World War I.

Shasu. A proto-Israelite people who some scholars believe were the ancestors of the Hebrews.

shawarma. Meat—usually lamb, veal, or turkey—grilled on a rotisserie. Shawarma is served in pita (pocket) bread with a choice of hummus, tahini (sesame) sauce, chopped vegetables, and condiments, such as tomatoes, onions, pickles, parsley, paprika, salt, and pepper. Shawarma and falafel are Israel's iconic fast foods served by street vendors and restaurants.

Tel Dan Inscription. A ninth-century-BCE inscription in Old Aramaic, chiseled into a black basalt stele, referencing the "House of David." The inscription is one of several extrabiblical archaeological finds that confirm the existence of the nation-state of Israel.

Tanakh. The Hebrew name for the Hebrew Bible/Old Testament.

Ultra-Orthodox Judaism/Jews. The oldest branch of mainstream Judaism whose adherents follow the strict teaching of the Torah, the first five books of the Hebrew Bible. These teachings include admonitions to only worship the one true God of Israel, kosher dietary restrictions, and a host of male and female norms of public and private behavior, found primarily in the biblical book of Deuteronomy.

(al)-Ummah al-Arabiyyah. The greater "Arab Nation" (i.e., the Arab world).

United Nations Palestine Partition Plan. On November 29, 1947, the United Nations General Assembly passed Resolution 181 calling for the establishment of separate Jewish and Arab states in Palestine. Because of Jerusalem's significance to Arabs and Jews, the partition plan stated that it would not be allowed to be controlled by either the

Arab or the Jewish state. The partition plan stated that Jerusalem would become an internationally administered city, without specifics as to the organization and makeup of the administering body. Jews accepted the plan, but Arabs rejected it. Consequently, a Jewish Israel was created, but a Palestinian-Arab state was not.

UNRWA (United Nations Relief and Works Agency for Palestinian Refugees). A United Nations agency established to care for, feed, house, medicate, and educate Palestinian-Arab refugees.

UNTSO (United Nations Truce Supervisory Organization). The first United Nations peace-observer ("peacekeeping") force established to monitor the truce between Egypt and Israel following the 1956 Sinai War / Suez Crisis.

usury laws. Laws enacted in Medieval Christian Europe prohibiting Christians from lending money for profit (i.e. with interest). European Jews were not prohibited from lending under these laws, which propelled them into the banking business. Ironically, the usury laws were based on Old Testament (Hebrew Bible) restrictions, which were Jewish prohibitions.

value-added tax (VAT). The de facto Israeli sales tax on virtually all products. Foreigners and tourists can receive a refund of the VAT upon departure from Israel's ports of embarkation.

West Bank. A thirty-by-sixty-mile geographical land area located west of the Jordan River. Palestinians, who number 2.8 million on the West Bank, are hoping to make the West Bank part of an independent Palestinian state, which would also include the Gaza Strip. Approximately 585,000 Israelis live in towns and settlements in the West Bank.

Western Wall. The last remaining outer wall of the Second Temple built by Herod the Great on the Temple Mount in Jerusalem, the same site on which Solomon built the first Jewish temple. King Herod's

Second Temple was looted and destroyed by the Romans during the First Jewish Revolt against Rome in 70 CE.

YHWH (Yahweh). The Latin-script transliteration of the Hebrew name for the Hebrew/Israelite God. (See footnote in chapter 1.)

Yiddish. A Hebrew-German hybrid language developed and spoken by Eastern European Jews in the Diaspora. At one point, Yiddish was considered as the possible official language to be adopted for the country of Israel because it was the spoken language of so many Jews immigrating to Palestine from Eastern Europe.

Yom Kippur War. The fourth Arab-Israeli war fought from October 6 to 24, 1973, between Israel and a coalition of forces from Egypt and Syria. Also called the Ramadan War and the October 6 War.

Zionism. The ideology that Jews have the right of independent self-rule in their ancestral homeland, the Land of Israel (Palestine). The word is derived from Mount Zion, one of the mountains on which Jerusalem is built.

Bibliography

Books

Archaeology Study Bible: An Illustrated Walk through Biblical History and Culture. NIV. Grand Rapids: Zondervan, 1984.

Baker, William G. *The Cultural Heritage of Arabs, Islam, and the Middle East.* Dallas: Brown Books, 2003.

Burnett, Joel S. *A Reassessment of Biblical Elohim.* Society of Biblical Literature, Dissertation Series 183, Atlanta. 2001.

Dunstan, Simon. *The Yom Kippur War: The Arab Israeli War of 1973.* Oxford: Osprey Publishing, 2007.

Ebban, Abba. *Heritage: Civilization and the Jews.* New York: Summit Books, 1984.

Ebban, Abba. *My People: The Story of the Jews.* New York: Berman House Inc., and Random House Inc., 1984.

Fisher, Sydney N. *The Middle East: A History.* New York: Knopf, 1960.

Friedman, Matti. *Spies of No Country: Secret Lives at the Birth of Israel.* Chapel Hills: Algonquin Books, 2019.

Freedman, Robert O., editor. *Contemporary Israel.* Westview Press, 2009.

Gilbert, Martin. *The Rutledge Atlas of the Arab Israeli Conflict.* 10th ed. Taylor & Francis, 2012.

Goldschmidt, Jr., Arthur. *A Concise History of the Middle East.* Boulder: Westview Press, 1983.

Gresh, Alain, and Vidal, Dominique. *The New A-Z of The Middle East.* I. B. Tauris,2004.

Halevi, Yossi Klein. *The Israeli Paradox: Letters to My Palestinian Neighbor.* Harper Collins Publisher, 2018.

Held, Colbert C. and John T. Cummings. *Middle East Patterns: Places, People, and Politics.* 6th ed. Boulder: Westview Press, 2014.

Hitti, Philip K. *The Arabs: A Short History.* Princeton University Press, 1949.

Hitti, Philip K. *History of the Arabs: From the Earliest Times to the Present.* 5th ed. rev. London: MacMillan and Co. Ltd., 1953.

Schack, Howard A. *A Spy in Canaan.* Birch Lane Press, 1993.

Laqueur, Walter, and Barry Rubin. *The Israel-Arab Reader.* Eighth revised edition, Penguin Books, 2016.

Lawrence, T. E. *Seven Pillars of Wisdom.* Book recording read by James Wilby. London: CSA Word Classic, 7.5 hrs. CD set, 2009.

Lewis, Bernard. *The Arabs in History.* New York: Oxford University Press, 1960.

Lewis, Bernard. *Islam and the West.* New York: Oxford University Press, 1993.

Lewis, Bernard. *The Middle East: A Brief History of the last 2,000 Years.* New York: Scribner, 1995.

Lewis, Bernard, ed. *Islam and the Arab World.* New York: Random House, 1976.

Lewis, Bernard. *What Went Wrong? Western Impact and Middle Eastern Response.* Oxford University Press, 2002.

Lipovsky, Igor P. *Early Israelites: Two Peoples, One History, Rediscovery of the Origins of Biblical Israel.* Lipovsky, 2012.

Lipovsky, Igor P. *Israel and Judah: How Two Peoples Became One.* Cambridge Publishing Inc., 2014.

Long, Jerry. *Saddam's War of Words.* University of Texas Press. 2004.

Miller, Aaron. *The Much Too Promised Land: America's Elusive Search for Arab Israeli Peace.* New York: Bantam Books, Random House Publishing, 2007.

Miller, Fergus. *The Roman Near East, 31 B.C.-A.D. 337.* Cambridge: Harvard University Press, 1993.

Schack, Howard H. *A Spy in Canaan.* New York: Birch Lane Press, 1993.

Shabtai Teveth. *The Tanks of Tammuz: An Eye Witness Account.* Lume Books Publisher, 2018.

Shanks, Hershel, ed. *Ancient Israel.* "*From Abraham to the Roman Destruction of the Temple.*" Co-published by Prentice Hall, Upper Saddle River, New Jersey, and Biblical Archaeology Society, Washington D.C., 1999.

Shlomo Aloni. *Six-Day War 1967: Operation Focus and the 12 Hours that Changed the Middle East.* Ospry Publishing, 2019.

Sultan, Wafa. *A God Who Hates: A Courageous Woman Who Inflamed The Muslim World Speaks Out Against the Evils of Islam.* St. Martin's Press, 2009.

Williamson, G. A. *Josephus-The Jewish War: A New Translation.* Aylesbury: Hunt, Barnard & Co, Ltd, 1959.

Professional Journals

Faust, Avraham. "How Did Israel Become A People? The Genesis of Israelite Identity." *Biblical Archaeology Review.* November/December 2009.

Garfinkel, Yosef. "The Birth & Death of Biblical Minimalism." *Biblical Archaeology Review.* May/June 2011.

Rainey, Anson. "Inside Outside: There Did the Early Israelites Come From?" *Biblical Archaeology Review.* November/December 2008.

Rainey, Anson. Shasu or Habiru: Who Were the Early Israelites? *Biblical Archaeology Review.* November/December 2008.

Shanks, Hershel. "When Did Ancient Israel Begin." *Biblical Archaeology Review.* January/February 2012.

Online References and Articles

Ahern, Raphael. "Ministers say Israel Close to Retaking Gaza, Hamas Leaders' Days are Numbered." *Times of Israel.* November 21, 2018 https://www.timesofisrael.com/the-daily-edition/.

Ahern, Raphael. "Paraguay Reverses Jerusalem Embassy Move; Fuming Israel Shuts Asuncion Mission." *Times of Israel*. September 5, 2018. https://www.timesofisrael.com/the-daily-edition/.

Ahronheim, Anna. "2017 in Numbers: Terrorists Kill 20 Israelis, 3,617 Palestinians Arrested." *The Jerusalem Post*. December 20, 2018. https://www.jpost.com/arab-israeli-conflict/.

Allen, John L. Jr. "Israel Honors Priest Who Promotes Arab Enlistment in the Army." *Crux Catholic Media Inc.* 2018. https://www.cruxnow.com/author/john-allen/.

Anthony, C. Ross et al. "The Human Cost of the Conflict." *Israel-Palestine Times*. December 14, 2018. https://www.israelpalestinetimeline.org.

Avnery, Orit. "How did the word '*Jew*' become the name most identified with the Jewish people. *Shalom Hartman Institute*. January 1, 2010. https:www.//hartman.org.il/.

Black, Ian. "Mordechai Vanunu Gets 18 Years for Treason-Archive, 1988." *The Guardian*. March 28, 1988. http://www.theguardian.com/world/.

Bowen, Jeremy. "1967 War: Six Days That Changed the Middle East." *BBC*. June 4, 2017. https://www.bbc.com/news/world-middle-east/.

Byman, Daniel L. "The Oslo Accords at 25, the Second Intifada at 18. Will There Be A Third?" *Brookings*. September 12, 2018. https://www.com/brookings.edu/blog/order-from-chaos/.

"Crime Index by Country: 2019 Mid-Year, 2009–2019." *Numbeo*. 2019. https://numbeo.com/crime/rankings-by-countrty/.

Connolly, Kevin. "Dead Sea Drying: A New Low-Point on Earth." *BBC World News*. June 17, 2016. https//www.bbc.com/news/world-middle-east/.

Currivan, Gene. "Zionists Proclaim New State of Israel." *New York Times*. May 15, 1948. https://www.nytimes.com/library/world/480515israeli-state-50.

"The Declaration of the Establishment of the State of Israel." *Knesset*. May 14, 1948. https://www.knesset.gov.il/docs/.

Farrell, Stephen. Israel Admits Bombing Suspected Syria Nuclear Reactor in 2007, Warn Iran. *Reuters World News*. March 20, 2018. https://www.reuters.com/article/us-israel-syria-nuclear/.

"Fatalities in the First Intifada." The Israeli Information Center for Human Rights in the Occupied Territories. *B'Tselem*. September 28, 2000. https://www.btselem.org/statistics/first_intifada_tables/.

Ferguson, Corrie, and Grupp, Amy. "Constantine and Christianity." *The Web Chronology Project*. 2016. https://www.thenagain.info/WebChron/EastEurope/Constontine Converts.

Friedman, Thomas. "After the War: Israel; US to Give Israel $650 Million to Offset Costs of the Gulf War." *The New York Times*. March 6, 1991. https://www.nytimes.com/1991/03/06/world/after-war-us-israel-give-israel-650-million-offset-costs-gulf-war.

Frohlich, Thomas C. "The Most Educated Countries in the World." *USA Today*. September 13, 2014. https//www.usatoday.com/story/money/business/2014/09/13/24-7-wall-st-most-educated-countries/.

"Future Government of Palestine." United Nations General Assembly 181. *United Nations Special Committee on Palestine*. November 29, 1947. https://www.un.org/unispal/document/auto-insert-187994.

Goldberg, G.J. "The Life of Josephus." *The Flavius Josephus Home Page*. 2012. https://www.josephus.org.

"Government: Political Parties in Israel." *Israel Science and Technology Directory.* 2018. https://www.science.co.il/gov/Parties.php.

Gunay, Niyazi. "Arab League Summit Conference, 1964–2000." *The Washington Institute.* October 19, 2000. https://www.washingtoninstitute. org/policy-analysis/arab-league-summit-conferences-1964-200.

Hasan, Hanaa. "Remembering the First Intifada." *Middle East Monitor.* December 9, 2017. https://www.middleeastmonitor.com/specials/first_intifada/.

"Headline: Revealed-The Secrets of Israel's Nuclear Arsenal/Atomic Technician Mordechai Vanunu Reveals Secret Weapons Production." *The Sunday Times.* October 5, 1986. https://www.thesundaytimes. co.uk/article/from-the-archive-the-secret-of-israels-nuclear-arsenal-revealed-vp3fdssqrpq.

Hosein, Hanson R. "The Dying Dead Sea: Levels Falling Precipitously as Rivers are Diverted." *NBC News.* October 10, 1999. https://www. nbcnews.com/id/wbna3072095.

"1947: The International Community Says YES to the Establishment of the State of Israel."

Israel Ministry of Foreign Affairs. 2013. https://www.mfa.gov.il/ jubilee-years/Pages/1947-UN-General-Assembly-Resolution-181.

"IRGC Commander: Israel Will Disappear." *The Iran Observer.* October 2015. https://www.iranobserver.org/iran-maintains-its-threatening-rhetoric.

"Israel." *The Central Intelligence Factbook.* 2019. https://www.cia.gov/ the-world-factbook/countries/israel/.

"Israel Elections: Overview & Explanation." *Jewish Virtual Library.* *1998–2021 American-Israeli Cooperative Enterprise.* 2021. https://www. jewishvirtuallibrary.org/overview-and-explanation-of-israeli-elections.

"Israel GDP 1960-2019 Data." *Trading Economics.* 2019. https://www. tradingeconomics.com/israel/gdp.

"Jewish Biographies: Nobel Prize Laureates." *Jewish Virtual Library.* *1901–2020. American-Israeli Cooperative Enterprise.* 2020. https:// www.jewishvirtuallibrary.org/nobel-prize-laureates.

"Jewish Nobel Prize Winners." *Jinfo.org.* 2002-2018. https://www.jinfo. org/Nobel_Prizes.

"Jordan." *The Central Intelligence Factbook.* 2019. https://www.cia.gov/ the-world-factbook/countries/jordan/.

Katz, Joseph E. "Memoirs of Khalid al-Azm, 3 Volumes, Beirut, 1973. "A Collection of Historical Quotations Relating to the Arab Refugees." *Eretz Yisroel.org.* 1973. https://www.eretzyisroel.org.

Katz, Joseph E. "1948 Khaled al-Azm on Palestinian Refugees." *Center for Online Judaic Studies.* 1998-2021. https://www/cojs. org/1948-palestinian-refugees-khaled-al-azm/.

Killgore, Andrew. "For Israel, Southern Lebanon Means the Litani River." *Washington Report on Middle East Affairs.* September/ October 2006. https://www.wrmea.org/006-september-october/ for-israel-southern-lebanon-means-the-litani-river.

"The Land: Geography and Climate." *Israeli Ministry of Foreign Affairs.* 2013. https://www.mfa.gov.il/mfa/aboutisrael/land/pages.

"The Lebanon War: Operation Peace for Galilee (1982)." *Israel Ministry of Foreign Affairs.* 2013. https://www.mfa.gov.il/mfa/aboutisrael/ history/.

Mackie, Kyle S. "Why Israel's Model Minority is Leading the Protest Against the Nation-State Law." *Haaretz.* July 26, 2018. https://www.haaretz.com/israel-news/. premium-why-israel-s-druze-community-is-up-in-arms.

Nawaz, Maajid. "Israel must be a secular state for all citizens." *The Guardian.* June 16, 2009. https://www.theguardian.com/ commentisfree/2009/jun/16/israel-must-remain-secular.

Nelson, Thomas. "Constantine and the Helena Churches." *The Bible Journey.* 2018. https://www.thebiblejourney.org/biblejourney1/21-theromanojewish-world-of-the-new-testament/constantine-the-helena-churches/.

O'Reilly, Bill. "More Countries Following Trump in Moving Israel Embassy to Jerusalem." *Fox News.* July 9, 2018. https://www.foxnews. com/politics/more-countries-following-trump-in-moving-israel-embassy-to-jerusale/.

"Passover Massacre at Israeli Hotel Kills 19." *CNN.* March 27, 2002. https://www.cnn.com/2002/WORLD/meast/03/27/mideast/.

Pensak, Miriam. "Fifty Years Later, NSA Keeps Details of USS Liberty's Attack Secret." *The Intercept.* June 6, 2017. https://www.theintercept. com/2017/06/06/fifty-years-later-nsa-keeps-details-of-israels-uss-liberty-attack-secret/.

"Population of Cities in Israel (2021)." *World Population Review.* 2021. https://www.worldpopulationreview.com/countiries/cities/israel.

"Population of Cities in Palestine (2021)." *World Population Review.* 2021. https://www.worldpopulationreview.com/countries/cities/palestine.

"Prices of Regulated Consumer Goods." *Ministry of Economy and Industry.* October 2, 2016. https://www.gov.il/departments/dynamiccollectors/food-price-control-search.

"Profile: Hosni Mubarak." *BBC.* March 24, 2017. https://www.bbc.com/news/world/middle-east.

Rogoway, Tyler. "Operation Desert Storm by the Numbers on Its 25th Anniversary." *Foxtrot Alpha.* January 16, 2016. https://www.foxtrotalpha.jalopnic.com/operation-desert-storm-by-the-numbers-on-its-25th-anniv.

Safi, Michael and al-Tahat, Jassar. "Jordan could 'look positively' one-state solution if Palestinian-Israeli rights equal." *The Guardian.* July 21, 2020. https://www.theguardian.com/world/2020/jul/21/jordan-could-look-positively-on-one-state-solution-if-palestinian-israeli-rights-equal.

Patrick, Neil. "The Sea of Galilee or "Jesus Boat." *The Vintage News.* June 29, 2016. https://www.thevinagenews.com/2016/06/29/sea-galilee-jesus-boat-ancient-fishing-boat-1st-century-ad-discovered-1986/.

Pressman, Jeremy. "The Second Intifada: Background and Causes of the Israeli-Palestinian Conflict." *The Journal of Conflict Studies Vol 23 (2).* February 21, 2006. https://www.journals.lib.unb.ca/index.php/JCS/article/review/220.

Mamama, Mohamed. "Sisi Says Military Economy is 1.5% of Egypt's GDP, But How Accurate Is It?" Mada, November 2, 2016. https://www.madamasr.com/en/2016/11/02/feature/economy/sisi-says-military-economy-is-1-5-of-egypts-gdp-but-how-accurate-is-this/.

St. Clair, Jeffry. "Israel's Attack on the USS Liberty: A Half Century Later, Still No Justice." *Counter Punch.* June 8, 2018. https://www.counterpunch.org/2018/08/israls-attack-on-the-uss-liberty-a-half-century-later-still-no-justice/.

Tabutin, Dominiqui. "The Demographics of the Arab World and the Middle East from the 1950 to the 2000s." Table A.2 – Land and Density in 2000, and Population from 1950–2040. *JSTOR*. 2005. https://www.jstor.org/stable/4148186?seq=1.

"1974: Teenagers Die in Israeli School Attack." *BBC*. May 15, 1974. https://www.news.bbc.co.uk/onthisday/hi/dates/stories/may/15/newsid.

"They Came in Peace." *Defense Intelligence Agency*. October 22, 2013. https://www.dia.mil/News/Articles/Article-View/Article/566917/they-came-in-peace/.

"Timeline of Jewish History: Modern Israel & the Diaspora (1970–1979 & 1980–1989)." *Jewish Virtual Library 1998–2018. American-Israeli Cooperative Enterprise*. 2018. https://www. jewishvirtuallibrary. org/modern-israel-and-the-diaspora-timeline-table-of-contents.

"Total Population by Country (2018)." *World Population Review*. 2018. https://www.worldpopulationreview.com.

"Treaty on the Non-Proliferation of Nuclear Weapons (NPT)." *United Nations Office For Disarmament Affairs*. July 7, 2017. https://www.un. org/disarmamet/wmd/nuclear/npt.

Turner, Ashley. "After US Embassy Makes Controversial Move to Jerusalem, More Countries Follow its Lead." *CNBC*. May 17, 2018. https://www.cnbc.com/2018/05/17/after-us-embassy-move-to-jerusalem-more-countries-follow-its-lead.

"Who We Are: United Nations Relief and Works Agency for Palestinian Refugees in the Near East." *UNRWA*. 2018. https://www.unrwa.org/who-we-are#.

"Wave of Terror 2015–2018." *Israeli Ministry of Foreign Affairs*. January 10, 2021. https://www.mfa.gov.il/mfa/foreignpolicy/terrorism/palestinians/pages/wave-of-terror-october-2015-aspx.

Winer, Stuart and Newman, Marissa. "Iran's Supreme Leader Touts 9-Point Plan to Destroy Israel." *The Times of Israel*. November 10, 2014. https://www.timesofisrael. com/iran-supreme-leader-touts-9-point-plan-to-destroy-israel.

Wootliff, Raoul. "Final Text of Jewish Nation State Law Approved by the Knesset on July 19." *Times of Israel*. August 2, 2018. https://www.timesofisrael.com/final-text-of-jewish-nation-state -bill-set-to-become-law.

Yaqub, Salim. "The Daring Move that Crippled the Middle East Peace Process." *The Washington Post*. November 20, 2017. https:// www.washingtonpost.com/news/made-by-history/wp/2017/11/20/ the-daring-move-that-crippled-the-middle-east-peace-process/.

Index

Less familiar foreign words and significant names are selectively italicized. Major headings are indexed and appear in bold.

A

Abbasid dynasty/caliphate 27, 105, 137, 138, 144, 214

Abdullah I 50, 205, 213

Abdullah II 154, 178

Abiru/Apiru/Hapiru/Habiru/Aviru 5, 8, 13, 205, 228

Abraham xiii, 1, 2, 3, 5, 13, 23, 152, 162, 163, 164, 165, 166, 196, 197, 201, 210, 227

Abraham and the Hebrew-Israelite narrative 1

Abrahamic 49, 85

Abu Mazin (see *Mahmoud Abbas*) 142, 152, 153, 184

Achille Lauro 69

AD 1, 28, 163, 164, 218, 221, 234

Aegean Philistines 139

Aegean/s, Aegean Sea 4, 97, 139, 164, 221

Aelia Capitolina 22, 205

Afghanistan 101

Africa 4, 92, 93, 108, 117, 137, 138, 141, 165, 201

agriculture 1, 92, 106, 144

Ahmed Yassin 155

air force (see *Israeli Air Force*) xi, xv, xviii, 55, 57, 58, 59, 60, 64, 115, 125, 129, 130, 131

Al-Aqsa Mosque 50, 77, 85, 205

Al-Azm, Khalid 48, 81, 205, 232

Alexander the Great 18

Al-Kubar nuclear reactor 118

Allah xviii, 118, 126, 128, 149, 151, 154, 155, 157, 212, 213, 214

Allahu Akbar 149

Al Qibla 173, 205

Ammonites 139

Anglo-French airborne force 52, 221

annex/annexation/annexed 49, 60, 68, 102, 128, 143, 152, 177, 178, 179, 181, 198, 199, 202, 211

annihilation of the Jewish State 44, 52

Anno Domini 1

Apartheid 183, 201

Aqaba 36, 94, 111, 173

Arab and Palestinian mistakes and missed opportunities 182

Arab coalition 130, 131, 133

Lehi 113, 175, 215
Levites 8
Liberty, USS 62, 63, 82, 216, 233, 234
Libya 27, 137
lingua franca 6, 18, 32
Litani River 125, 126, 128, 135, 232
Lithuania 29
"Little Satan" 154
low-level wars/conflicts xii, xvii, 36, 43, 108, 123, 192

M

Ma'alot school massacre 124
Maccabean/s/Maccabean Empire/ Revolt 18, 19, 21, 22, 80, 205, 206, 209, 212, 214, 216, 218, 219, 224
Maccabee Beer 18
Madrid Conference 152
Mahmoud Abbas 142, 152, 153, 184
Mahmoud Ahmadinejad 154
mandate/s, British/French 27, 30, 35, 37, 39, 40, 41, 42, 51, 52, 53, 54, 67, 68, 84, 90, 96, 97, 116, 128, 173, 174, 175, 206, 207, 210, 211, 215, 218, 221
manufacturing and industry 106
Mark Twain 175
Masada 19, 20, 21, 216
maternity leave 110
McMahon, Henry, Sir xiii, 36, 37, 140, 172, 216
1915 McMahon-Hussein Correspondence 36

Mediterranean Sea 3, 6, 16, 57, 59, 91, 92, 93, 94
Merneptah/Israel Stele 8, 9, 10, 210, 216
Mesopotamia 1, 2, 3, 17, 18, 162, 210
MiG aircraft 125
Military xi, xiv, xv, xvii, xviii, 3, 7, 9, 10, 26, 27, 28, 30, 37, 40, 41, 51, 52, 53, 56, 57, 58, 60, 61, 62, 63, 65, 69, 70, 71, 73, 74, 75, 76, 77, 78, 79, 80, 87, 88, 91, 96, 101, 102, 105, 107, 108, 109, 110, 113, 114, 118, 120, 124, 125, 127, 128, 129, 131, 132, 133, 142, 145, 146, 147, 150, 151, 154, 155, 162, 167, 175, 176, 179, 182, 192, 193, 194, 210, 211, 212, 214, 215, 217, 221, 234
military coup 51, 80, 211, 217
military service xi, 87, 110, 113, 114
Minimalist/s 9, 11, 207
Ministry of Defense (MOD) 58, 102, 132
Mirage aircraft 67, 68, 206, 215, 218
Moabites 139
Moldova 29, 104
monotheistic 26, 85
Mordechai Vanunu 119, 121, 229, 231
Moshe Arens 130
Moslem Brotherhood 77, 79, 80, 217, 220
Mount Hermon 92
Mount Mariah 84
Mount of Olives 26, 84
Mount Zion 31, 224

Phalange Christian Militia 180, 220
Pharaoh Merneptah 10
Pharaoh/s 10
Philistia 7, 219
Philistines 4, 7, 22, 139, 164, 219, 221
Phoenician/s 2, 139, 165
physical features xvii, 91
Picot, Francois 37
Pillcam 88
PLO (see *Palestine Liberation Organization*) 69, 123, 124, 125, 126, 127, 161, 175, 176, 183, 206, 207, 211, 219, 220
pogroms 29, 30, 31, 109, 219
Poland 29
Pope Urban II 27
Popular Front for the Liberation of Palestine (PFLP) 69, 124
pork 106
Portugal 27, 84, 221
Potash 93, 106
pro-Israeli 191
pro-Palestinian 191
proto-Israelites 5, 7
Ptolemy, Ptolemaic Empires 18

Q

Qatar xviii, 130, 144, 156
Qumran 19, 219
Qur'an (Koran) xviii, 105, 166, 220

R

rabbinical court/s 89, 215
rabbi/s 32
Rabin, Itzhak 220

Ramadan 70, 71, 75, 79, 190, 220, 221, 224
Ramadan War (see *Yom Kippur War*) 70, 75, 79, 82, 190, 220, 221, 224, 225
Ramallah 142, 195
Rashidun caliphate/dynasty 6, 18, 27, 51, 137, 138, 139, 211, 212, 216
Raytheon 132
Red Sea 36, 92, 93, 94, 111, 115, 155, 173, 195
Red Sea–Dead Sea Canal Project 94, 195
refugee camp/s 49, 127, 141, 180, 219
Religion/s xvii, 4, 6, 7, 9, 11, 16, 17, 26, 33, 49, 84, 85, 90, 137, 138, 139, 162, 165, 166, 196, 203, 208, 210
revolt 18, 19, 21, 22, 80, 205, 206, 209, 212, 214, 216, 218, 219, 224
roadblocks 124
Roman Empire xiii, 18, 19, 25, 26, 138, 208
Romania 104
Roman/s xiii, xvii, 4, 6, 7, 13, 17, 18, 19, 20, 21, 22, 23, 25, 26, 31, 42, 105, 138, 139, 165, 205, 208, 209, 212, 214, 216, 217, 218, 219, 224, 227
Rusalimum 12
Russian Jews 83
Russian pogroms 30, 109

S

Sabbath 32, 89, 90, 220

US embassy annex (Beirut)
   attack 128
US Marine Corps barracks (Beirut)
   64, 81, 126, 127, 128, 176,
   214, 232
US military base ("facility") 107
USS *Liberty* 62, 63, 82, 216,
   233, 234
usury laws 29, 223
Uzi 108

V

value-added tax 223
vehicle assault (ramming) 150, 183

W

Wailing Wall 84
War of Independence (Israel's) xiv,
   xvii, 18, 22, 47, 48, 49, 52,
   53, 54, 55, 57, 58, 59, 60, 61,
   62, 63, 65, 66, 67, 68, 69, 70,
   71, 72, 73, 75, 76, 77, 78, 79,
   82, 83, 85, 86, 88, 89, 90,
   91, 92, 93, 95, 96, 98, 101,
   102, 103, 104, 105, 106, 107,
   108, 109, 110, 111, 112, 114,
   115, 116, 117, 119, 121, 126,
   127, 130, 131, 132, 133, 145,
   146, 147, 149, 153, 154, 156,
   157, 161, 162, 167, 169, 176,
   177, 178, 179, 180, 181, 182,
   190, 193, 194, 195, 197, 198,
   199, 200, 206, 211, 213, 215,
   216, 217, 218, 220, 221, 222,
   223, 231, 233, 234
Water Concerns xvii, 92, 195

West Bank 5, 6, 8, 43, 49, 60, 61,
   65, 66, 68, 71, 74, 83, 91,
   102, 141, 142, 143, 146, 147,
   149, 150, 152, 166, 176, 177,
   178, 179, 182, 184, 194, 195,
   198, 199, 200, 202, 211, 219,
   221, 223
Western Wall 49, 65, 84, 223
West Jerusalem 49, 60, 61, 102,
   103, 152, 195
White Paper on Palestine 41,
   172, 208
World War I xvii, 31, 35, 36, 37,
   38, 39, 43, 83, 140, 172, 173,
   174, 206, 207, 213, 215, 222
World War II 43, 52, 53, 73, 74,
   84, 91, 115, 118, 209
World Zionist Organization 44
Wye River Summit 152, 184

Y

Yamaka (see *Kippah*) 89
Yemen 101, 108, 119, 155, 156,
   165, 214
Yemen Civil War 119
Yeshiva 3
YHWH 2, 224
Yiddish 32, 89, 224
**1973 Yom Kippur /Ramadan /
   October War** 70, 71, 75, 79,
   190, 220, 221, 224

Z

Zion/Zionism/Zionist/s xiii, 30, 31,
   38, 39, 44, 45, 76, 96, 172,
   179, 212, 224, 230